Fínn McCool's

FOOTBALL CLUB

FOOTBALL CLUB

THE BIRTH, DEATH, AND RESURRECTION OF A
PUB SOCCER TEAM IN THE CITY OF THE DEAD

STEPHEN REA

PELICAN PUBLISHING COMPANY
GRETNA 2009

The word "Pelican" and the depiction of a pelican are trademarks of Pelican Publishing Company, Inc., and are registered in the U.S. Patent and Trademark Office.

Library of Congress Cataloging-in-Publication Data

Rea, Stephen.
  Finn McCool's Football Club : the birth, death, and resurrection of a pub soccer team in the city of the dead / Stephen Rea.
    p. cm.
  ISBN 978-1-58980-641-2 (hardcover : alk. paper) 1. Finn McCool's Irish Pub (New Orleans, La.) 2. Soccer teams—Louisiana—New Orleans. 3. Irish Americans—Louisiana—New Orleans—Social life and customs. 4. Hurricane Katrina, 2005. 5. Hurricanes—Louisiana—New Orleans. 6. New Orleans (La.)—Social conditions. 7. New Orleans (La.)—Environmental conditions. I. Title. II. Title: Birth, death, and resurrection of a pub soccer team in the city of the dead.
  GV943.6.F47R43 2009
  796.334'620976335—dc22
                                        2008046591

Printed in the United States of America
Published by Pelican Publishing Company, Inc.
1000 Burmaster Street, Gretna, Louisiana 70053

To my grandfathers, Billy Meharg and David Rea.
They taught me that soccer can bridge any
generation gap, knowledge I still use today
with the younger members of our team.

Contents

Acknowledgments

I would like to thank the following people.

My family: Nicola, my mum Linda, dad Billy, grandmothers Sadie and Jean, Carol, Anne, William, Rachel, Tavares, and Sandra.

In Northern Ireland: Matthew Crozier, Doug and Victoria Ferguson, Patrick Griffin, Simon Lowry, Neil and Sharron McKeown, Conrad and Julie Smyth, Neil Warburton, and Brian and Lorraine White. I think about y'all often.

In the USA: Martha Heckman, Denny and Michael Guarracino, Joe and Sam Guichet, Mike Inez, Patricia and Tom Schoenbrun, Mark Southworth, Leslie and Richard Wilson, and Beatriz and Ray Ziegler. You helped us settle. Special mention for Dawn and Gordon Sheals.

Around the world: Lizzy and Peter Acheson, Jo and Paul Bolton, Gloria and Terry Butler, Tony Dennis, Gurbir Dhillon, Dave Feldstein, Fay Gould, Ange and Pete Licalsi, Roger Lowry, Brian and Harvey McKibbin, Ozzy and Sharon Osbourne, Jason and Sara Patterson, Rachel and Steve Scully, Joe and Louise Thompson, and Keith Willey. Thank you for enriching my life and opening your homes.

Gone but not forgotten: Randy Castillo, Mark Putterford, and Bobby Thomson.

For your kindness after Katrina: Jackson Collins, Anne Marie Fraback, Bill and Karin Hamilton, Kenny McClure, and Kevin Palmer. We will never forget it.

Extra-special thanks to Annie Cunningham, Blair Harvey,

Sharon Miles, and my fairy godmother Lynn Seager-Putterford for your confidence and inspiration.

Not in the book but in Finn McCool's: Hubie Collins, Aidan Gill, Ashleigh Gros, Janel and John Lamkin, Patrick Pocock, Daithi and Michelle Robb, and Lynda Woolard, who took the back-cover photo. Where would I go if you weren't there? And the best bar staff in the world: Carolyn, Dawn, Joann, Katie Jean, Keith, Marie, and Taemee. I'd particularly like to offer sincere heartfelt thanks to Stevie, Stephen, and Pauline — without "youse" there would be no book.

Thanks to Ian McNulty who took the photo of the flooded Finn McCool's at the beginning of this book.

To all Finn McCool's FC players, coaches, and fans from the past, present, and future, thank you for carrying the torch. I am extremely grateful to all of you who graciously gave up your time to be interviewed, and I want to single out Benji, whose match reports were an entertaining and invaluable source of reference.

Lastly but most importantly, I owe more thanks than anyone can ever imagine to my beautiful wife, Julie. The irony of her incredible support as I wrote a book about a game she hates is not lost on me.

So this book is for Julie. She advised me, backed me, supported me, encouraged me, believed in me — and only occasionally told me to get a job.

Prologue

8:55 A.M.
Saturday, August 27, 2005

I arrive at Finn McCool's Irish pub on Banks Street in Mid-City.

It's a typical summer's day in New Orleans. A cloudless cobalt sky. Not yet nine and already in the eighties. During the ten-minute drive from my home on the edge of the Garden District, our twelve-year-old Ford Escort had creaked and groaned as it strained to cope with the air conditioning blasting at full power. The oppressive heat will creep up all day, reach 98 degrees in the late afternoon, then mercifully cool down slowly, like a saucepan lifted off the burner.

Finn's is a remodeled wooden Creole home in a residential area. It's not much to look at from the outside. Parking is sometimes tight. It's a "mixed" neighborhood. In Northern Ireland, where I'm from, that means an area inhabited by both Protestants and Catholics, but here it refers to blacks and whites. There are a few Hispanic families too.

The surrounding streets might euphemistically be labeled "sketchy." At night you'd want to be careful. Two weeks ago someone tried to rob our towering Dutch player Frank "the Tank" Komduur. He must have been out of his head on crack. No clear-thinking mugger would tackle giant Frank.

The front door is three steps above street level, the usual defense against flooding in the city. Inside it's cool and dark. My eyes take a second to adjust after the blinding blue

11

outside. I fan my polyester Chelsea replica shirt, already damp from sweat.

Finn's is a million miles from the Disney-fied version of many Irish bars in America. There are no needlework harps, Guinness tea towels, or plastic green leprechauns. It's more like a Belfast workingmen's social club than Rosie O'Grady's in Orlando. I could be in Dundalk or Donaghadee, County Down, or County Clare. Finn's is the real deal.

Stephen Patterson, one of three owners, glides back and forth behind the twenty-foot-long polished wooden bar like a shark. He never stops and is always serving people or washing glasses or emptying ashtrays. He grabs a frosted beer mug from the tall white fridge behind him, which has a couple of magnets stuck to the door. Next he reaches for a bottle from the hard liquors alongside. There's a decent two-shelf range but it's not the showy glass pyramid of obscure vodka brands you find in flashy yuppie joints. Above him a framed drawing of a smiling World War II GI holding a steaming mug asks, "How about a cup of shut the f—k up?" A handwritten sign on a strip of cardboard reads, "Wee pizza—$3." Packets of Tayto potato chips imported from the old country hang drunkenly from a display. One of those big old black rotary phones is mounted halfway up the wall.

He pours coffee into a small brown porcelain cup for me. Some of the lads start drinking as early as 6 A.M. when they watch games, but there's no way I could face alcohol at this hour. He hands me milk in a small plastic to-go cup. The staff also use them when you have been bought a drink you aren't ready for: they are placed upside down on the bar to signify you have one "in the well" and often you'll have three or four stacked up in front of you. Regulars can keep them until the next visit, as they keep a record behind the bar.

There are about eight customers and I sit between our soccer team's assistant coach Robert "Big Rab" Nelson and forward Benji Haswell. Big Rab, thirty-seven, is a ship designer from Scotland who is six feet, four inches tall and weighs almost three hundred pounds. He's been "on the wagon" for a week and is the only one following the Scottish soccer game between Rangers and Hibernian on one of the two TVs above the bar.

My team Chelsea are playing Tottenham Hotspur in the English Premiership on the other set. South African Benji, thirty-four, is a landscape gardener who supports Tottenham (known as "Spurs"), and although he already looks drunk, he claims his bloodshot eyes are because he stayed up until 3 A.M. watching rugby.

This half of the building is long and narrow. Facing the bar are two electronic gambling machines and a jukebox, and this part of the room is so tight that if someone is picking a song while a drinker is on a stool at the bar opposite, you have to excuse yourself to squeeze past. There's also a black metal table and four plastic chairs, and some Saturday nights a beautician sits here and will do your nails for ten dollars. Today there's just a pack of leaflets about pension rights for British ex-pats.

As the Chelsea game kicks off, I head to the men's restroom in the corner of the pub. As there's only one toilet, you often have to queue outside the rickety door and along the side of the bar, but it's free at the moment. I've no time to write a taunting soccer message on the blackboard above the sink.

Another blackboard above the front door advertising forthcoming events reads: "September 17 — Halfway to St. Patrick's Day Party." On the way back to my seat I pass two small black-and-white photographs of the Giant's Causeway in Ulster's County Antrim on the wall at eyelevel. They're maybe six inches by four inches and I didn't notice them for months.

Our team captain Paul Medhurst is standing beside my chair when I return. The rotund forty-two-year-old bank manager is another Spurs fan and is talking to fellow Londoner Steve Scully. Because there are so many regulars called either Paul or Steve, these two are known as Medhurst and Scully. Scully follows the London club Arsenal but is rooting for Spurs today because he wants title favorites Chelsea to lose. He'll be thirty-three on Monday and when he gets drunk he does a funny little dance in front of the jukebox. When I say he should be ashamed of cheering for his bitterest rivals he replies, "My enemy's enemy is my friend."

Also sitting at the bar is our English midfielder Paul Daley, a twenty-nine-year-old oilfield manager from Nottingham, and our pocket-rocket star striker Billy Dwyer, a school counselor and (unusual for our team) a New Orleans native. He's hung over; he turned thirty yesterday and was out celebrating until late last night. It hasn't stopped him this morning from going straight for the beer though.

Stephen carries a box of glasses from the other side of the pub, a large space about twenty feet by forty feet with doors for the ladies' restroom and the storeroom. There's a dartboard, a Foosball table, a pool table, and a bunch of tables and chairs. If there is a large crowd for an important match, Stephen pulls down a roll-out big screen. Posters and flags hailing the Scottish club Celtic are scattered around the walls, as Stephen is a fanatical fan still smarting from the previous week's defeat to archrivals Rangers.

A corkboard hangs on the pillar between the two parts of the pub. Pinned onto it is a poster listing the games for the Shell Shockers (the city's minor league soccer team), a schedule for the bar kickball league, news about the book club, and a few snapshots of laughing barmaids and dressed-up drinkers. The obituary of a regular clipped from a newspaper seems almost comic in this incongruous setting. The dominating item is a blown-up photograph of Finn McCool's Football Club taken four months earlier after our first-ever match. We all look incredibly happy.

We watch Chelsea and Spurs while discussing our own game against local team Olympiakos at 6 P.M. tomorrow. We've entered the second division of the Southeastern Louisiana Adult Soccer Association and the season starts in two weeks. It'll be the first competitive eleven-a-side game many of us have played in years — in some cases decades. At training just thirty-six hours ago we filled the last two places in our twenty-two-man squad. We can't wait for the kickoff.

But some of the boys are apprehensive about taking on Olympiakos. They have ex-professionals, semiprofessionals, and professional coaches. And never mind the second division; they've been first division champions for the last six years. Our forty-six-year-old defender Dave "the Rave" Ashton challenged one of their players to the game in a drunken moment of bravado, but our goalkeeper is out of town and we're missing other key players. The fear is we'll be heavily defeated. But Medhurst is bullish. He reckons they haven't started preseason training and we'll catch them cold.

Then Billy says: "With this hurricane the game will be called off anyway."

I mean to ask him to explain, but I'm distracted by a Chelsea goal and a red card for Spurs player Mido. At halftime our stocky midfielder Graeme Shand, like Big Rab a Scottish ship designer, arrives. He comes over to me and enquires, "Stevie, can you sing?"

"Why?" I say.

"Because I thought you might like to sing me 'Happy Birthday'."

He's thirty-seven today but refuses my offer of a beer because he was hammered last night and is determined to stay sober. Big Rab congratulates him then leaves to get a haircut. Stephen will tape the second half of the Rangers match for him to watch when he returns.

On his way out he holds open the door for our English midfielder Andy Smith, thirty-four, an oilfield engineer from Grimsby nicknamed the Ginger Whinger because he's constantly moaning. He orders a Harp and says, "I've just been helping the girlfriend evacuate her horse. Would you believe it cost six hundred bucks?"

Should we be worrying about the approaching hurricane? It has crept up on us, come in under the radar. Even my wife, Julie, normally ultracautious about storm warnings, hadn't mentioned it this morning and had gone shopping. Benji has lived here longer than me and his wife, Shawn, is from Louisiana so I ask him.

"It's going to be fine, dude. I have friends that will tell you there's no way New Orleans will ever get hit by a hurricane; it's all to do with the mouth of the Mississippi and wind direction and stuff. Shawn is out of town this weekend and I'm not going anywhere. It'll be alright. If those pussies Olympiakos don't turn up then it means we win."

I turn my attention back to the soccer. Ulsterman Ivan Sproule's hat trick for Hibernian to defeat Rangers has yet another Scot, Celtic supporter Steve "Macca" McAnespie, rubbing his hands in glee. Cackling Macca is the Shell Shockers player-coach and will be training us for five dollars per person per week when our season starts.

The rest of us watch Chelsea cruise to victory. A great start to the weekend and it's not even 11 A.M. Medhurst, Benji, and Scully complain about the referee. I gloat for a bit—I followed Chelsea for two decades before they won a trophy, but now I'm wallowing in their recent success—then we carry on talking about our match tomorrow.

Big Rab comes back and settles down to watch the remainder of the Rangers game. He's unaware we all know they lost 3-0. Every so often Macca innocently asks him what the score is. "Rangers are losing 1-0 . . . It's 2-0 now . . . Hibernian have just gone 3-0 up." Each time, Macca cracks up behind his back and we all laugh at the windup.

Physiotherapist Dave the Rave turns up in time to see his hometown team, Manchester City, play against Portsmouth in the English Premiership. He's just finished work and half-watches the game as we continue to discuss our match.

I leave at halftime. I promised Julie I'd be back by lunchtime in case she needs the car. I double-check the details for tomorrow. Meet at the pub at 5 P.M. If Olympiakos doesn't show, then we'll hold a practice session.

Benji orders another beer. He says: "We'll be there okay. We've nowhere to go, dude. We're a whole team of transplants and foreigners—where are we going to drive to? Ireland?" He laughs. I smile and pat him on the shoulder. I tell everyone I'll see them tomorrow.

But forty-eight hours later Finn McCool's was under water. Macca was fighting for his life on the roof of a flooded house.

And one week later we had no way of knowing if more than half of our squad was still alive.

Finn McCool's

FOOTBALL CLUB

CHAPTER 1

Macca

For months he had nightmares. Her screams woke him in the dead of night. He heard her cries in his sleep. Her name was Lauren. She was eighteen.

"I'll never forget the sound of her voice. I'll take it with me to my grave. During the night she suddenly went quiet. I kept shouting and shouting and shouting but I never heard from her again. It haunted me for a long time."

Macca never saw Lauren. Like him, she was trapped on a roof in the Lakeview area of New Orleans. She was two streets away and started yelling and crying the day the levees broke. He kept shouting to her and reassured her over and over help would come. He coaxed her into talking about herself and urged her to keep her spirits up.

Someone would rescue her soon. She just had to hold on a little bit longer. But she fell silent in the pitch-darkness of a drowned and abandoned city. He repeatedly called her but she never answered back. He never did find out what happened to her. But right then he knew — he just knew — she was gone.

Ex-professional soccer player Macca was thirty-three when Katrina hit and had been in Louisiana two and a half years. He won the League Cup in Scotland with Raith Rovers before being sold to English club Bolton Wanderers in a record move worth the equivalent of nearly $2 million. Former England national team coach Kevin Keegan then signed him for the London outfit Fulham, but when Frenchman Jean Tigana took over, Macca left for the lower league club Cambridge United and was looking for a new challenge when his contract ended.

He found that the game in England was like an old boys' club and he had burned too many bridges as a hotheaded player to get a job in the close-knit world of top-level coaching. So in 2002, believing soccer was set to explode in the States, he flew to South Carolina intending to sign for the Charleston Battery. The deal collapsed and he returned home, but on the trip he met Irishman Kenny Farrell, who persuaded him to join a minor league team starting in New Orleans.

When he arrived in February 2003, the Shell Shockers didn't even have a name. He was unveiled as their first signing and helped get the club off the ground, combining playing for them with coaching roles at youth teams in the city. Finn McCool's was one of the first bars Kenny took him to and Macca, who likes to drink, immediately made it his local. As a Celtic supporter who grew up in sectarian-split Glasgow, he relished being able to indulge in friendly banter with Rangers fans while watching explosive "Old Firm" battles between the two teams.

When our pub team started we wanted him to manage us in the Shell Shockers' off-season. He was initially reluctant because of his paid coaching commitments and thought it would be a short-lived joke.

"But being around the guys all the time and seeing the excitement grow was an eye-opener for me. I realized it was more serious than a muck-around on a Sunday and you wanted to take it a step up from just having a drink and a laugh. It's that British mentality of wanting to win all the time: it's okay to have fun but it's no fun when you are getting beat. And it was because of that attitude I said I'd do it."

Even amongst the hardened drinkers who hang out at Finn's, Macca is famous for his benders. That Saturday when I left him at the bar, he was just getting started and he stayed there all afternoon and evening.

"With hindsight people think I was an idiot, but at the time I was laughing and joking over a few beers with the boys. The Weather Channel was on and we were keeping an eye on the hurricane as it was getting closer, but we were trying to avoid thinking too much about it and were discussing other things."

Later he met friends in a hole-in-the-wall bar near Bourbon Street and kept drinking. Then drank some more. He was still in the French Quarter on Sunday afternoon as the news reported gridlock on the I-10 Interstate out of New Orleans. He finally panicked as one after another of the restaurants, cafes, and bars shut down.

"I was at my wit's end. By now it's 5 P.M. and I realized it was too late to go anywhere. I made my way along Bourbon to Canal Street to get a cab, but there was nothing around, so I started walking home and from nowhere the wind picked up and was whipping around me at an incredible speed.

"It was pouring with rain and I was soaked, but then a taxi driver stopped and asked me where I was going. He wasn't working but gave me a ride to the top of Canal, and when he dropped me off I legged it as fast as I could to the house. By the time I got home and got bunkered in, it was a raging gale."

He hadn't prepared for a storm. No hurricane stockpile. No supplies. No emergency kit. Television showed Katrina drawing a bead on the city. The local channels signed off. Then the power died.

Complete blackness. The wind screaming outside and the

rain battering the house. Within minutes a window blew out. Pictures and photos crashed off the walls. Windows rattled and shook. Storm shutters were ripped loose and banged incessantly against the building.

"The noise was driving me nuts. There was nothing I could do but go to bed. The sound was unbelievable, unbearable, like being on a battlefield. I plugged my ears with toilet paper but couldn't sleep. I was just hoping and praying it would pass in an hour or two. It was bedlam, like five hundred people all having a party in your room.

"I could sense the roof straining as if it was going to be ripped off at any second. I thought, 'Bloody hell, if this goes I'm done for,' and I crawled into the walk-in closet and shut my eyes. The pressure was crazy."

In the early hours, dehydrated from a weekend on the booze, he got an orange juice from the fridge and saw through the patio doors that rainwater had flooded the garden up to the back step. On his next visit to the kitchen it was over the step. The third time it had reached the deck, and the back fence had blown down.

An hour later the garage roof had been clawed off and the doors torn from their hinges. The contents floated around the garden and porch and the barbeque set was repeatedly clanging against the glass. He considered going out to get it but went back to bed instead.

"I must have managed to doze off, but then I woke with a start and saw there was water right up to the bed. I said, 'Holy s—t, what's going on here?' and jumped up and waded across the room to the chest of drawers. On top of it was a zippered waterproof wash-bag with my passport in it, and I don't know why but I had the presence of mind to snatch it and stuff my mobile phone in there as well.

"I couldn't believe how fast the water was flooding

in — even in the seconds it took to grab my stuff it'd risen higher. I waded out of the bedroom and saw a broken window where the water was pouring in. I clambered onto a chair to escape through it and was halfway out when the current yanked me away."

He was swirled down the street by the force of water gushing through the rupture in the nearby levee. He can't swim and thought he was about to drown, flailing helplessly as the torrent tossed him about like a cork on the ocean.

"It was chaos. I couldn't see anything, but I could hear trees falling and there was stuff everywhere. Tiles and bits of roofs were being blown about and I was trying to protect my face with my hands, but I couldn't tell if anything was coming towards me.

"I could hear things landing in the water all around me and I was trying to keep a clear head and get my bearings but I was scared s — tless. I was being slammed into electricity cables lying in the water and didn't know if they were live so I was trying to duck under without touching them.

"I was sliced open from being pounded into fences and railings and street signs. The water was so high it was above the stop signs, so they were hidden and you didn't even know they were there until you hit them. I was only wearing a tee-shirt and shorts and my legs were cut to ribbons. Eventually I managed to cling onto the edge of a roof, scramble up, and climb to the highest point.

"I was knackered. It was only maybe one hundred yards from the house but it felt like miles. I was trying to hang onto the chimney stack but there was nothing to grip and I felt like the wind was going to blow me back into the water at any minute. I was also convinced it was going to break off and I remember thinking, 'If this gives way then I'm f — ked.'

"I was trying to shelter myself from the worst of the gale but it was coming from all angles, and I could hear trees breaking apart and bits of buildings cracking. It was absolutely terrifying."

The storm eased as the morning wore on and the driving, stinging rain—like needles on his body—finally stopped. He caught his breath. Possessions drifted past. The middle-class Lakeview neighborhood had been reclaimed by the sea, and Macca saw firsthand the awesome devastation caused by the catastrophic collapse of the levees.

He shouted to Lauren and heard other trapped survivors dotted about the district. By late afternoon the wind died down, the clouds dissipated, and he was drenched in an eerie silence. It was as if he was alone in the world's largest swimming pool. He spent the night clinging to the roof.

"At dawn I just thought, 'Well, here we go again.' I was getting more and more dehydrated and exhausted but couldn't lie down to sleep because of the pitch of the roof. I kept telling myself that a boat or a helicopter or something is going to come and rescue me. Even if I had been able to swim there was no way of knowing what dangers were in the water."

Helicopters buzzed high in the sky on Tuesday as the rescue mission trundled into gear and America struggled to comprehend the scale of the disaster that had almost obliterated one of its most famous cities from the face of the Earth.

The southern summer sun beat down relentlessly. There was no hiding place. Macca, partially clothed, fair haired, and pasty skinned, was being baked alive. He made contact with a couple in their eighties a few houses down. They'd spent the night hugging each other as they balanced on a chair in their upstairs bedroom with the water up to their necks.

"At this stage I was delirious. I'd had nothing to eat, nothing to drink, no sleep, and I was getting sunburned to death. I'm not a religious person but I was reliving all the things I'd done wrong in my life. All the times I've been an ass, all the times I've pissed people off . . .

"But the main thing I was thinking about was my five-year-old daughter, Marissa, in Scotland. I wanted the chance to see her again and I said to myself that if I get out of this then I'll never act so stupidly again. When you are given that much time to think it is a huge bloody lesson, believe me."

By late afternoon the Coast Guard choppers were flying lower, and every time one passed he'd scream at it and frantically wave his white top. On a low sweep a pilot spotted him and hovered so close he could shout over the noise of the blade.

He asked, "Are you alright?"

Macca answered, "I am now. Where have you been?"

Macca told him to evacuate the elderly couple first and watched them being winched to safety. The pilot signaled he'd be back in ten minutes. Two hours later he still hadn't returned.

"I thought, 'Are you kidding me?' I couldn't believe it. I was being teased. That was the breaking point, and I can't tell you how deflated I was. It was about 7 P.M. because the sun was setting and I knew they'd be stopping the rescues for the night. I don't think I would have survived another night.

"But just as I was about to give up, they reappeared and a guy came down, tied me onto the rope, and I was pulled in. 'It's okay, you'll be safe now,' he said and I burst into tears.

He gave me water and I was dying to drink it, but my lips were so burnt it stung and all I could do was dab it on them. I just cried and cried like a baby."

CHAPTER 2

Frank the Tank

Frank the Tank didn't evacuate either. He was one of seven Dutch nationals his government listed as missing after the hurricane. But while Macca battled to stay alive as he was battered about like a shipwrecked sailor, Frank was tucked up in bed. Fast asleep.

The thirty-eight-year-old colossus spends half the year in Holland growing pot. He harvests in three-month cycles and his crop must be good, because when Katrina hit he held the silver medal for the second-best cannabis in Amsterdam. For fifteen years he's been coming to New Orleans to work at the hippy India House hostel less than a mile from Finn's.

"In 1990, I was at a summer camp in New York and bought an Amtrak pass to go down south to find the Blues. At the station in New Orleans there was a large-breasted girl with a sign reading, 'India House—$8 a night.' She didn't tell you that you slept on a mattress on the floor!

"I came every year for Jazz Fest and got to know the owners [of India House], Aaron, John, and Mark. I bought a car from them for $375 to drive to Florida, but it broke down, so I called and said I had no money and asked if I could come back and stay and they agreed.

"Aaron is English, and in March 2005 the police arrived looking for his brother Angus. He'd the same initials so they took him instead, and it turned out he had an expired visa because though he married an American, he never did the proper paperwork.

"He was in Angola [a notorious Louisiana prison] for

two months then deported and barred from coming back. He got very depressed and kept calling the hostel saying, 'I've no money, can you send me some?' and we had to tell him, 'No, we've had a hurricane and we are closed. Can you send us some to fix up the place?'

"John was from Ireland and in 2004 he was killed by a plum pudding. He cooked it using his grandmother's special recipe, and it was so super rich and he ate so much of it the doctor said it gave him a heart attack.

"There's only Zimbabwean Mark left. He used to just sit on the porch all day drinking and smoking, but now he has to do all the work."

Frank started training with us in May 2005 after a Finn's bartender told him about the team. The six-foot-three-inch mobile brick wall loved to throw himself into lunging tackles and I think it was only through the utmost self-control he didn't go flying in with both feet off the ground just to get a drink of water at halftime.

"It'd been four years since I played, but I enjoyed it a lot and the players were better than I had imagined. I felt appreciated and wanted, and it was great to be able to talk to other Europeans who sometimes have a better grasp of world affairs than Americans. You could say it was love at first sight."

Mark left for Katrina but asked Frank to stay, as he was the hostel maintenance man. Eight other staff and friends also decided not to evacuate, and their first job was to kick out the one hundred or so guests still in the three-building complex.

"We said, 'The bus leaves at noon for the Superdome' and at 11:30 A.M. we swept the place to throw them all out. Not everybody watches the news—some were really stupid anyway—and many left their luggage, expecting to be back the next day. I had been through a couple of hurricanes and was convinced the hostel would hold up okay, so we boarded up the windows and then I went to bed on Sunday night.

"I'd had a drink and a smoke so I fell asleep, although I kept getting woken up by the water splashing beside me every time the roof sprang a new leak. I'd move my mattress but always get back to sleep okay and the others hated me for it.

"When the storm died down the next day, we had five broken windows and a few inches of water in the hostel, but by the afternoon the water had crept up to a height of about three feet. We spent the day carrying stuff upstairs, and although we hadn't expected it to be so bad we were having fun and there was nothing to do but have another drink and another smoke."

For five days Frank and his friends partied and found inventive ways to amuse themselves as the water rose. "We danced on top of submerged cars, some belonging to guests who decided to go to the Superdome rather than drive away. We shrink-wrapped a mattress, lay on top of it, and tested how far we could paddle. We only got to the corner of the road when it sank and we had to swim back. We had an ugly couch everybody hated and we set it alight, pushed it off the porch, and watched it float down the street. We should have been better prepared, but we had the key to the candy machine so although we couldn't heat any food, we had plenty of brownies and cookies.

"We also watched Dr. Ed, who lives in a one-story house opposite the Canal Street church where the Coast Guard was airlifting people to safety. He closed his practice rather than give it to his wife after a really messy divorce and became very strange and likes to self-medicate a bit too much. Never talk politics with him because he's a fanatical right-winger. Or is it left-winger? He's a fanatical winger of some sort, anyway, and at times you just have to say, 'Hey now, Dr. Ed, it's time for you to go home' and he'll leave.

"Well, the water was up to his ceiling so he got all his important papers, taped them down on top of his roof, and covered it with a tarpaulin. But nearly every time the helicopters came, they blew it off and all his documents ended up in the water. Three times in one day we saw it happen! He's crazy anyway and this sent him over the edge, so next thing he has a handgun and whenever a helicopter appeared he would shout, 'Looters! Looters!' and wave it about and threaten them. He did this for two days and then they sent in a SWAT team and took him out at gunpoint. But three days later he was back."

They listened to radio reports, but they focused on rescue missions and alleged atrocities in the Superdome and not on what was happening in Mid-City. As living conditions rapidly deteriorated inside India House, relationships unraveled, nerves frayed, and arguments developed. The disintegrating law-and-order situation on nearby Canal Street ratcheted up the tension as they watched armed gangs in boats loot stores.

"The first couple of days weren't too bad, but it was really humid and the hostel had taken such a beating that nearly every room had a leak. We'd stored all the mattresses in one room and they turned into one giant sponge and you couldn't even go in there. Other rooms were soaked because of the broken windows, and we spent all day on the balcony and then slept there at night.

"The water got dirtier every day and as there were no working toilets, you had to use a bag and throw it out the window. When the bags started floating back in, it was time to get the hell out."

By Thursday the water had crested and they knew it would take weeks, not days, to disappear. They decided to wait twenty-four hours to see if the level fell, but the next morning Frank was shaken awake and told some were leaving for the Superdome. He wasn't invited.

"The five who left didn't like the fact that we were partying and having fun. Two of them were not very successful recovering drug addicts, you see. And we did have fun—but what were we supposed to do? We were stuck on a f—king balcony for five days!

"We gave our one life vest to a girl who couldn't swim and forty-five minutes later we sat on the balcony and waved them off. As soon as they disappeared around the corner I heard, 'Right, let's go raid the ATM machine.'

"We talked about it and were worried about security like the ink bombs you see in movies, but they removed it from the wall and put it in the water with a blanket over it. It was held together with just four hinges, and an old rusted hacksaw easily cut through them in twenty minutes.

"There was nearly three thousand dollars in twenty-dollars bills and we split it three ways. That was great because the day before the storm I paid sixty dollars to put my car in the parking lot, which left me with $2.75 in my pocket. The funny thing was afterwards we discovered Mark had been trying to call to tell us to break into it! Once we had cash we thought we should get the f—k out of there, as looters were hitting every shop in the neighborhood and we thought we might be next."

They taped together three large coolers, put their belongings inside, and at noon on Friday, September 2, stepped off the porch and warily swam through eight feet of murky, lukewarm water towards Canal. They were heading for the West Bank, across the Mississippi river, and three blocks towards the French Quarter, Frank's feet touched the ground. By the I-10 bridge the water was chest high. They resembled pallbearers as they inched forward carrying the makeshift raft like a coffin and were frequently dunked into the cloudy water as they struggled to keep their footing.

"I was scared of everybody. There weren't many people around, but occasionally guys in boats would stop and confidently stare at you to intimidate you. We saw fifty people in the water straight ahead, and as it's not a great area at the best of times, we decided to zigzag to the right, away from Canal.

"We passed three dead bodies. The first was a man in white overalls floating face-down in the water. I eased it to the side. I wouldn't let the girl with us stop to look at it and pushed her in the back to keep her moving. I saw his photo later in some of the special Katrina magazines and books. The next was a black man with a hood over his head in a wheelchair. The third was a man halfway in the water.

"Man, it was hard work walking. We just focused on surviving. We never allowed ourselves to stop and just kept moving. You couldn't see anything in the water but could feel all the hurricane debris, and every time you lifted your foot, it got stuck in something—downed cables, trees, chairs, signs and stuff floating in the water. The only time we laughed was when we found a big box of bubble bath and opened it, frothing it up and joking we were doing our bit to clean up New Orleans."

For five spooky hours they walked, waded, and swam through a near-deserted New Orleans in an increasingly agitated attempt to escape the modern-day Atlantis.

"The back streets were empty, although when you came

across a shop there were usually looters. People were just taking all kinds of stuff they didn't even want. We met a very friendly looter and he walked with us for a bit and had all the typical looter things like food and beer. After a while he said, 'Well, I'm heading back to the store now so I'll send you on your way.' He was really nice. He told us to go to the Superdome to get a bus out, but that was the one place we didn't want to go.

"At the I-10 Claiborne entrance we tried to get onto the interstate, but the military police said there was no shelter, water, or food that way. We told them we didn't want anything, but they said it didn't matter and ordered us to turn around.

"We went back down into the water, headed west towards Kenner, and up another interstate ramp—we were desperate to get onto dry land—but we got turned around there as well. Those mother-f—kers couldn't stop you at the entrance but made you walk a mile before they sent you back.

"The third time we found a ramp near a jail and the police were unloading prisoners in orange suits and shackles all chained together, and the cops said we couldn't pass. So once more we went down into the water and found ourselves back near Claiborne Avenue.

"We met a French girl who stayed with us for a time but then she got tired and just sat down, and there were a few people close to the Superdome who didn't want to go in because they heard all the wild stories. We also found a soldier who told us to sit beside him and he'd guarantee our safety for as long as he was on duty but warned that after that we were on our own.

"By now I felt terrible, really depressed. It was early evening and there was no way we'd be able to walk out before nightfall. I didn't want to be wandering about in the dark and was about to go back to India House. The soldier had told us that if we didn't go to the Superdome, we wouldn't be on the register and in line for an evacuation bus. No one knew we were even in the water.

"But then we saw a strange thing in the Central Business District, down a back street near Loyola: a school bus with a nervous-looking driver talking to a couple with a dog who had gone to the Superdome but then left when they'd been told to release their pet, as it wasn't allowed in. Standing beside them were six girls in pink, frilly dresses and high heels who had got stranded in the city after coming in for a bridal shower the night before Katrina.

"The driver had stolen the bus and was waiting to meet twenty of his family to drive them to Baton Rouge, and we negotiated with him and handed over one hundred dollars each to get aboard. Man, I can't tell you how happy we were! I was ecstatic.

"One of the girls had a huge family villa near Baton Rouge — they were very rich people — and we crashed there for two days. I had my own room and they totally looked after us and gave us food, beer, everything. One of their friends even brought us weed. Man, it was awesome."

CHAPTER 3
Coming to America

I first saw Julie in a bar in London's Victoria Station on December 2, 1995. I still remember the thick green turtleneck sweater she wore. I'd flown over from Belfast for a friend's birthday party the following day, and I was meeting a few old school mates for a drink. They had invited some female American students they'd bumped into on a recent trip to Dublin. The girls were at Kingston College in London on a three-month exchange program and had visited Ireland for the weekend.

So these Northern Irishmen who lived in England went to the Republic of Ireland and met some Americans who were also living in England and visiting the Republic of Ireland, and they arranged to meet back in England when another Northern Irishman (me) who didn't live in England but lived in Northern Ireland was coming to visit England. When people ask how we met, it's easier to pretend it was on a world cruise.

Julie returned home to Charlotte, North Carolina, and we kept in touch although it was six months before I saw her again. After a three-year intercontinental love affair, I booked a trip to the colorful and exotic walled city of Cartagena in Colombia, on the shores of the Caribbean, to ask her to marry me. I imagined dropping to one knee on the soft sand at sunset as the sun sank into the shimmering sea, palm trees swaying and whispering in the gentle breeze while waves rolled onto the white beach and birds circled lazily in the soft dusk light.

Unfortunately, our plane developed engine trouble taxiing at London's Heathrow Airport and the vacation was canceled. Plan B: Crawfordsburn Beach in Northern Ireland. In winter. Freezing temperatures. A howling gale.

After a lot of coaxing I finally convinced her to leave the house for a Sunday afternoon drive. We parked; I said I had to use the bathroom and went to hide the engagement ring under a shell. I came back and suggested a romantic walk along the beach. She wouldn't get out of the car.

It is a proven scientific fact that Julie is the most cold-blooded individual in the history of the world. If the temperature falls below 85 degrees, she wraps herself in four layers of clothing, curls up in a blanket, fills three hot-water bottles, and makes a cup of steaming chicken soup. When I said we should take a dander on this refreshing, bracing day she looked at me like she thought I'd smoked a year's supply of Frank's "wacky baccy."

She was adamant it was too cold, and no amount of persuasion or bribery would change her mind. I lost my temper twice. Eventually I simply abandoned reasoned argument, prized her fingers from the door, and dragged her out of the vehicle to the beach. By the time we got there I'd forgotten where I'd hidden the ring.

She stood shivering, bundled up like the explorer Scott of the Antarctic, while I scrambled around in the sand and simultaneously shooed away a curious Jack Russell determined to pee on me. When I finally found it, she quickly agreed to be my wife, mainly I think to get away from the biting wind. And the smell of dog urine.

Her acceptance was fortuitous because I was coming under increasing pressure from pals itching to go on a bachelor party. We'd set up a monthly direct deposit into a savings account two years before because I wanted something more elaborate than a night in the pub, and now they were getting impatient and demanding a definite date. If Julie had said no, then I would've had to manufacture a whirlwind romance to escape a lynching. Or ordered a Russian bride.

I can't remember why I chose New Orleans. I'd enjoyed my previous visits and I suppose I just reckoned it would be a good place for a party. A couple of the lads asked, "Why the hell are we off to New Orleans? What's there to do there?"

My bachelor party lasted two weeks. After three days in Reykjavik to see Northern Ireland play Iceland in a World Cup qualifying game, it continued with three days in New York, then finished in the Big Easy, where we paid four thousand dollars to rent a mansion for a week. Six did the whole thing and six others flew in for parts of it. Never in my wildest dreams did I think I'd be back to live in Louisiana, but that house is just five streets away from our home. I see it nearly every day.

Perhaps I ended up in New Orleans because after four years as a newspaper journalist in England, when I left school I returned to Belfast to buy a travel agency at the ripe old age of twenty-one. At the time, my friends were buying beer. I desperately wanted to see the world and was scared I'd grow old like the lead character in the British movie *Shirley Valentine*, who regrets never traveling to all the places she planned on seeing when she was young. I was determined not to end up like her, although admittedly there was only a remote chance I'd turn into a bored, middle-aged Liverpudlian housewife.

For twelve years I booked cheap weekend breaks to Scotland, beach trips to Greece, and theatre breaks to London. I slapped stickers on tens of thousands of brochures and shuffled them from shelf to shelf attempting to keep the office looking fresh. Twice a week I'd pick last-minute vacation offers to make into posters for the window.

When not obsessively trying to keep the displays vibrant and attractive, I'd unblock the toilet, vacuum the floor, and replace fluorescent bulbs. Invariably, while balancing precariously on top of the counter, I'd crush the light in my hand and the glass would shatter and rain down onto our computers. It was so predictable the staff rushed for the brush and dustpan every time a bulb blew, and we spent our lives gingerly picking razor-sharp slivers and shards of glass out of the keyboards.

As a cub reporter it was drummed into me that the general public are not stupid. Never patronize them. Don't talk down to them. Always treat them with respect. I now know this to be a load of bull. The general public are stupid. In fact, their stupidity scales heights you cannot imagine. Ask anyone who deals with them face to face on a daily basis. This is one of many similar conversations I had in the travel agency.

Me (breezily): Can I help you there?

Man in flat cap and woolly jumper with distracted look: Here, how much is it to go to one of them places?

Me (patiently): Where are you thinking of?

Man: You know, foreign like. You know, across the water, to the sun like.

Me (helpfully): Majorca, for instance?

Man: Who?

Me (explanatorily): Majorca. It's an island in the Mediterranean.

Man: Aye, that'll do. How much is that?

Me (accommodatingly): It depends when you go, how long you go for, where you stay. For instance if . . .

Man: Aye, right, but just tell me, how much is it gonna cost me like?

Me (with a soupcon of irritation creeping in): As I was saying, it depends on what you want. If I can show you on the screen here . . .

Man: Hang on, would I need one of them things to go there? 'Cos I haven't got one.

Me (confused): Things?

Man: You know, one of them things that you need before they'll let you go to them places.

Me (questioningly): Do you mean a passport?

Man: Aye, that's it. Do I need one of them?

Me (confirmedly): Yes, you do.

Man: Jesus! I can't be bothered with all that.

Me (gravelly): You can't travel abroad without a passport.

Man: Well, I see. Forget that then. But how much would it cost me anyway?

Me (resignedly): There's a deal on now for . . .

Man: Hang on; do you need all that funny stuff as well if you go to them places?

Me (baffled): Sorry?

Man: That what's-the-name, funny money and all. Do I need that?

Me (educationally): Yes, they have a different currency on the continent. But it's not a big deal to . . .

Man: Jesus, I can't be bothered with all that! But how much would it cost anyway?

Me (through gritted teeth): This morning I found an offer for . . .

Man (now angry): It's not me, you know. It's her.

Me (scanning the shop, bewildered): I'm sorry? Who?

Man (shouting): Her! It's her! She wants to do this, not me. I couldn't care less. I want to spend the money on the hut.

Me (surreally): The hut?

Man (throwing his arms up in exasperation): Yes, the hut! For my chickens! The chickens! They need a new hut! But how much would it cost to go to them places anyway?

Of course we also had hundreds of friendly and likeable customers who were a pleasure to help, but after years of selling charter tours to Spain and flights to Stansted and boats to Stranraer and buses to Scunthorpe, I was worn out and my enthusiasm sucked dry. But I had seen the world. All seven continents, every U.S. state, all the sovereign territories in Europe bar one, more than 100 countries.

I saw elephants crashing through trees to drink at a watering hole at twilight in South Africa and killer whales circling icebergs in Antarctica at midnight. In Australia I climbed Ayers Rock to watch the sun rise and in Beijing I saw it set over the Great Wall of China. I went to mystical religious sites like Angkor Wat in Cambodia, Peru's Machu Picchu, the pyramids at Giza, and Tikal in Guatemala.

I frolicked with seals in the Galapagos Islands, got up close and personal with whale sharks in the Philippines, and swam with hammerheads in Papua New Guinea. I dived on the *Rainbow Warrior* in New Zealand, World War II Japanese ships in the Solomon Islands, and with giant manta rays in Costa Rica.

With a peculiar sense of adventure, I visited the world's trouble spots. I repeatedly prodded my nodding cabby to keep him awake on a four-hour drive in Libya during Ramadan when he was not allowed to eat or drink during daylight hours. I had a bizarre conversation about Irish politics with a Bosnian border guard, and I flew to Jordan in the Middle East three days after 9/11.

I went to Beirut for a long weekend with my friend Roger Lowry and we were escorted off the plane by the army then stopped at a nighttime roadblock by armed militiamen. I saw a tank in a Pizza Hut parking lot and a man in jeans and a tee-shirt at a bus stop with an RPG rocket launcher casually slung over his shoulder. On a plane inbound to a country where they were kidnapping and imprisoning Westerners, there were seventeen of us aboard a huge jet, and the in-flight movie? *The Shawshank Redemption.*

In the space of three months I visited Ushuia in Argentina, the southernmost town in the world, and Alaska's Point Barrow, the northernmost point of the American mainland. I climbed down to the Valley of the Moon in Bolivia and up to the Temple of the Sun in Mexico City. I ate the best steak of my life in Uruguay, found insects in a pizza in Belize, and got food poisoning in Vietnam.

I was a busy man. But one ready for a new challenge in the New World. Although Julie liked living in Northern Ireland (and still claims to miss it), she yearned for more than a fleeting glimpse of the sun. Waking up to a drizzly, miserly gray sky for months on end depressed her, and in the seven years she lived on and off in Belfast, she wore shorts once: an August day in 1999 when she put them on, went outside, trembled uncontrollably, said, "What the hell was I thinking?" and ran back inside to change.

We spent six months on an around-the-world trip (I came back early to see Chelsea play in the European Champions League semifinal in London), then sold, gave away, or dumped nearly everything we owned. We shipped the invaluable items we couldn't possibly live without to Julie's parents, and after repetitive, ruthless pruning we had a dozen boxes containing CDs, board games, and photographs. Oh, and my Subbuteo collection, a prized childhood table-soccer game. That last box caused a fight.

We were ready to hit the Land of the Free. It was time I got to see my wife's legs again.

CHAPTER 4

Living in America

A few years ago Julie and I had a long layover in Miami and we bought a map of the States to pick somewhere to live. I suggested New England, but she ruled it out because of their harsh winters and blew on her hands, rubbed them together, then put on a third cardigan as the temperature dipped into the eighties.

She wanted to live in the south, but I vetoed North Carolina as I wasn't moving to a new continent only to set up home down the road from the in-laws. We compromised on New Orleans, an oasis of decadence in the sober desert of the Bible Belt, a city we'd both visited and enjoyed. In June 2004 we flew to Charlotte, loaded up Julie's old car with two suitcases of clothes and a box of CDs, and coaxed the wheezing Escort seven hundred miles south.

We checked into a yucky motel twenty miles from the French Quarter and spent a week looking for somewhere to rent. It's tough when you don't know the going monthly rate, the good neighborhoods, or even the city layout. We started with apartment complexes, but they were either too far from downtown—no point moving to unique, evocative New Orleans and living in the suburbs— or wildly expensive.

We zeroed in on a district three miles west of the Quarter, called "Uptown" because it is upriver from the original city. It is also built on higher ground. We were unaware of this detail at the time, but the following year everyone was an expert on the city's topography. By day five of our search, we were fed up, discouraged, and ready to jump at anything.

We viewed an apartment in a block on prestigious St. Charles Avenue, the city's second-most famous street, with narrow, dark, depressing corridors like a cheap hotel in a Manhattan murder mystery movie. The agent banged on the door to make sure the current art student occupant was out, as apparently she was usually still in bed when prospective tenants turned up at 3 P.M.

Inside, hundreds of rose petals were scattered on the floor. "Looks like there was something romantic going on here last night," said the agent perceptively. Nothing romantic about the so-called view though, a two-foot-square barred window overlooking a wall where two pigeons sat in their own filth. Ours for just $1,400 a month.

We kept looking. We were constantly getting change to use phone booths to set up appointments, as we didn't have a cell phone, and in desperation, we resorted to going to a rental company. We left after five minutes because we couldn't stand the smarmy staff. "Now this place here, oh! It will be so good for you! It's ideal for you two, exactly what you guys want."

I wanted to scream: "How the hell do you know what we want? We've just walked in and you haven't asked us anything. You've only just met us. You don't even know our names!" But I didn't.

We extended our motel stay and continued searching. We got lost and ended up outside a one-bedroom apartment with a For Rent sign, which turned out to be the first privately owned and fully furnished place we'd found. We wouldn't need to buy a bed, a microwave, or anything and took it on the spot.

Or at least we tried to. In Belfast we had converted our

savings to two U.S. currency drafts worth tens of thousands of dollars drawn on a New York bank, but Julie's bank in North Carolina told us there would be a seventy-dollar fee to cash them.

At another branch they said the first branch was talking nonsense and they wouldn't charge us anything. But the New York bank might. How much "might" they charge us, we asked. They had no idea but suggested we deposit the money into an account with them and wait and see. Err, no thanks.

So we took them to New Orleans only for the Hibernia Bank to quote us $224 to open an account! The New York lot wanted $100 per check, and Hibernia would levy a $12 charge on each as well. I couldn't believe it. Here we stood with our life savings, ready to start a relationship with a financial institution from whom we one day would be getting a mortgage, loans, whatever, and they refused to waive even one of the $12 fees.

I pompously said that on principle I would rather return home to cash them than pay such outrageous charges, an obvious, stupid lie, though it would have been cheaper to fly back to Charlotte and cash them there for seventy dollars. Thankfully our neighbor Mary Flynn put us in touch with another bank around the corner who didn't charge us a cent, so we paid the rent and signed a one-year lease.

Once we settled in and got over the giddy excitement of having found an apartment, we realized the bizarre Mexican owner had stuffed it with a lot of furniture and clutter. An awful lot. It was crammed with every cheap ornament, plastic religious icon, and general bit of useless tat she'd ever come across in her life.

She lived alone but owned eleven chairs, with an additional four on the front porch. We suspected she was head of a Hispanic coven, and she did indeed turn into a witch when she sued us the following year (but that's another story). Any misplaced piece of furniture around the city in 2004 wound up in that house. If you mumbled to yourself that summer, "I'm sure I left that patio chair here somewhere . . .", then that's where it is now.

A plastic daffodil skyscraper last seen in *The Day of the Triffids* dominated the dining table, forcing us to look at each other sideways during meals. After a week we both had necks like Stretch Armstrong. The cupboards smelled musty, the toilet broke the second day, and there was dog poo under the table and bed. But it was home.

We had a to-do list that lasted for weeks and we practically lived in Wal-Mart. The biggest difference between the shops in the U.K. and the U.S. is their return policies. At home I'd psych myself up for days to take back an item, then call friends to track down a bag belonging to the store where I bought it, make sure the receipt was in pristine condition, and wrack my brain to come up with a valid reason why I was entitled to my money back. No matter what you returned you had to steel yourself for the inevitable Gestapo-like interrogation: "What's wrong with it? Did you take it out of the package? Was it at room temperature the whole time? I'm sorry, sir; our rules are that unless you bring it back dipped in liquid gold and smelling of lavender then we can't possibly refund you the 58 pence . . ."

In New Orleans you march in, hand it over, and get the cash back, no questions asked. You often have up to ninety days to do it, and that policy is something I abuse regularly. When my little brother William and little sister Rachel visited, I bought a table-tennis table and DVD player to keep them occupied then returned them when they left. Wal-Mart is like a big, wonderful library.

If the best thing about shopping in the States is the slack return policy, then the worst thing is dealing with sales assistants. They are sniveling, creepy liars. All of them. They make sleazy used car dealers in Britain look like Mother Teresa. Does anyone ever believe anything they tell them? No really, do they? When they say things like "Those pink baggy jeans and yellow belt make you look really slim" or "I have this very bidet at home and it keeps me minty fresh" has anyone in the history of the world nodded and replied, "Really? Well you look like an honest fellow, so I'll take it"?

We stored the porcelain angels, blow-up Jesus, Julie's thirty-two sweaters, and nine of the chairs and hunted for a sofa bed. The furniture showroom staff were so slimy, I showered every time I got home. They insisted on telling you their life story or swearing this particular fabric was created for the king of Siam and would change your life.

After weeks of this we met a harassed salesgirl who kept rolling her eyes and complaining to us about the owner's granddaughter in for work experience. When we asked for a delivery discount because we only lived a mile away, she threw her hands in the air and yelled: "Whaddya want me to do? This thing's cheap!" We found her honest attitude refreshing and snapped it up.

You cannot buy anything in an American store without a salesperson trying to sell you something else. We picked a computer and then fought a two-hour pitched battle with salesmen, managers, cashiers, and God knows who else before managing to escape. It was like a scene from *Night of the Living Dead* as we backed towards the exit while they attacked in waves, thrusting ink cartridges, boxes of paper, and surge protectors at us.

If you make the rookie mistake of standing still for two

seconds after making a purchase, they pounce on you with the dreaded phrase "extended warranty."

"Will you be taking our extended warranty with this purchase, sir?"

"No thanks."

"You should consider it, sir. It's piece of mind for just $12.99 a month."

"No thanks, I'm intending to eat this apple quite soon."

"But anything could happen, sir. You might drop it when you leave the store."

"Then I'll pick it up and give it a brush."

"But it may have been contaminated with a life-threatening disease, sir. With this insurance you'll be covered for such an eventuality."

"I'll take my chances. Look, I've been eating it while you were speaking. I'm almost finished."

"But you could still choke on a seed, sir. We have seed-induced-coughing-fit cover for $9.99."

"No thanks. All done. See?"

"Then how about our apple-core-disposal policy? If you can't find a trashcan within one hundred yards we'll pay you $10 and . . ."

As if moving continents wasn't hard enough to deal with, even in America, New Orleans is considered a law unto itself, and what should have been simple tasks turned into tedious Tolkien tales of epic endurance. Like when I had to get a Louisiana driving license.

The Office of Motor Vehicles' Web site was hopeless, so I drove to their office, but there was no information desk and to ask a question I had to join the line. Here you don't get a designated driving test appointment but queue up for a slot, and as it was August the office was packed with students wanting to sit the test. The queue snaked out the door and into the parking lot, so I tried the next day, but it was just as crowded. And the next. And the next. I joined the line that now stretched so far it met me as soon as I got out of my car.

Eventually I discovered I couldn't transfer my U.K. license and had to do the local test, so I filled out the forms and returned the next morning. I queued up again. I took the eye test, but I had waited so long they were closing and said to come back tomorrow for the theory and road sign exams. I returned the next day. I stood in line again. I failed the road sign exam.

It started easy, things like: You see a white sign with a large P in the middle and a red line through it. Does this mean: a) No parking b) No peeing c) No push-ups d) No Portuguese. But then came questions on types of roadside reflectors and the difference between dotted white lines and solid yellow lines and all kinds of stuff I had no idea about.

I probably should've read the book they gave me. And the test instructions. I found out later you're allowed to skip questions you don't know the answer to. This would explain why the staff were scratching their heads and calling over colleagues, as I don't think anyone had ever failed it before.

So I had to go back, queue up again, and retake it. Then I had to return to sit the actual driving exam, and I distinctly remember asking if there was anything I needed to bring. I was told I needed nothing. I returned the next day, queued up again. At the desk they asked if had my insurance with me. No I didn't. I went back the next day. Queued up again. NASA trains astronauts faster.

When I finally sat the test, it was so quick I thought I'd failed. I literally drove around the block and then had to park between two white lines so far apart Stevie Wonder could have done it. I scored 96 percent, losing marks for not pausing long enough at a stop sign. The examiner advised me to count to ten in future. In Louisiana you'd be lucky to find a driver who knows all the numbers between one and ten, never mind one who stops at intersections long enough to count them off.

We had completed such official rites of passage, and we were getting used to the permanent sweat sheen, giant cockroaches, and smell of dog poo when I looked out the window one day in August and saw three different neighbors loading up vehicles. I investigated and found out they were evacuating from Hurricane Ivan, which explained why those blokes down the road had been hammering plywood over their windows. I'd assumed they were having a bonfire and were protecting the glass.

New Orleans had hurricanes? It was news to me. The traffic was mental and it took seven hours to crawl to a bed and breakfast 120 miles away. Ivan jogged east and crashed into Mississippi, with our wind damage limited to a few leaves on the porch. I joked about the terrible destruction natural disasters could inflict and swore to never hightail it out of Dodge again. Funny how these throwaway remarks come back to haunt you.

By November, Julie had a job, I was a house husband (but one who couldn't cook or iron, so not too much "house" and really just a "husband"), and the presidential election was in full swing. Dozens of Democratic campaigners gathered on the neutral ground along St. Charles every evening in all kinds of weather, and in the midst of rush-hour traffic they jumped up and down, waved placards, and yelled at drivers to vote for their man.

Although I admired the dedication of these political cheerleaders, did they believe they'd change voting intentions or that their actions would be the tipping point for wavering citizens? Did any Republican-leaning redneck roll down his truck window, lean out to spit, tip back his baseball cap, turn down Lynyrd Skynyrd, and say to himself: "Dang it, I was gonna vote for George W. but darn! That poster-waving mob makes a convincing argument. To heck with policies and campaigns — I'm going with the chanting crowd bouncing about in the rain!"

It cooled down, cooled down, and then cooled down some more. New Orleans' first Christmas snow in fifty years was a wonderful fairytale sight. Of course, viewing the apartment during the wax-melting, searing summer, we hadn't thought to ask about the heating. There was none. After sweating like hooded rapists in a disco for months, we were now bundling up at bedtime like Arctic adventurer Ranulf Fiennes.

Julie was simply delighted by this turn of events, and I don't exaggerate when I write that she slept in three layers of clothing, a wooly hat, scarf, and gloves. The only exposed skin was the very tip of her nose, and when she needed to breathe it would pop up from underneath the covers like a submarine periscope.

We were so miserable we checked into a bed and breakfast, the Fairchild House, on Christmas night. The electric heaters from Wal-Mart were worthless in a home with twenty-foot-high ceilings designed to keep the room cool, but we cranked them full-blast anyway and huddled around like picketing Yorkshire miners warming their hands during a harsh winter in Northern England. By the end of the year we'd had enough and decided to buy a house. I returned the heaters to the library.

CHAPTER 5

Let Me Play, Buddy!

Four weeks after immigrating, I met my friend Jason Patterson in Pittsburgh to see Chelsea on a three-game U.S. tour. In a bar after the game, we got to chatting with a local who had lived in New Orleans for a year, and I said I found the southerners friendlier than the folk up there.

He replied: "Yeah, but it's a kinda false friendliness. It's like they seem friendly but they don't really become your friends. There's just something, I don't know, it's hard to explain . . ." and he trailed off. Six months later I knew what he meant.

I should say right now that I'm a pretty rubbish soccer player. I have no flashy tricks or fancy stepovers. I have one move: I pretend to kick the ball, and when the opponent reacts to the dummy, I drop my shoulder and prod it past him. I'm so one-dimensional, my mate Richard Wilson calls me "Mono."

But I love playing and would rather have a kick-around than do just about anything else in the world. In Belfast, I had indoor five-a-side at Monday lunchtime, seven-a-side outdoor on Monday night, seven-a-side again on Tuesday night, back indoor Wednesday lunchtime, outside once more on Thursday night, and then indoor on Saturday afternoon. Playing that much, it is a miracle I stayed so useless.

I was apprehensive I would not be able to find a game in New Orleans and imagined I'd have more luck in a city with a large ex-pat community like Los Angeles. It's hard to find anywhere on Earth with an environment more hostile to European "football" than Louisiana, where the definition of "sport" is animal murder. The state license plate reads, "Louisiana—Sportsman's Paradise," a reference to hunting and fishing.

Wal-Mart's sports department sells guns, ammunition, and camouflage jackets but no soccer boots or shin guards. The staff even wear fatigue vests, probably so when the inevitable AK-47-firing doomsday militiaman storms in blazing, they can escape by blending into the stock. One day (after returning a one-dollar tape measure I had no further need of) I checked the racks for soccer magazines, but the choice was *Shotgun Weekly*, three paintball publications, and innumerable periodicals devoted to monster trucks.

The twenty-four pages of sports in the city's newspaper, *The Times-Picayune,* are hogged by the gridiron team the Saints, who play in the Superdome. If the Shell Shockers are featured, it's usually a miniscule report of a home match, and a headed goal was once described as, "He head-butted a point." Soccer is a wuss's game played by kids, girls, and foreigners. Down here, you talk sports with a rifle in your hand.

But I knew somebody somewhere was playing the game. It was a good sign the three parks in New Orleans (Audubon, Lafreniere, and City) all had well-tended pitches, but I only saw children on them and I felt a bit of a pervert watching in my playing gear like some kind of pedophilic soccer groupie.

I trawled the internet, emailed every organization I found, and asked anyone I met if they knew of any pickup games. I got excited by a newspaper advertisement looking for members to join a co-ed squad until Julie explained it meant there were girls on the team. I'd never heard the term in my life, and she took it as an attack on her sex when I reacted with horror and revulsion to the idea of playing competitively with females. Later I'd hear Americans say, "Look at those hot co-eds" when they were talking about a group of girls, but surely if the term stands for "co-educational," then by its very name it implies males and females educated together. If there are no males around, are they not just "eds"? No wonder I was confused.

I'd been told there was a Tuesday evening game at Lafreniere Park and drove over to find a thin man with wispy blond hair placing tiny training goals on a field. I asked if it was a pickup game and he hemmed and hawed as if it were the final question on *Who Wants to Be a Millionaire.* "I suppose it is, but it's kind of a practice for the team I run. You might be able to play if not enough of them turn up." Gee, thanks mister!

I attempted to chat about his club, but I may as well have been speaking Swahili for all the interest he showed. Some of his squad arrived; a few Hispanic kids milled about; I hung around awkwardly. A match developed, and if you wanted to take part you ran onto the field and tried to kick the ball like you were ten and it was recess at school.

For the next couple of weeks, I was the new kid obviously desperate to play but too shy to ask. The following Tuesday about six Latino youths and I (the sole English speaker) lined up against Wispy Hair's full team. Not only were we outnumbered, but we also had to score in the two-foot goals while his side attacked a full-size net because, "I want my guys to get some practice shooting on goal." It was ridiculous.

Unfairly stacking the teams was a repeated pattern all over the city. It may be a cliché about the American win-at-any-cost mentality versus the British sense of fair play, but every pickup game was the same: guys angled to get on the same side as the best players, without the merest nod to choosing two evenly balanced teams. It was more important to crush the opposition than to create an enjoyable contest.

The first two times I attempted to chitchat and a couple of lads asked where I was from and what I was doing here, but it was hard going. The third week I did my stretches and loitered on the periphery—and was roundly ignored by everyone as they started playing.

I wasn't naïvely expecting to be greeted like the Prodigal Son, but I imagined the reverse situation of an American in Belfast appearing at our game. We'd have included him on one of the two (even) teams, asked how he was finding Northern Ireland, and welcomed him the next week when we'd have kicked the ball to him as we warmed up.

I watched for a bit and then two Caribbean blokes running sprints nearby felt sorry for me and kicked me their ball to play with. When they asked for it back, I fell in with a Mexican goalkeeper and took shots at him for half an hour because none of his club had turned up for training. I resolved to never again make the twenty-six-mile round trip to stand like an idiot and watch Wispy and his boys.

So, though not keen on the twice-weekly training world of organized competitive soccer, my options were running out, and I answered a newspaper ad for players to join a league team. A Honduran was putting a squad together and we arranged to meet at Lafreniere. He arrived with a sumo wrestler who turned out to be his goalkeeper.

"So you're gonna join our team. Great!" said Mr. Honduras. "That'll give us four players. It's sixty dollars for the shirt. You can give me the money now." I told him I didn't have it on me. "Then just give me thirty dollars, but you'll only be allowed to play the first half." I thanked him for his time and made a break for the car. I think he shouted after me that if I gave him a dollar I'd get on for a minute and a half.

I was disheartened and gaining weight with every passing week. One morning about 11:30, I said to Julie, "I'll head out for a run now. It heats up in the afternoon but it's a bit cloudy and I'll be done by 12:30." I ran six miles, staggering back home like a shot cowboy in a Western, convinced I was about to expire from exhaustion. My first—and last—run in New Orleans was a painful lesson in underestimating the summer afternoon heat.

Next I heard about a relatively new indoor center called Riverside and rang the Trinidadian owner, Colin Rocke. He said the season was half-over but I could enter my team in the next one. I told him I didn't have a team. He said I needed to find a team.

He asked me where I was from, then said, "You're European? Why didn't you say? In that case you can join my first-division side. We have an important play-off game on Sunday." I replied that although I was European, I wasn't very good. He said I needed to find a team. I said I hadn't managed to find one since he mentioned it thirty seconds ago.

I went to look around the six-a-side facility anyway and it was impressive: two pitches (the larger about the size of an ice-hockey rink with hi-tech artificial Astroturf), proper goals, spectator grandstands, an electronic scoreboard, and referees. The receptionist said a team needed players and I signed up.

They were called SOP, which stood for either Sons of Perversion or Songs of Persuasion. Or a mixture of the two. I never did find out, because the only person who seemed to know was an African-American in his early twenties, and despite asking him three weeks running and concentrating harder than any person has ever concentrated on anything in the history of the world, I still couldn't decipher his answer.

Even after years here I still struggle with some black people's southern drawl, and many can't understand a word I say either. At a furniture warehouse the African-American foreman asked, "What are you, Australian?"

"No, I'm from Northern Ireland."

"Huh?"

"Irish."

"From Scotland?"

"No, Ireland."

"Right, right. You one of them Vikings?"

Verbal communication with the octogenarian black homeowner opposite our house is impossible. Just after we moved in, I saw him in the street as a car alarm shrilled and I remarked, "Annoying alarm, eh?" He looked at me as if I'd asked to have sex with his cat. I repeated it, he stared at me, and then after an embarrassing pause he said something. I had no idea what it was and looked at him. He knew by my confused face I hadn't got it and said it again. I gawked at him blankly. We stood facing each other for maybe ten seconds in a friendly but silent Mexican standoff, then I said, "Well, nice meeting you. Bye," and waved. He raised his hand in acknowledgment and we both contentedly toddled off.

So every Tuesday I played for SOP, or more accurately POS, as in Pile of Shite. It was four lads in their late teens or early twenties and a few Johnny-no-mates like myself without a team. The youngsters were really, really, really terrible. They were unable to pass, shoot, or tackle, and a couple couldn't even tie their laces properly and spent much of the match chasing after their escaped shoes.

It wasn't just that they were useless (I'm no Pele), but what was so annoying was their aversion to passing the ball. On the extremely rare occasions I'd run the length of the pitch, lay it off, and scream for it back, they'd either run into a defender and fall over or just kick a boot into your stomach.

Every single week I told them the same thing: talk. Yell if you are in space and tell me if there's a man behind me. I don't recall any of them ever saying anything on the field, and if they wanted a pass, they'd either clap like a seal or hoot like an owl. It drove me nuts.

Before one game I gave them positions and explained that as I was the grizzled veteran, I'd "sit" in midfield and they needed to do the running. "Just how old are you?" asked one.

"I'm thirty-four."

"Dude . . . That is old," he nodded sagely.

The state-of-the-art sports arena had all kinds of facilities but just one shower in the dressing room. Another Irishman and I were the only customers who ever used it. I couldn't figure it out; the Americans are hardly a shy, retiring race and surely they don't get embarrassed undressing in front of each other. Once, I was naked and about to shower when an African-American teammate walked in to use the toilet. You've never seen a more shocked expression, and when I spoke to him, he looked at the floor, mumbled something, and almost broke down the door in his rush to get out. Maybe I was the first nude white man he'd ever seen and assumed I'd suffered a terrible penis-shortening accident.

The first season we lost every game bar one; for the second campaign we had a few (slightly) better players and finished halfway up the table, which got us into the play-offs. Somehow we scraped through to the final, where we cruelly lost in sudden-death overtime after playing two games back-to-back. We won tee-shirts reading "Finalists 2005" and one dishonest youth stenciled "Winning" along the top.

The next season it regressed to weekly ritual humiliation, and after one particularly galling game with the headless chickens, I packed it in. My quest for a game resumed.

Ironically it ended less than three miles from home at Audubon Park. The park is split in two by Magazine Street, with an entrance on leafy St. Charles opposite Loyola and Tulane universities. That part features a golf course, pond, playground, and circular running track winding through the shade of the ubiquitous lofty oaks.

On the other side of Magazine is the zoo, with the railway tracks and the levee holding back the Mississippi behind that, and sandwiched between the trains and the water are four pitches. I'd sniffed around them a few times but only ever seen kids, not realizing that hidden in a corner was a baseball diamond with pickup games on Monday and Wednesday evenings.

Silly me: I'd been looking for a soccer field instead of a baseball field. It even had floodlights, although you had to scale a fence and swipe at the switch with a stick to turn them on. This section, called "the Fly," became my soccer-playing hangout for much of the next year.

The standard of play was fairly high, with a smattering of Latinos, a handful of players my age, and a host of skillful college-age Americans. You might think soccer is a universal sport, but it was hard to believe such a simple game could have so many interpretations. It took me months to adapt. Even with eleven-a-side we used the small training goals, and if a defender planted himself between the posts it was impossible to score. There were no corners, so get in trouble deep in your own half and you could simply boot the ball out across the sideline. It wasn't just the variety in tactics and rules; the whole style of play was alien to me. It was much more physical, and opponents (some beefed-up all-American boys) stuck out their hand and held you at arm's length as you tried to tackle.

But above all soccer is a team game and, just like the indoor squad, many here had never learned that. Remember the greedy boy at school who never passed? Sometimes at the Fly that was every player on both sides. It was maddening when someone glided past three opponents only to be dispossessed trying to score rather than pass to a better-placed teammate, and time and again I'd give the ball and look for it back, but the player would be running headlong into a crowd of opponents.

I watched four regulars play keepy-uppy one night. In the U.K. you stand in a circle and kick or head the ball to the person next to you, he flicks it on to the next in turn, and so forth. These guys got the ball and tried a trick before passing, and right there, in that little snapshot, the contrast between the two soccer philosophies was summed up for me. At home get the ball and pass it, here get the ball and show what you can do with it.

Is this symptomatic of American society in general? I think you learn more self-reliance here than in Britain, and you stand on your own two feet or you don't stand at all. Although there are welfare benefits in the States, they are nowhere near as generous as at home with our subsidized housing, free healthcare, and unemployment checks. Culturally, people in the U.S. don't buy rounds of drinks and restaurant bills are often divided up to the penny. Maybe this individualistic view permeates American soccer, and the way Americans play accurately reflects their nation's every-man-for-himself attitude, which overrules the collective team conscious.

Or is it merely that when they were young, they didn't have good coaches and never grew up with the basic understanding of soccer that comes to those where it is a national pastime? They've never experienced big-match fever gripping the country and didn't rush excitedly into the streets with their friends, spending hours pretending to be soccer heroes like George Best, Gerry Armstrong, or David Healy.

Although frequently frustrating, playing at the Fly had one fabulous benefit: the location. It was just yards from the Mighty Mississippi, and when the ball went dead or a teammate was attempting to barge his way through eight players, I'd stand and gaze out over the water. Huge tankers ploughed up and down the river, replica paddleboats languidly cruised by, and little tugs puffed and churned their way to the sea. I'd listen to the ding of their bells and the blast of their horns and see their lights shimmy through the heat haze at dusk. It was beautiful.

Anyway, after meandering more than the Mississippi, I'm back to that conversation with the drinker in Pittsburgh. After playing with the same group twice a week for months, I hadn't made it past "Hi" or "Bye" with anyone. They weren't particularly unfriendly but it was a case of everyone arriving, playing, leaving. Occasionally, if it was *very* hot, some of us might sit on for a while, catch our breath, and make small talk, but nobody seemed to want to make friends and get beyond being casual acquaintances.

When I did try and chat, I picked the guys with Attention Deficit Disorder. Their pupils would drift away and you'd sense their minds wandering, and when they couldn't be bothered listening anymore they'd just walk off mid-sentence and leave you babbling half-heartedly to the insects and mosquitoes. I'd garble away at breakneck speed just to finish a sentence without being either interrupted or ignored.

A few, however, were friendly enough to point out I was sitting on top of a fire ant nest, that their bites were particularly painful, and that I should move right away. This happened three times, my back was plastered with ugly red blotches resembling a strange version of the measles, and I wondered if they thought I was deliberately sitting on the mound of earth just to get a conversation going. Maybe subconsciously I was, although I'm inclined to think I'm just an idiot.

Twice I swapped numbers with lads I thought I clicked with, and at different times I called both inviting them out. One was busy while I left a message for the other, but he never called back. Despite playing dozens of times with the same guys, I hardly knew any of their names, never mind counting them as pals.

But everything was about to change for the better.

CHAPTER 6

I Like to Watch

Although I was worried I might not be able to find a game of soccer to play in America, I knew from previous visits I'd be able to watch more televised English Premiership matches than at home.

The day we signed our rental lease, Julie called the local cable provider, and as she listened to the myriad of choices, packages, and special offers she interrupted: "Listen, just make sure we have Fox Soccer Channel. That's all my husband cares about." I've taught her well. She was also keen to get off the phone because the company was called Cox and our address was Peniston, so she'd laugh every time she had to spell it.

Exploiting the desperation of ex-pats to follow soccer, the company only provided FSC if you bought an expensive digital bundle featuring crap like the Extreme Monopoly Network, the Naked Napkin Folding Channel, and the Send Money to This Minister or Go to Hell Channel, but getting it had been one of my conditions for moving stateside. However, the Sunday 4 P.M. game was always a twenty-dollar pay-per-view event and the season opener on August 15, 2004, was a biggie—Chelsea versus Manchester United—the two best clubs in England. I rang every Irish pub, English bar, and sports grill in the city to find out if it was on for free and was told to try Finn McCool's.

I emailed their Web site and received a reply from Stephen Patterson: "Yes mate, this is THE place in New Orleans to watch football. Come on down on Sunday and meet the lads." The ten-dollar cover charge made it half the price of ordering it at home, and Julie pulled on a scarf and gloves and ran me to Banks Street around 9:30 A.M.

We'd only been here six weeks and hadn't explored beyond the Quarter's tourist traps and Uptown's elegant wine bars, and I was a bit wary arriving at the slightly skuzzy street in Mid-City. But I went in, paid Stephen the ten dollars, and settled down in front of the big screen with a coffee.

Within minutes I was chatting to a sparkly-earring-wearing supporter of the English team Middlesbrough. With his spiky blond hair, Stephen Cullen was a twenty-year-old student from Craigavon in Northern Ireland who'd arrived just thirty-six hours earlier on a scholarship program for students to spend a year at American colleges. He'd been sent to Dillard University, one of New Orleans' two black institutions, and was the only white male out of more than eleven hundred students.

His grandfather knew Stephen Patterson's father and passed on the pub's address, and Stephen had skipped that morning's orientation meeting after pretending he had to attend an important family gathering. I don't blame him; I would've shot my granny to watch Chelsea and Manchester United.

Homesick and lonely, he'd spent the previous day crying in his room, and when he returned home to Northern Ireland, he said meeting me that day was one of the highlights of his time in New Orleans—evidence of his acute isolation, as I was almost his father's age and the sort of old fogey he'd normally have avoided like the plague. We became pals and were known as "the two Irish Stephens." The two male Finn's owners were also Irish Stephens (Patterson and Collins); there were two English Stephens as well, Londoner

Scully and Fisher from Preston, and with Scottish Stephen McAnespie, there could be seven Stephens in the pub at one time.

To tell Stephen Cullen and me apart, the regulars called me Big Stephen and him Little Stephen, even though he was taller. I was delighted; at five feet, six inches I'd never had the adjective applied to me in my life! Less flatteringly (and more commonly), I was Old Stephen and he was Young Stephen.

He had no African-American friends (for reasons that would take another book to examine properly), and he'd often come over to watch games, stay the night, or go for a pizza. He was also a talented, speedy soccer player and was immediately roped into my citywide hunt for a game (everyone we approached would ask, "Wait, you're both called Stephen?"). He joined me at the Fly and then on the indoor squad, though this led to the one bust-up we had.

For once we were winning easily against a team of teenagers (eight goals ahead with two minutes to go) when their goalkeeper lunged clumsily at Young Stephen. He jumped out of the way, and although he could've been hurt if there had been contact, he sidestepped the challenge and the game continued. Young Stephen went ballistic.

He raced to harangue the team's coach about the tackle, shouting and screaming and swearing, oblivious to the game carrying on around him. It left us a man short and I yelled at him to sub out, but he ignored me and kept up the tirade until the match ended and then stormed off in a huff. In the changing room I said he'd overreacted and tried to calm him down, but he was still ranting and raving and in fruity Anglo-Saxon terms told me to mind my own business. The next day he phoned to apologize.

Two days later we walked the length of Magazine Street,

six miles of eclectic shops, funky boutiques, and hip bars and restaurants stretching from the Quarter to Audubon Park. For hours we strolled down one side and back the other, wandering around stores, drinking coffee, and trying free samples from chocolate shops.

I preached like a wizened Jedi master. I told him once upon a time we were all young and fiery, and though it was good he had fire in his belly and was passionate and committed, he must learn to channel his aggression. We'd been cruising comfortably during the game and his actions had left us a player down and harmed the team. If he did it in a close game, it could cost us the match. He could have even been suspended for next week. I droned on and lectured him all day, and he admitted he'd been stupid and promised to control his temper.

The next indoor game was less than two minutes old when a chasing opponent grabbed me around the neck. I turned and swung a punch at him and was sent off. It took a while for Obi Wan to live that one down.

I also met Medhurst that first day in Finn's. The Londoner came to Los Angeles in 1986 to visit a friend and stayed nine years bartending and selling real estate. He moved to New Orleans with a Louisiana girl and worked at a now-defunct English pub before embarking on a banking career in 2000. (As I was a Chelsea supporter, he kept his Tottenham Hotspur allegiance quiet and claimed to be a fan of another London outfit, Leyton Orient, just like the joke about the boy who says his father works as a stripper in a gay club because it's less embarrassing than admitting he plays for Spurs.)

He spotted me as a new face in the bar and introduced himself. He asked if I wanted to join the Finn McCool's membership scheme for two hundred dollars, giving unlimited yearly access rather than paying a cover charge every week. I explained I had FSC at home and didn't think it'd be worth it, but he urged me to think it over and pointed around the room. "That guy over there used to come and sit and watch games on his own. So did he. And him. But now we're all mates together, and sometimes what starts out as a quick trip down to the pub to watch a match ends up as a full-scale, all-day bender."

It was a blatant attempt to appeal to the stereotype of a hard-drinking Irishman and I agreed to consider it. He said he'd keep track of the money I paid and would stop charging if I hit two hundred dollars. I wrestled with joining for weeks but ultimately decided against it for three reasons.

The first was financial. Neither Julie nor I were working, and as we were already paying to have soccer piped into the house, I would have felt guilty handing over another couple of hundred dollars before we were on sound monetary footing. And that was just the membership fee—I'd spend more at the bar every weekend.

Secondly, it didn't feel right to make a habit of heading down to the pub before 9 A.M. At home when you go to your local bar to watch a game it's in the afternoon or evening, and it's usually dark, miserable, and raining outside. Bloody weather. You don't fall out of bed on Saturday, eat breakfast, and then go to the bar when the sky is blue, the birds are singing, and the sun is blazing.

The weather was still new and exciting, and I'd wake up, look out the window, and think, "Great! It's a lovely day and the sun is shinning. We should go and do something . . ." In Ulster this is the reaction to the infrequent and thus cherished balmy summer's day, and this conditioned response is deeply ingrained in us. I didn't want to waste my weekends in a dark room with the curtains closed to stop sunlight from reflecting on the TV screen.

Of course after a couple of months you realize the sun shines everyday and you are desperate for any excuse to stay in the shady, cool inside. Bloody weather.

But the biggest factor was a gut feeling it just wasn't the right thing to do. I'd moved to New Orleans to start a fresh new chapter in my life, meet new people, and experience new things. I was determined to make American friends and integrate into the community. It seemed too easy to go to an Irish pub, sit with a bunch of ex-pats, and slag off the USA while talking about how much better things were back home, an attitude I'd experienced elsewhere in the States.

Apart from anything else, it's rude to come and live here then spend your life complaining about it. I'm not saying immigrants aren't allowed to criticize their adopted homeland, and God knows there are plenty of things wrong with America, but there are plenty of things right with it as well. If you're whining and miserable, then go home. Nobody forced you to come here. Actually, my wife did kind of force me . . .

The point is that I assumed Finn's would be full of cliquey Yank-bashers and I intended to go there infrequently. I pledged to ration my soccer-watching pub-going to once a month and suggested the one hundred dollars we'd save over a ten-month season would pay for a Chelsea bedspread. Unfortunately Julie already had all our spare cash earmarked for thermal underwear and hats.

What I didn't know was that the Irish satellite company Setanta, which takes 80 percent of the cover charge, insists that licensed premises double the entrance fee for international games between countries in the World Cup qualifying competition. So in September I watched Poland beat Northern Ireland and with more World Cup games the next month, I thought I'd be kissing goodbye to the bar until the New Year.

But Medhurst offered me the chance to see the October ties for free in return for collecting cash at the door. He knew I wanted to see them but that money was tight, and his generous gesture was typical of the club's welcoming, inclusive attitude. He even took over in the afternoon, allowing me to watch the games undisturbed, and come January I'd spent sixty dollars and was on target to stay within my budget. I was also beginning to appreciate the community spirit of the Finn's crowd.

Some matches I listened to via the radio commentary broadcast over the internet. When Northern Ireland went to Azerbaijan, I tuned into Radio Ulster and called my pilot pal Gordon Sheals with updates, meaning my mate who lived in San Diego and was on a runway in Denver about to fly to San Francisco knew what was happening in Baku from me in New Orleans via a Belfast station.

He returned the favor as I ate with my visiting friends Conrad, Julie, and Oliver Smyth in the Riverwalk mall's packed cavernous food court when we played Wales. He rang to say we were leading 2-0 and I leaped up, punched the air, and shouted, "F—king yes!" which rather shocked the hundreds of Southern Baptists surrounding us on a lunch break from their conference at next door's Convention Center.

For two weeks I subscribed to ESPN Deportes, the Spanish-language version of ESPN, solely to see Chelsea play the Spanish giant Barcelona in a Champions League tie. The Spanish-language commentary made an enthralling contest even more exciting, as every goal kick or foul was treated like the second coming of Christ. When someone actually scored, the commentator exploded into a yell of, "GOOOOOOOOOOOOOL!!!!!" which made your throat raw just listening to it and lasted longer than some teams' participation in the competition. If I could have afforded it, I would have kept the subscription for the hysterical Latino soundtrack alone.

But mostly I was reduced to watching Chelsea on the internet. A high-speed connection and a nine-dollar annual charge allowed access to a Web site offering "streamed" live games. I don't know who was behind it and I presume it was illegal, but every match day they posted a list of upcoming televised games and a link redirected you to the applicable site.

Often there were seven or eight choices per game and sometimes the link told you which country's coverage you were dropping in on. They were nearly always Asian but occasionally something obscure like Slovenian or Moldovan, and a few, such as Hong Kong's Star TV, even had English commentators and ex-professionals summarizing at halftime.

But as you'd imagine with such a cheap option there were both technical and psychological drawbacks. The clarity and quality could be topnotch, and if I got an English-language channel from the Far East, it really was like watching a miniature TV. This was the best-case scenario, but I still had to hunch forward and squint at the three-inch screen like a short-sighted surgeon.

More often than not I'd click the link, nothing would happen, and after a few minutes I'd get an error message. So I'd try another URL address, pause expectantly, have my hopes dashed by a "site has reached capacity" missive, sigh, try the next one, and so on and so forth until finally by halftime I had admitted defeat and was following BBC Web site updates. After two months of this I read a forum posting urging users to "hold the stream early"—i.e. guarantee access by securing the link hours in advance. This was when the psychological problems arose.

In theory, once I was satisfied the picture was up and running, I'd minimize it on my monitor and get on with my life, doing things like (for instance) writing that book that I promised my wife was occupying my time while I lazed around the house as she was out working her fingers to the bone and buying sweaters everyday. For instance. But in practice, of course, it was different.

I would sit and torture myself that one of the other links had better quality. Maybe there's a touch of ghosting on the Bulgarian nature channel I've tuned into. As users can only hold one stream at a time, should I gamble and release it in favor of that Taiwanese station, which is normally pretty good? Or do I stick with what I have?

Sometimes the signal had great color, contrast, and clarity but a Cantonese commentary. Do I give it up and search for an English-language broadcast? Or is there someone huddled over a computer in Outer Mongolia right now, blowing on his fingers and twitching like a Wild West quick-draw gunslinger, poised to nab my spot as soon as I sign off?

Other days I locked on a high-definition perfect picture two hours before kickoff, but due to the unreliable scheduling information of the guerilla-like Web site, I wasn't watching Chelsea play Liverpool, but a less-than-fascinating examination of the history of the Philippine post office. In Serbo-Croat.

With a crushing inevitability this led to my becoming hooked on Chinese soap operas. Part of me secretly rejoiced when instead of watching a white-hot top-of-the-table clash featuring Chelsea, I was treated to the latest gossip from the Beijing equivalent of *Desperate Housewives*.

True, the dialogue was a smidgeon hard to follow at times, but in a world where characters stalked, stormed, or slinked their way around the set it was easy to tell the goodies (wearing white, happy smiling faces, girls small and demure, men strong and handsome) from the baddies (dressed in black, permanent scowl, females conniving crones, males shifty baldies). And talk about drama! If the camera zipping from startled freeze-framed face to face wasn't enough of a clue something major had happened, there was always the wild, screeching orchestral music threatening to blast apart your computer speakers. The plot nuances may have escaped me, but I could still shake my head and mutter to myself, "Poor Wan Li. Will she never realize Sun Wah doesn't love her? Why can't she see she should be with Goi Ka?"

I was saved from this growing addiction by an excited call from Young Stephen one Monday morning in February. He said: "Hey old man, I was at the pub on Saturday and guess what? Finn McCool's is starting an over-thirty-five football team and are looking for players. Even crap ones like you."

I'd turned thirty-five nine weeks before. The timing was perfect. But I never did find out what happened to Wan Li.

CHAPTER 7

Finn McCool's

I knew that Finn's was unique as soon as I walked in. It was bedecked in Glasgow Celtic flags, the Republic of Ireland's tricolor, and traditional (Catholic) Irish motifs and emblems. And sitting at the bar were two drinkers with Loyalist (Protestant) tattoos and Glasgow Rangers shirts.

I was stunned, and for a few seconds I thought I'd stumbled into an elaborate practical joke and tried to spot the hidden cameras. I'd be surprised if you could find a similar scene anywhere in the world, definitely not in Glasgow and never in a million years in Belfast. In fact, at times during the Troubles, Protestants who found themselves in a "Catholic" pub—and vice versa—were shot dead. It even happened to strangers merely suspected of being the "wrong religion," and I grew up with horrific tales like this on the news.

But 2004 New Orleans was thousands of miles and decades away from the dark days of terrorist-torn Northern Ireland, and the three Celtic-supporting owners were determined to make everyone feel welcome. Even Rangers fans.

Stephen and Pauline Patterson, both thirty-eight, from Craigavon and Belfast, thought they had few prospects in a country apparently bent on violently cleaving itself in half. They first visited New Orleans in 1988, then worked in New Jersey for three consecutive summers. But it seemed half of Belfast was there too, and Stephen, tall and broad with sculptured sideburns down to his mouth, and Pauline, short with a cherubic smile, grew sick of seeing the same old faces and situations they were trying to escape. Stephen suggested looking up a contact in the Big Easy and called Stevie Collins because their fathers worked in the same factory back home.

Lurgan-born Stevie, forty-two, is taller, thinner, and quieter than Stephen. The epitome of the term "silent partner," he's happiest perched at the end of the bar smoking, content to read the paper or watch TV alone. Cliché-like, when you get to know him you discover his wicked dry sense of humor.

He immigrated to Florida in 1989, then wound up in Louisiana with friends who had answered an advertisement for an Irish band to play on Bourbon Street. Some learned to play instruments on the journey over and when they arrived they boasted a repertoire stretching to all of four songs.

Pauline was an art college graduate and Stevie got her a job with him in the heraldry department of O'Flaherty's, an Irish store and bar in the Quarter. The Pattersons found the first couple of years hard. Stephen struggled to find employment, money was tight, and they relied on friends' generosity, as they could barely afford groceries. They had little or no social life and would go six months without leaving the Quarter. They had overstayed their holiday visas so they dared not go home, as they'd be banned from reentering the country, and they had no cash to fund a move to another city. Stephen's grandparents died and he couldn't go to the funerals. They were trapped.

But caged in the heart of the city, they fell in love with New Orleans, and by 1992 they had green cards and Stephen was also working at O'Flaherty's as a barman. The highlight of his month was the arrival from New York of a three-hour video costing twenty dollars and featuring edited English soccer matches. They would all throw in a couple of bucks and excitedly pile into the back room of Ryan's, another Irish bar in the Quarter, to watch action weeks out of date.

American interest in soccer was nudged to life by the success of the 1994 World Cup Finals, which the country hosted, and the odd game like the Champions League final began to guiltily sneak onto national channels like ESPN. The next tournament in France four years later stirred it further awake, and Stephen and a few others bought a satellite dish for O'Flaherty's to tune into British games every weekend. They became the New Orleans Celtic Supporters Club, though Englishmen like Medhurst had no interest in Scottish soccer, and even more bizarrely a founding member was Big Rab, the dyed-in-the-wool Rangers fan from Paisley.

Stephen says, "You'd get a few guys in for a game and then not see them again for months. The Quarter can be a pain in the arse for locals, as parking was always difficult, the drink was too dear, and the vibe wasn't conducive to making friends. But it was all we had at the time." Medhurst reckons he'd blow fifty dollars every visit.

Come 2002, Pauline was working in an Irish pub called Mick's but had branched out into selling real estate, Stephen was still at O'Flaherty's, and Stevie was behind the bar at The Kerry, yet another Irish watering hole in the Quarter. They were renovating buildings together and kicking around the idea of opening their own place when a client asked Pauline to find him a bar to buy. She offered him a dive on Banks Street called Joe's 19th Hole but he declined, and the trio considered purchasing it, but then they passed too.

In the spring the price was reduced and they took the plunge, jumping straight into a frantic race against time to renew the out-of-date liquor license, which would expire for good if not reactivated within six months. The permit was granted five months and thirty days after lapsing.

Stevie says, "It was an easy decision to make but a harder decision to live with. The place was a s—t-hole with a terrible reputation. We had to kick out the hookers—it was 'liquor' out front and 'poker' out back—but we wanted to give all the customers a chance to start with a clean slate, and to be fair we never had anyone mess with us."

They gutted the structure, tearing down the walls, installing more windows, demolishing the low-hanging ceiling, and stripping the frame back to the studs. They opened on Friday, July 26, 2002, and shortly afterward Stephen left O'Flaherty's to concentrate fulltime on Finn's.

The following year they bought dishes and TVs, and the Celtic club, which had been suffocating at O'Flaherty's with membership dwindling to single figures, now had a secure, sympathetic home. Stephen actively promoted it and sent out a weekly email listing upcoming televised games, and Medhurst volunteered to collect the cover charge and control the finances. By the summer of 2004, Finn's was the only venue with the Euro Finals and had cemented its place as *the* "football" pub in New Orleans.

So, what's so special about Finn's? For a start, it's the friendliest pub I've ever been in. And I've been in a lot.

Stephen says, "We don't have the best location in the world, so we have to try hard to convince people to come here because very few of our customers live close by. In O'Flaherty's there were a couple of head bangers who wanted to start trouble but we weeded them out of here. The football is the most important thing and because we aren't a large community we all have to band together to survive.

"Whether it's Rangers and Celtic or British and Irish, it doesn't matter. There are no politics here. We've fought hard to enforce that rule: wear your colors with pride, and if anybody has a problem with it, then it's their problem. The great thing is that we own the pub and we make the rules."

Stevie nods in agreement. "Down here it's not like in New York or San Francisco where there are twenty different Irish bars with a Galway pub, an Armagh pub, and so on, and where you've every rural parochial paper from Cullybackey to Cork. We never liked that and wanted Finn's to be a reflection of New Orleans and its diverse mix of people.

"The majority of our regulars are local and we're not just an ex-pats' pub, though if you want to come along on a Saturday just to watch the football and we don't see you again until the following weekend, that's fine too."

Secondly, the clientele is eclectic and eccentric, a polite way of saying they're a bunch of weirdoes. I doubt there's ever been such a concentration of characters anywhere at any time as there usually is at Finn's on a Friday night. Everyone is christened with a nickname.

You've already briefly met Dave the Rave, the self-confessed world's oldest teenager tragically trapped inside a forty-six-year-old's body. With a porn star moustache. He's been here since 1996, when he fancied working in the States, heard a newscaster mention the cool-sounding name "Baton Rouge" in a story about an election primary, and immediately decided that's where he'd go. The agency dealing with his job application talked him into going to New Orleans instead, and he first stepped foot in Finn's in May 2003 when it was jammed to the rafters for a big European club final.

He's often found drinking with fellow Englishman Mushroom Mike Castro. One night Dave ate a sweet Mike gave him, went to the bathroom, and came out to find the bar had turned turquoise. He said to himself, "What's happened here? Why has Stephen Patterson turned green? And his hair purple?"

One of those Northern Irish Rangers fans at the start of the chapter is prone to bouts of heavy drinking and depression. When he dropped off the radar for five days, the regulars feared he'd killed himself, until someone thought to try the jail. Sure enough he was sharing a cell with crackheads who were buying drugs from the guards and shooting up with their own concoction made from mixing floor cleaner and Kool-Aid. Luckily another Finn's regular, lawyer Loophole Larry, got him out.

I tell you, all human life is there.

In a city hopelessly racially divided in every imaginable way, Finn's is also the only New Orleans bar I go to where, at least to some degree, whites and African-Americans mingle. Stevie says, "We've even had friends ask, 'Why do you let the blacks in?' We go out of our way to ensure that anyone who works here always welcomes and greets customers no matter who they are or what color their skin is."

It's hardly an earth-shattering contention that immigrants with similar upbringings and interests will gravitate towards each other. I was determined not to get caught in the ex-pat whirlpool but was sucked into the Finn's vortex, spiraling down helplessly and landing elbow-to-elbow at the bar with fellow Paddies and Brits. At least that's my excuse to Julie.

It may well be a friendly locale, but after Dave said he had lots of American buddies and never hung around with ex-pats until he started going to Finn's, it got me thinking: Has Finn's had a damaging, isolating effect on us immigrants? Does going there stop us from properly integrating into American society? My teammates think not.

Medhurst explains, "There are American bartenders and a

lot of the customers are American and you go there because you are made to feel very welcome. If anything, it's opened us up to meeting more Americans, because although I went for the football at first, I got to meet all these locals I wouldn't have met otherwise."

Paul agrees. "Football started our relationships but we're such a diverse group it's easy to relax and make friends. There are people from all over the place, and the tone you pick up as soon as you enter is that this is a bar for everybody and you need to leave politics outside."

Dave adds, "It's an oasis within America, just a tiny piece of Britain and Ireland offering snugness and familiarity, little things to let us know our culture is alive and kicking so we can keep our national identity while living in their country."

South African Benji, in his typically blunt manner, makes the same point slightly differently. "Foreigners here will stick together. Even if we have our differences there's a cultural familiarity, and because we're all in the same boat we'll deal with that s—t. Even if it means hanging out with a load of jerks."

Benji first went to Finn's for the 2003 Rugby World Cup. "I'd just watch the rugby and leave because I imagined it'd be the same as O'Flaherty's, where they overcharged you for flat draft beer and treated you as a second-class citizen because you weren't Irish. But I made an effort to talk to some people and they weren't total jerks like I expected.

"The World Cup was a defining point because my buddy Jonathan and I are both arrogant jerks and we went in there shouting the odds and acting like a-holes, but we never got thrown out and people actually seemed to enjoy us. It was a lot of fun and I thought, 'Man, they're a pretty cool bunch of people,' and I started going there purely socially."

But there must be more to it than a shared background and a collective interest in soccer. There are at least four other Irish pubs in the Quarter alone, and everyone agrees the difference in atmosphere between Finn's and O'Flaherty's, for example, is night and day.

Big Rab says, "Watching matches there, it was always quiet and nowhere near as warm or friendly. Even if there are only two or three of us in Finn's, you still enjoy the game, and you probably aren't even exclusively concentrating on it, but sitting back and chatting about all kinds of things."

In contrast Billy likes not having to talk all the time. "The beautiful thing about Finn's is that you can go in at 9 A.M. and everyone is staring at the TV. They are following the football and they know you're there, but they're happy just watching the game and don't feel they need to indulge in small-talk. That's awesome."

Shell Shockers coach Kenny trained soccer clubs in the city after arriving in 1995 following a career in the League of Ireland and four years at college in Massachusetts and was in Finn's the day it opened, although, "I'm scared to walk about there at night!" However, he says, "The pub gives you the environment and the owners go out of their way to make you feel comfortable, but you're there to enjoy the atmosphere the people create. It's like having a great time at a wedding—it's neither the food nor the drink that make it memorable, but the guests."

If going to Finn's is like going to a wedding, I was about to attend an awful lot of ceremonies . . .

CHAPTER 8

And So It Begins . . .

I was home.

After months with guys who barely acknowledged me, I knew from the first training session with Finn's it was where I belonged. I could pinpoint accents, tell which clubs the lads supported, and didn't have to explain why a club team like Chelsea wasn't playing against countries like Brazil in the World Cup.

I'd emailed Stephen about the team and he answered, "Yes, we are getting a squad together, mate, but it's a bit disorganized at the minute." On the contrary, this was the most organized game I'd been involved in since arriving.

We met at the pub then caravanned two miles to the aptly named St. Patrick's Street, where a parched pitch shared a field with a rutted baseball diamond. I rode with Stephen Fisher, thirty-three, an English computer programmer from Preston called "Captain Morgan" because of his resemblance to the pirate on the rum bottle. He'd been sent to New Orleans nine years ago by a recruitment company: "I wanted to explore America and it was just the luck of the draw where you went. The chance to live here seemed like a challenge, a fantasy, like something you see in the movies, and New Orleans was a fun place with a great climate."

We stretched, jogged, and then ran through a variety of warm-up exercises led by Eric Althouse, a thirty-four-year-old furniture maker from North Carolina with a coaching license. He looked like a Harley-Davidson rider with his beard, thickset build, bandana, sleeveless shirt, and arms plastered in tattoos, and it didn't take much to psych him up. Sometimes in the pub after a few drinks he'd try to force you to punch him in the face ("Watch out. Eric's on the loony juice," Medhurst would warn).

Big Rab handed out bibs and we had a game. Though it was early February and supposed to be winter, it was roasting and the frequent breaks had us diving for water like we'd walked across the Sahara. Some lads had talent but were badly out of shape, others had only turned up for a bit of fun, and a handful had obviously never kicked a ball in anger in their life. I was confident I'd found my level and didn't need to worry I'd be humiliated by some lightning-quick college kid, and because I was fitter than nearly everyone, I scored four goals, enjoyed it immensely, and we all adjourned to Finn's.

On my first visit to Finn's, I'd asked Medhurst why there was no pub team and he said they played kickball, so what had changed since August? I need to backtrack a little and introduce you to Adrian Simpson.

Chunky Adrian, christened "Chucky" by Benji after the waddling doll in the *Child's Play* film, had worn sunglasses the whole first session and confessed he tried to kick me all day after taking an instant dislike to me because of my ponytail. In a Finn's world inhabited by larger-than-life figures, Scouser Adrian, thirty-four, says he's the largest of them all. He'll also tell you it was his idea to start the team. He has a limitless supply of stories, most of which end, "But you can't put that in the book." When he gets warmed up, he's hard to stop.

"At university I got the chance to come to the States to study history, and I literally got a pin and stuck it in a map and the closest place I'd heard of was New Orleans. So the nearest I could get was Baton Rouge, and the night before me and my mate Angus were due to leave we had a huge party with all our mates and all our families and everything, and it was great and when we woke up the next morning I said, 'F—k it, let's not even go.'

"But we did go and Louisiana State University was magic and everything was paid for and we just had to pass ten classes, so after about three weeks we were hammered every night. We'd drink with all the professors and I was dead set on trying to shag a bird of every different color.

"It wasn't a high intellectual standard—I'll never forget the first day of this World War II class when the lecturer asked if there were any questions before he kicked into it, and this bird stood up and said, 'Yes, who won World War II?' I thought she was talking about some deep philosophical interpretation, but no, it was just a reflection of the level of education. She honestly didn't know who'd won the war.

"Everyday we'd go for lunch from about 11 A.M. until two in the morning and there'd be loads of people around our table, and one day a local entertainment reporter came over and wanted to write a story about Angus and me. In the newspaper we were described as the biggest thing to hit Baton Rouge since the Sex Pistols.

"We'd get invited to lots of parties and movie openings and be very pretentious and do acid trips and lived this rock 'n' roll lifestyle and never do any work, so near the end of term I was one class short, which meant I would've got into trouble with the student exchange body.

"Then I was out of my head one night and sang 'You'll Never Walk Alone' [a traditional Liverpudlian soccer anthem], and this teacher said he'd give me an A if I promised to sing it at his wedding in a few weeks. So that was okay. I never did it, though, because we all got s—t-faced one night and he got arrested and taken to this place called Tent City, where we had to pay money into a little account for him so he could buy fags and stuff and I felt really guilty.

"We went to New Orleans to stay with a mate's sister for a couple of months and b.s.'d our way into jobs as roofers. They asked if we could build scaffolding, and we said, 'Oh yeah, no problem,' and when we didn't have a clue what to do, we pretended the stuff was all different here to what we were used to back home.

"After a day they said, 'You've never done this before, have you?' but they were cool and we were the only two white boys on the crew. We were living in the Quarter and they showed us the city and we got second-degree burns working on a hospital roof and I went to a transvestite's funeral after meeting a guy dressed as a nun and we had a fantastic time.

"I went back home after a year and got a good job in the corporate world but was always interested in returning, and I came back in 2000 for a sabbatical and hooked up with a buddy running a coffee company. He asked me to work for them and sponsored me for a green card and I flew back here on September 11, 2001.

"I first went to Finn's to watch the English FA Cup Final in May 2003. I missed having a local but didn't want to hang around with English people all the time, but you realize you are only trying to run away from yourself. It's a big decision to go and live in a different country and create a life here and you can't beat yourself up about going to Finn's and spending time with people you have a big connection with."

I told you he could talk.

Things were always happening to Adrian. In England he'd worked for Coca-Cola's marketing department and ran a competition for youngsters to win mountain bikes.

It was a big event attended by lovable children's TV star Mr. Blobby (described by Adrian as "a right c−t") and ended with Adrian on stage in front of the media and lots of excited kids. When he announced the winner of the first bike, the crowd parted to reveal a disabled child in a wheelchair. Embarrassed and panicking, Adrian whispered to the father that they'd give him the cash value instead, but the parent, misinterpreting the offer as a slight to his son, began to shout and scream and had to be restrained from attacking Adrian.

Another time he was on the judging panel of a kids' talent show contest with the local mayor at a Butlin's holiday camp in Wales. One entrant had a learning difficulty and alternated playing the fiddle and telling jokes, and the mayor, who'd had a few drinks, leaned across to Adrian and said, "You know, I think this lad's a bit ta-ta." Adrian smiled indulgently at his drunken colleague just as the video director flashed a closeup of the judges on the screen above the stage. It looked like Adrian was making fun of a disabled child, and before he knew it he was pinned to the wall by the father with the menacing question, "Were you laughing at my son?" Adrian made sure the boy won first place.

He'd been involved in trying to twin New Orleans and Liverpool, two ports with other common links such as dockland regeneration, and had spent months in meetings before someone thought to check the records. Turned out Liverpool was already twinned with New York. However, he was awarded the title Honorary Citizen of New Orleans in recognition of his wasted work, and the certificate honoring him signed by the mayor and council members hangs above his toilet.

Adrian maintains the team was his idea, although Kenny

also claims the credit. But it had its genesis in the kickball league started by Finn's staff and featuring the likes of Medhurst, Dave, and Paul. The team spirit and camaraderie engendered a nostalgic desire to play soccer again, but they ruled it out, as they considered themselves too old, too unfit, or too old and too unfit.

But at a heavy weekend drinking session in January (my money's on the fifteenth, the day of a big game between Manchester United and Liverpool), someone suggested organizing a kick-around. Participants in this drunken discussion were Adrian, Kenny, Dave, Medhurst, and Big Rab, and according to Adrian, "We were all s—t-faced," so we'll probably never know who mentioned it first.

What's not disputed is that they met at St. Patrick's the following Saturday afternoon. It was an inauspicious beginning. Kenny brought bibs and cones and led the one-hour session, which started with a gentle jog around the pitch to get the blood flowing. After that a couple of the guys said, "Okay, no thanks, that's enough for me," and went back to the bar.

Paul says, "We hadn't even started and we'd lost two already! Even though training was at a slightly raised walking pace, many of them were doubled over in pain."

Young Stephen was also there. "I remember the grunts and groans from players stretching muscles which hadn't been stretched in a long time. We tried to do a drill in which a player in the middle hits the ball around the circle but nobody could pass that far. It was the biggest disaster I'd ever seen in my life."

Kenny says, "I was worried that someone would keel over, and some were nervous and shaking and pulling out gear they hadn't worn for twenty years. I wanted to make sure it was not a muck-around and get a little serious, but we also wanted everyone to feel they could get better so they'd come back. That day a lot of the lads realized the other sports they'd been playing were just a poor substitute for football."

So when I showed up the team was a week old. That first day I cadged a lift back to Finn's from Mike McInerney, a thirty-nine-year-old portly computer technician known as "Mike Mac," whom Young Stephen and I had met at Riverside in embarrassing circumstances. We were chatting before our game, a rematch against a Brazilian team we'd had a previous fiery encounter with when they'd lost their tempers, spat at us, and had a man sent off. We knew one of their players was sitting beside us but poked fun at them anyway, confident he wouldn't speak much English and even if he did he'd be unable to decipher our quick-fire Ulster accents.

Suddenly he turned to us and asked in a Limerick brogue, "So where are you boys from?" Mike Mac was the only non-Brazilian and had been recruited by his son's friend's father, but thankfully we hadn't offended him and he happily jacked in the Samba Boys for Finn's.

After training we were dirty and stinky and sweaty and smelly, but at Finn's no one cared. Pizzas arrived and were passed around, and I never bought a drink the whole day, as players practically wrestled each other for the chance to stand a round for the team.

Julie arrived to pick me up and as she removed her hat and scarf, I introduced her to the lads. "Don't be tiring him out—he's a good player," said Adrian. It was the greatest compliment of my soccer career.

CHAPTER 9

Marði Gras

We trained every Saturday. Some guys showed for a week or two then quit, blaming work commitments or a twinge from an old injury, and pub regulars, friends, and acquaintances revolved in and out. Dave said after a couple of sessions he could already tell who'd stick at it ("players with history"), while a year later Eric recalled, "I remember those days as the best times of all."

Young Stephen was an ever-present despite his tender years, and my third practice was abruptly curtailed when I had to rush him to the hospital. He'd poked the ball through Dave's legs, and our old warhorse hadn't taken kindly to the move by the boyish buck and threatened to "break his f—king legs." At a corner shortly afterwards, they'd both attacked the ball like their lives depended on it and Dave's head cracked into Young Stephen's left eye socket and split it open. Blood gushed like Old Faithful in Yellowstone Park and play was stopped—so we could one up each other in a comedic commentary.

Luckily, Jonathan Walsh, a thirty-three-year-old lawyer from New Jersey, had medical training from his part-time Coast Guard service. He handed over a bright red tee-shirt to press against the gash and camouflage the blood. Dave maintained it was an accident, while Young Stephen was adamant the cut on the back of Dave's head proved he had turned away and chickened out of the challenge. Young Stephen needed six stitches and still has the scar.

The four-hour emergency room tedium was enlivened by

a heated altercation between a white visitor in his thirties and a middle-aged black patient. The white guy warned the black man to stop chatting up a teenage girl sitting with her mother, but the black guy told him to mind his own business, as he wasn't hitting on her but just being friendly.

Two armed guards arrived to sort it out, my first experience of pistol-toting security officers in a medical facility. Fresh from playing soccer with a group of lads from the British Isles, it was a stark reminder New Orleans is a long way from home, and not just geographically. Then again, maybe the guns weren't much different from life in Belfast.

After practice we'd go to Finn's to relive the session, swap histories, and make new friends. If I thought Julie's and my decision to come to New Orleans was a touch arbitrary, it was nothing compared to the randomness of some others. Big Rab had applied to work in America in 1994 and didn't know he was headed to New Orleans until his plane ticket arrived two days before he left. Paul decided after two years in Aberdeen he wasn't prepared to face another Scottish winter and would accept the next job offer no matter where it was.

Mike Mac's wife, Marian, had been offered nursing posts in Louisiana and Savannah and they chose by flipping a coin. Mike had got a job selling meat from the back of a van and on his first day was told to go door-to-door in the small Mississippi town of Pass Christian. Before he could sell anything, someone called the cops on him, and with no driver's license or vehicle break tag he was arrested. After two hours at the police station he drove back, parked the truck, and walked away, but they stayed in New Orleans.

Silver-haired Galway native Sean Kennedy, forty-three, and his wife, Carmel, applied for U.S. and Australian visas in 1991 and decided to move to whichever country responded first. They came to New Orleans for no other reason than Carmel's cousin, who lived in the region, suggested it during a visit to Ireland, and just like the Pattersons, they'd found it tough at first.

Sean remembers, "We had some awfully lonely nights. It was very hard to get a job because although I was reasonably skilled and on decent money at home, our credentials counted for nothing here. I got a job I was massively overqualified for, but once I got a start and Carmel got her nursing exams, the American Dream was very good to us."

We often analyze why we had so much fun with Finn's but failed to build relationships with American footballers. He tells me, "After our first training session I said to Carmel, 'I'm as happy today as I've ever been since coming to the States.' I loved it and wish it'd happened years ago.

"I'd not laughed so much in a long time because there were a lot of quick-witted, entertaining funsters. The effort and skill impressed me, but more than that we'd great fun during and after, and right away you knew a lot of us had something in common.

"The very first game I ever played in America I really enjoyed but I swear to God, I didn't even have my shoes and socks off and I looked up to see that everyone had gone home and I was sitting alone in the middle of the field.

"We're from a society where we see our mates on a Friday night and we're all missing that because having dinner with the wives isn't filling that vacuum. I experienced a great spirit for the first time in fourteen years and it was wonderful to be a part of it. Before we started I'd only drink in Finn's occasionally, but now I go a lot more and if none of the lads are there it's not the same."

I also became good friends with Benji, who had moved from Baton Rouge with his African-American wife, Shawn, because they were a mixed-race couple. He said, "That town's way too conservative and it's also really lame, so when she got offered a job here we were happy to move.

"The subculture in New Orleans is that you can be a freak and no one cares because there are so many other freaks, and we are freaks because we are an interracial couple. There are racists here as well, but it was never going to work out in Baton Rouge."

Opinionated Benji left South Africa in 1996 to see the world but ran out of money after four months in Europe, and not ready to return home he went to Baton Rouge to work as a rugby coach because his father had started the university team there. He was intending to stay only a few months but never moved back.

Though he grew up in South Africa, he'd been born in Baton Rouge and jokingly considers himself "African-American." As he was the only African-American on the team, we nicknamed him "Token."

He says, "I was stuck in Louisiana financially but also politically. At home I'd been involved in politics and worked for a newspaper, dodging bullets in townships, which was exciting but dangerous. Most of my countrymen are shy and reticent and not outspoken like me, so I freak them out and that's why I spent most of my time in jail or getting shot at!

"Here I had a great lifestyle, I was making enough money as a gardener to get by, and I spent my time partying and chasing chicks. When I went back to visit in 2000, I realized that I had changed, the country had changed, and I was no longer a South African but an American.

"I was very dismissive when I heard about the football team and thought it was for losers. I'd tell them, 'F—k you, soccer jerks—I play rugby,' so no one ever invited me to play. I'd hear talk about an over-thirty-fives team, but I assumed as I wasn't English they wouldn't want me, but finally Adrian asked me along because he thought I'd make the team."

Just as Benji started coming to training, we broke for Mardi Gras. For months neighbors and Julie's workmates had gripped our arms excitedly and gasped, "Your first Mardi Gras. Oh my God! I'm so excited for you! You're going to love it!" We'd smile patronizingly and think what a load of simpletons the locals must be to get so worked up over a couple of parades.

My friend Neil McKeown once worked for a tourist office in Donaghadee, a small seaside town in Northern Ireland, and I went to see their summer parade. They had seven floats, one of which was a bus. A regular, run-of-the-mill, boring old bus. It wasn't cunningly crafted into the shape of a cat, it hadn't been decorated with thousands of twinkling lights, and it didn't have disco music pumping from a PA perched precariously on the roof. It was just a bus. It wasn't even a double-decker. It hadn't been washed. It was only because of the yellow Float Five sticker I knew it hadn't blundered into the parade by accident. So I envisaged that Fat Tuesday would be about as exciting as the Lord Mayor's show in Belfast: a few floats rolling through the neighborhood followed by a night on Bourbon Street with excited girls flashing their breasts and drunken guys tossing them beads.

In fact the celebrations are truly wonderful, last for weeks, and are almost exclusively family orientated. Everyone should experience Mardi Gras in New Orleans at least once, and if I were a politician I'd lobby for it to be mandatory for all citizens. A kind of national service.

In a city where the tourist industry is built on visitors getting wild and crazy, Mardi Gras is the party that New Orleans throws for itself in residential areas miles from the Quarter. The streets heave with adults and kids for the nightly parades and shops sell specially adapted, seven-foot-tall highchairs for the children. They sit in them and yell and wave at the floats, shouting, "Throw me sumthin', mister!" so masked riders ("krewe" members) will lob them presents ("throws").

The riders can be elderly women, carefully and deliberately peeling off one plastic bead necklace at a time and gracefully dispensing it with a wrist action reminiscent of the Queen Mother playing darts. Other floats rock with dozens of beer-swilling members who sing along to loud music and hurl their bounty to the outer reaches of the spectators.

It can cost thousands of dollars to ride with a krewe and you'll spend the same again on throws, but even so most have long waiting lists. Members pay for everything out of their own pocket and there's no corporate sponsorship like, "This Mardi Gras float brought to you commercial free by Pepsi." Some krewes hold post-parade parties in the Superdome, the largest building of its kind in the world, and it's upwards of one hundred dollars just to get in, no food or drink included.

Throws range from plastic bracelets costing a few cents to elaborate hi-tech musical medallions with flashing LCD lights. We caught thousands and thousands of beads, and I feared we would have to move to a bigger house to store them. Even now I try to fob them off on family and friends who visit, and when they decline any more because their cases are full to bursting, I'll sneak a few extra into their luggage or stuff a handful into their carry-on. We piled up an unbelievable array of booty, from squishy footballs (both European and American!) to wooden spears to teddy bears to Frisbees to miniature flushing Mardi Gras toilets.

As each float creeps closer, the crowd works itself into a frenzy in anticipation of grabbing a bouncy ball or a toy whistle. With their arms flailing, spectators lunge at the falling goodies, viciously elbowing grandmothers in the face and knocking toddlers into a crumpled heap. Some individuals sink to pitiful depths. But I honestly didn't see that old dear. And at her age she would've only needed that eye for another two years anyway. Three at the most.

Each parade starts with a shower of doubloons, shiny colorful coins embossed with mottoes and logos, that rain down from horseback riders like disintegrating rainbows, and the end is signaled by a fire engine, in its wake convicts in orange jumpsuits picking up the trash.

As we waited for one parade the heavens opened and a downpour drenched us. Most locals ran for cover but a few of us were too drunk to care (luckily Julie had prepared for inclement weather and brought a hooded top, an overcoat, a hat, and an umbrella), and on the near-deserted streets we made out like bandits as sacks of novelties were dumped upon us.

The best part of the festivities are the school marching bands with their thumping drum-heavy sound and crashing cymbals. They are led by baton-twirling girls: not the skinny, perfect-teeth, cheerleader types from high-school movies, but all different shapes and sizes, many overweight and plain looking, happy and proud to be marching and reveling in their role in the procession. But even in the midst of America's biggest street party, the racial divide is glaringly obvious—exclusively black school, exclusively white school, exclusively black school. Mixed-race bands are so rare that you do a double take.

Bizarre sights are the norm during Mardi Gras season, and one morning on our road I came across a neighbor in nothing but a dressing gown pulling a cart with a baby dressed as a cow, a dog wearing a wizard hat with a wand in its mouth, and a sign around its neck reading "Hairy Pawter."

Along the block some college kids moved their living room into the street for ten days. They dragged out sofas, chairs, a TV, and a barbeque and yelled, "Happy Mardi Gras!" every time you passed. Day and night for a week and a half they were there drinking and partying, but by 8 A.M. on Mardi Gras day only the hardiest remained, sitting silently, staring straight ahead like zombies. However, one did rouse himself long enough to encourage my mate Simon Lowry to, "Chug, chug, chug!" from a hosepipe of beer he'd waved at him.

On Mardi Gras day everyone gets into the party spirit and many couples and families dress up together. A family of skeletons. A priest and a boy scout. Mr. and Mrs. Shrek with a baby Shrek. Locals walk up and down St. Charles, waving, smiling, greeting friends and strangers, and sipping whiskey and drinking beer before breakfast.

I was the height of satirical elegance in a bright purple Japanese soccer shirt, bright green Northern Ireland soccer shorts, and bright orange shoes. None of this chromatic clothing was part of a costume but just things I had in my wardrobe. Julie bought a feather boa in Mardi Gras colors (purple, yellow, and green), wrapped it around her most festive balaclava, and we headed to the Quarter.

But my favorite Mardi Gras story features my school pal Joe Thompson, who was at a California college for a year in the early nineties. The Friday before Fat Tuesday he and three friends made a last-minute decision to go to New Orleans for the weekend, but with the flights full they were forced to fly to Baton Rouge.

They arrived in the early hours, and thanks to Joe's Irish charm and good looks he managed to persuade a car rental agent into releasing the last available vehicle in the state of Louisiana. Without a map, plan, or hotel room they drove to New Orleans and partied like crazy.

The first night he slept under a hedge. The second he stayed with a young lady (told you he was charming). The third found him asleep in a sorority house. The time passed in an alcohol-fuelled blur. When he sobered up on Monday morning and tracked down his friends, they were way behind schedule.

He drove like a lunatic to the airport, dumped the car, and ran pell-mell into the terminal, where the check-in agent said their flight had closed. Joe begged her to let him on. He explained he had to get back to college or he was in serious trouble. He pleaded. Close to tears and desperate, he told her he'd made a spur-of-the-moment visit to Louisiana to see a sick relative.

She listened to his anguished pleas, looked at him for a moment, and said, "Tell the truth. You've been partying in New Orleans, haven't you?"

Joe feigned shock. "No, no, I've been in Baton Rouge seeing my frail relative."

She nodded. "I suggest you go and look at yourself in the bathroom, sir."

A puzzled Joe slunk off to the restroom and looked in the mirror. He had a red and green dragon painted across half his face.

CHAPTER 10

Home Is Where the Heart Is

By March I'd spent another ten dollars watching Chelsea win the final of the Carling Cup competition, and at training the water breaks were becoming less frequent. But we encountered a problem familiar to kids around the world: no one wanted to play in goal. Then, to mix sporting metaphors, one Saturday I arrived to find Jonathan had stepped up to the plate and donned the goalkeeper's green jersey. Our injured Young Stephen hadn't returned his red one.

Pitch-side, Eric shook his head. "Look at this lot; they can't help themselves. There are gonna be a lot of strains here today." Five or six giddy players, giggling like girls, had not been able to resist the siren-like lure of shooting at a real-live target. Without running through the endless stretching and limbering-up exercises crucial to men our age, they were lining up to fire shots at Jonathan from twenty yards. A big bunch of kids. I rushed to get my boots on and join in.

Kenny's involvement with the team had lasted one session and Medhurst was the driving force who had taken control: washing the bibs, looking after the balls and cones, calling and cajoling players to attend, and generally keeping the momentum going. The practices were fun run-arounds, with little evidence of the over-thirty-five competitive team initially discussed, though Adrian claims he was a visionary even then: "At the pub we'd spend two hours dissecting a kick-about and I remember thinking, 'Who are all these people turning up and where are they coming from?' I said to Medhurst, 'This could actually go somewhere and we should join a league,' but he was having none of it."

Young Stephen had been enjoying it so much he turned down a trip to Florida rather than miss training, even though the drastic age difference meant he spent most of his time trying to avoid being kicked by the geriatrics. "There was a great enthusiasm and buzz with everyone talking about football all the time. The amount of hours devoted to discussing things like who should play where and the pros and cons of different players was just incredible. When one week's session finished, we carried on talking about it until the following Saturday."

The day Jonathan went in goals I joined Young Stephen on the injury list. Phil the Power, a marathon-running attorney, had just started playing soccer. He probably reckoned American girls impressed by footballers was a neglected socioeconomic group he could exploit, as at Finn's, he would be either on his cell phone or trying to impress girls with his ability at pool. (Ever since I met him he's called me Sean and it's now gone on so long, I don't have the heart to correct him.) As he proved, fit and keen but lacking any shred of skill could be a dangerous combination. Like when he tackled me, for instance.

I was tiring in the afternoon heat and when I toed the ball a little too far ahead of me, Phil pounced. He charged at me with the speed he normally reserved for unescorted blonds at the bar, crashed full-tilt into my right leg, and I collapsed screaming. I initially thought I'd broken it, and Big Rab heard the crack from his shady bench on the other side of the field. At Finn's, Pauline fussed over me with a bag of ice and I bravely sat in the corner, stoically accepting drinks from the boys, who'd used the incident as an excuse to end training and go to the pub.

My knee ballooned to goldfish-bowl size and I kissed goodbye to soccer for weeks, but for once I didn't feel like slitting my wrists, as I'd plenty to keep me occupied. For starters there was the St. Patrick's Day parade, which was much like Mardi Gras, only with fewer drunks (New Orleans must be the only American city where residents can say, "We have a lot of intoxicated people on St. Patrick's Day but we have *more* on . . .). It kicked off in ancient traditional Irish style with the African-American mayor Ray Nagin riding in a yellow convertible sports car. But then it got strange.

Inebriated old men in tuxedos with green devil horns stuck on their heads staggered past, kissing any girls who didn't dodge them fast enough. Bagpipe-playing Louisianians squealed out Cajun tunes as boozed-up marchers of Middle Eastern descent handed out Irish tricolor badges and porcelain pixies. Float riders threw green and white beads, Irish Spring soap, and the ingredients of Irish stew — potatoes, cabbages, and carrots. It was like the distribution of food stamps crossed with a Celtic *The Price Is Right*.

With all its eccentricities, New Orleans has a way of burning into your skin. Though we'd only planned to stay here for a year, we decided to plant some roots. Between Julie's twenty-eight sweaters, eight tons of Mardi Gras beads, and 132 cabbages we'd too much stuff to move anyway.

It reminded me of Belfast in the way it felt like a small village rather than a large city, and I'd often meet people I knew in shops or bars. (I reunited with my friend Ray Ziegler whom I'd lost touch with and hadn't seen in seven years when I bumped into him on the street.) I also loved the informality and the lack of pretense: the first time we met our Porsche-driving neighbor, Rob, he was in his garden wearing nothing but a pair of boxers, holding a beer, and cooling himself off with a garden hose.

We broke free from the smelly excrement-littered icebox and bought a house. There was debris to be removed from the attic, handles to fix on the closets, and switches and knobs to be tamed. I'd never owned a dishwasher, a garbage disposal unit, a central air-conditioning system, or a spice rack and needed schooling on operating them all as Julie treated me like a thawed relic from the Ice Age. Through necessity I successfully mastered pulling out the spice rack. I needed somewhere to store my Band-Aids. I still haven't cracked the other stuff.

The crawl space obsessed me for days. Here many houses are raised around four feet for two reasons: it's the only major American city below sea level and is in constant danger of flooding so the height lends some protection from the water, and secondly the design lets air flow underneath the home to cool it, which was more important a century ago in the days before fancy air-conditioning systems that husbands can't work. Our crawl space was littered with bits of pipes and metal and bricks and other building material, and I filled bag after bag with rubble and skulked around the neighborhood the night before trash day depositing them in garbage cans.

Some homes had the crawl space blocked off with latticework, and I asked my elderly next-door neighbor if it was a good idea. Yes and no. He told me there was a crazy cat lady opposite — I once counted seven on her porch — and that they liked to get under our houses and "mess" (the cats that is, not him and the crazy cat lady). In stifling heat and humidity it often meant a pungent and overpowering odor, which closing up the area would stop. The bad news was that if the cats can't get under your house, then they can't chase away the rats. We'd see rats scurrying along the power lines looping through the trees, and the crazy cat woman's pets were probably keeping them away from our kitchen. Block up your crawl space and you create a Kurdistan-like safe haven for the plague-spreading pests that New Orleanians accept as part of everyday life.

At one house I viewed, the realtor told me about receiving a frantic call from her new Yankee neighbor who screamed, "Oh my God! There's a huge rat on your roof!"

She replied, "Yeah, I know; he lives there. We're four blocks from the Mississippi and you're surprised we have rats? Jeez!"

Then she likely put down the phone, continued fanning herself, sipped a cocktail, and said, "Lordy, Lordy, Lordy, I do de-clare."

In the end I plumped for defecating felines over disease-ridden rodents and left the underneath of the house open. The smell was indeed a drawback, especially as the same neighbor who complained about the crazy cat lady had bird and squirrel feeders in his backyard right beside our fence. Patient pigeons sat on top of it with their rears overhanging our yard waiting for a chance to nip between raiding squirrels. Between the stink of cat feces and bird droppings, it was like we'd bought a cell in the H Block of Northern Ireland's Maze jail in the eighties when prisoners were wiping the walls with their bowel movements during the so-called Dirty Protest.

Our neighbor was frighteningly security conscious and had more latches, locks, bolts, alarms, and motion-detecting lights than Fort Knox. He'd installed a six-foot metal gate across the shared alleyway between our houses and kept hinting—or more accurately, shamelessly suggesting—we should pay half the cost. As he'd erected it months before we moved in, I didn't feel any such responsibility, but rather than say that, I just cowered inside when I sensed his presence and only foraged outdoors when he wasn't around.

If he did trap me I broke for the safety of the living room whenever there was a whiff the conversation was being steered towards security, gates, or indeed any metal object, but one evening I was ambushed placing my soccer boots on the porch and had to listen to why he'd put up the gate. "A couple of black kids" had run down the alley and stolen his bike from the backyard. He had heard their footsteps but didn't see them because they'd fled by the time he had unlocked the forty-six bolts and gotten out his front door. I sympathized and then feigned death before he mentioned money.

It only occurred to me later, how could he tell the thieves were black? Do the feet of African-Americans have a different tone when they hit concrete? In fairness, I should say the last time I saw him pre-Katrina he was boarding up a black neighbor's windows, and crime statistics show the robbers would most likely have been African-Americans, but I still find it an unsettling assumption.

The antipathy between the races in New Orleans was a major shock to me and even to southern-raised Julie. In Belfast, I grew up with civil unrest and sectarian violence between Protestants and Catholics and religious discrimination on both sides. But shops and offices in the city center were neutral territory and staff treated everyone equally, as they couldn't tell your religion from your skin color. Here skin color is a big deal.

New Orleans is not wracked by racial tension. It's not a hotbed of unrest with the threat of violence simmering beneath the surface. In all my time here I've never heard of one racially motivated attack, not a single mugging, stabbing, or shooting. In contrast there was a spell recently when BBC Northern Ireland reported a new hate crime against Eastern Europeans or Asians everyday. Instead there's an underlying animosity, a distrust, and whites and blacks show no interest in intermingling. Benji and Shawn are the only mixed-race couple I've ever seen. And by that, I mean I've never even *seen* another anywhere.

Julie works in a plush building on the edge of the Quarter with high-end shops like Saks Fifth Avenue. She was in an elevator with two teenage African-Americans when a few well-dressed whites got in, and the blacks pushed their way out, one muttering, "I ain't gonna get in any elevator with a bunch of white people."

I spoke to a white middle-aged homeowner when we were considering buying a house in his area, and when I asked if it was a safe neighborhood he replied, "Yes it is, but just be aware that 60 percent of this city is black."

Julie and I queued at Wal-Mart to ask an African-American assistant a question, but she ignored us and helped the black guy behind us instead. Then again she might have thought, "There's that dude that's always bringing things back. And that chick who's always buying scarves."

There can be a mind-boggling casualness to the racism. Soon after Ray arrived, he struck up a conversation with a guy in a shop who said, "Yeah, you'll like it here, it's okay. Despite the f—king niggers." It's astounding some locals nonchalantly say these things to complete strangers they assume share their prejudice. Ray could have had a black girlfriend, wife, or adopted child.

Suburbs like Kenner and Metairie in Jefferson Parish are wealthier than New Orleans and can fund better schools, so middle-class families move there (so-called white flight) chasing better education for their children. This increases Jefferson's tax base while at the same time eroding that of

Orleans Parish, where public schools don't have money for basics like toilet paper and soap, never mind books or high-quality teachers. (In thirty-five years in the U.K., I never met an adult who couldn't read or write. I met three in my first year in Louisiana.)

The vast majority of whites who stay don't trust the city's creaking, broken education system and send their kids to private schools. At the end of their childhood the black public school youths are spat out with little or no education, and New Orleans is locked in a downward spiral of polarization and mutual mistrust.

The day of the 2004 presidential election we watched news reports from polling stations across the city. In true dysfunctional, underfunded, and downright incompetent New Orleans fashion, voting machine problems meant that at places like the black college Xavier University people had to queue for hours to vote. Julie wrapped herself in three blankets, grabbed a book, and walked to a nearby school to cast her ballot. She was back in minutes. In our white middle-class district there was no line. If I'd read before I moved here that it was harder for blacks than whites to vote in Louisiana, I'd have dismissed it as the paranoid ranting of a mentalist. But I'm not making a political, social, or racial point when I state that in this one particular contest at least, that was the case.

Anyway, more important for me than the state of race relations in America was a trip to England for the England versus Northern Ireland World Cup qualifying game in Manchester. After that I went to Belfast, but my time there felt strange. Although we'd had a six-month around-the-world trip the year before, and I'd also been on holidays to Australia and South America lasting months, now I owned a house in a different country and didn't have a home of my own in Ulster. My ten-year-old sister Rachel asked if Belfast was still my home or was it now New Orleans. It was a good question.

Can you only have one home? I was born in Northern Ireland and lived there for thirty years, so it'll always be my home, but now I think of America as my home as well. In Belfast people asked when I was going "back," and I'd tell them when I was due to go "home" (even when I lived in England, the first thing everyone asked when I went back to visit was when I was leaving again).

It was amazing how quickly certain things had been wiped from my memory, and I couldn't recall phone numbers I'd known for decades and was confused as to whether shop chains were in the U.K. or the U.S. The entertainment landscape had shifted so radically I'd never heard of the top-rated TV shows or the leading pop bands, although I'd been clueless about those things before we left anyway. In the small town of Holywood where I'd lived for eight years I walked past a black man and thought I'd imagined him, as I'd never seen a black face on the High Street before. Northern Ireland's racial homogeneity was never starker than after nine months in Louisiana.

When I flew back to the States the immigration officer asked, "How long have you been out of the country?"

"Two weeks," I replied.

"Welcome home," he said.

My knee had healed and I returned four days before April 16, 2005, the first game ever played by Finn McCool's Football Club.

CHAPTER 11

Our First Game

"You cheating f—king c—t!"

Just twenty minutes into our inaugural match our captain was sent off. We were off to a stellar start.

In his defense, Medhurst claimed he was shouting at a player and not the referee. And at least one of the adjectives was accurate.

With the score tied at one each on a boiling-hot day on a rock-hard pitch in Chalmette, ten miles east of New Orleans, the opposition attacked down the right. Apparently the ball went out and left back Sean stopped chasing it, but the attacker crossed anyway and with our defense static, a forward scored. As it was supposed to be a good-natured, friendly game there were no assistant referees, and the referee, Finn's barmaid Shannon Chaney, awarded the goal.

Our defenders were incensed by the gamesmanship and Medhurst followed their right winger back to the center circle for the restart, yelling at him to tell Shannon the ball had gone out. Head bowed, the guy ignored him and pretended he couldn't hear anything.

I'd been on the edge of our penalty box and hadn't seen the incident, but watching him slink away I could tell he was guilty. Medhurst got more and more angry and finally launched his invective, and Shannon thought he was yelling at her and ordered him off.

We had begun the match like we were an under-eleven team from the Helen Keller School of Disabilities. (I originally wrote School for the Deaf, then realized a lack of hearing wouldn't impact your soccer abilities, and if anything not being able to hear your teammates' insults could be an advantage on our squad. Talking of the deaf, when I worked in Birmingham, England, we used to go to a pub beside a deaf college and sometimes it'd be packed but silent, as the drinkers communicated by sign language. The jukebox was crap though.) No one had a clue what to do and panicking players would wildly thrash the ball as far away as possible on the odd occasion we got near it.

Sean should've been wearing a Davy Crockett cap because it was the Alamo on his side of the pitch, with only Phil in front of him, and I was amazed we held out for ten minutes before they went 1-0 up. Sean said, "Jesus, you'd think we'd never played a lick of football in our lives."

Sean, Dave, Medhurst, and Michael Balluff, a thirty-six-year-old businessman from Chicago, made up the defense; Paul and Phil were on the wings; and I was center midfield with our most-gifted starter Colin Bates, forty-three, an English movie producer who'd starred for the professional club Brighton and Hove Albion's youth team. Adrian and Benji were our strike force, while a visiting South African friend of Benji's was roped into acting as our goalkeeper.

Young Stephen was one of three substitutes and was apoplectic after Medhurst said he'd "maybe" get fifteen minutes at the end. Young Stephen had a point because he never missed training and was fit and talented, but I also followed Medhurst's thinking that if we were going to build towards an over-thirty-five team, it was pointless playing a twenty year old who was leaving in three weeks. It did make sense. And I wanted his starting place.

As it happened, we agreed to "rolling" substitutes, allowing players to switch in and out an unlimited amount of times as a concession to aging sportsmen toiling in the

Louisiana heat, and our coach Big Rab brought him on after five minutes when he saw what a shambles we were. The other side's subs seemed to stretch for three blocks and reminded me of the U.S. army massing on the Iraqi border. Most looked like they'd only started shaving, and if you added up the age of every one of their squad, you still wouldn't have the combined total of our four defenders.

After fifteen minutes we settled down and started stringing a few passes together. I took a quick throw on the left to Young Stephen, he found Benji, who laid it back to me twelve yards out, and I scored the equalizer. Nobody was more surprised than me. I'd just put my head down, closed my eyes, and hoped for the best. A bit like having sex.

Then came their dodgy second goal, Medhurst's red card, and a halftime haranguing of Shannon as we reminded her whose side she was supposed to be on. Big Rab could have been legendary Scottish coach Jock Stein with his motivational speech, although admittedly I don't recall the former Celtic boss ever wearing a Rangers shirt and holding a beer bottle in each hand.

In the second half we started to stamp our authority on the game, and by "stamp our authority" I mean of course, kick the hell out of their players. Our tackles became increasingly robust, and Dave was responsible for two opponents having to be carried from the pitch, while another two hobbled away hurt, with one requiring hospital treatment.

The latter was Dave's colleague from Chalmette Hospital and responsible for arranging the game. He'd made a prematch speech warning there was no charge for the pitch but no insurance coverage, so we had to take it easy and not treat the friendly too seriously. I dread to think what it would've been like if he had wound us up and said to get stuck in. They'd be making a series of MASH about us. On Monday he confessed to Dave they'd tried to listen in on our team talk before the game, but none of them could understand a word we'd said to each other.

Whether it was due to increasing confidence, higher fitness, or sheer intimidation (I know which one my money is on), we began to dominate. My best pass of the day sent Benji tearing through the middle to score, only for Shannon to rule it offside, but with twenty minutes left he beat two defenders and passed to me on the edge of the box. Once again I put my head down and hoped for the best, and when I opened my eyes the ball was nestling in the back of the net for my second goal to make it 2-2.

We pressed and pressed but couldn't score a winner, and in fact nearly lost it at the death when Dave hared forward and I found myself at right back. The ball was chipped into the penalty area, and I lunged to clear it. Off balance, I toppled backwards and realized if I made contact I'd complete my hat trick with an own goal. I pulled my leg away and the forward gathered the ball but shot wide. The final whistle went seconds later.

The fourteen players, Rab, and Mike Mac (who'd come to watch the second half) lined up in the center circle for a photograph. In it, you can also spot Finn's regular Joy Sturtevant playing with her boxer dog Oban in the background behind Medhurst's shoulder. Looking at it now, with everything that has happened since, it feels like it was taken on a different planet. We all look so happy. I'm one of three barefooted players and my blistered toes felt like they had received a pedicure from Freddie Kruger. Four months later the field was under twelve feet of water. Many of those Chalmette lads lost their homes or their jobs. Some lost both.

So our debut ended even-steven. And years from now, when they reflect on the glorious and uplifting history of the team, my name will be writ large as the scorer of Finn McCool's Football Club's first-ever goals.

But afterwards all everyone talked about was how Medhurst would be famous as our first player sent off, while Young Stephen unilaterally made Benji the man of the match. I should have demanded a phone-in poll.

At Finn's the mood was euphoric. It had been the first organized full-pitch match many of us had played in a long time and every moment was replayed, every player rated, every attack analyzed. The later it got and the more we drank, the better we'd been.

Medhurst slurred, "I'm so relieved I can still do it because that first ten minutes of mayhem was nerve-racking. The second half we threw everything at them and shoulda won but hey, this is what it's all about. That was bloody brilliant."

"It was f—king great," agreed Adrian, "F—king great."

Looking back Benji says, "Man, we were s—t, we sucked, and we had some shockers on the side. I've played on better squads, but I immediately knew we had something and that I was part of a team who actually gave a flying f—k. There was a belief that we weren't going to lose and a sense of pride and togetherness.

"I don't know if we'll ever replicate that feeling of, 'These Americans aren't going to beat us.' As foreigners we've a healthy disrespect for their football ability and we had the mental strength to go, 'Right—this is our team and our game and you bunch of Yank homos aren't going to beat us.'"

For the first time we talked seriously about entering a league, and I was surprised to discover we didn't have enough qualified players to form an over-thirty-five team.

I'd grown accustomed to pickup games with college kids, so when I trained with Finn's it seemed everyone was as old as me. My Christmas presents had consisted of various leg supports, bandages and wraps, and there was so much Velcro in my sports bag that when I reached into it they attached to my arm like an extraterrestrial limpet. It was one thing to compete against squads with similar rusty joints and aching limbs, but surely we'd never be up to taking on energetic whippersnappers on a weekly basis?

But that was a debate for another time. In Finn's I talked everyone through my goals so often that by the time I left, the first was a dazzling solo run and the second a thirty-yard screamer. Julie had to drag me out and I collapsed into bed due to a combination of celebratory drinks, spent nervous energy, and jetlag.

But I only had a few days to recover before my English friend Keith Willey and two pals visited for Jazz Fest, a huge two-weekend music event that is nearly as big a deal as Mardi Gras. Held at the Fairgrounds in Mid-City, it features hundreds of bands, seven stages, and dozens of tents with handicrafts and food such as gumbo, jambalaya, and crawfish.

Artists throng every music venue in the city and bars and clubs run all-nighters, meaning some acts don't even go on stage until 5 A.M., and it's common to see morning commuters mingling on the sidewalk with bleary-eyed concert-goers stumbling out into the sunshine.

Two weeks of nothing but jazz and I'd be polishing my assault rifle and sharpening my Rambo knife, but thankfully it's always a varied musical lineup: B.B. King, the Black Crowes, Dave Matthews, and Steve Winwood all played in 2005. It was also a good excuse to call off training.

The following Saturday a win for Chelsea over Bolton

Wanderers would give them their first English Premiership title in fifty years. It was live on FSC but Young Stephen refused to come to my house to watch it because he was convinced I'd spend the day gloating. However, twenty minutes before kickoff, in the midst of a torrential downpour, he called from Finn's.

"The bar's been hit by lightning and they've lost power. Can you come and get me so I can watch the match at your place?" As thunder clapped and the wind howled, I cackled maniacally, rubbed my hands with glee, and told him I'd be right there.

CHAPTER 12

Our First Victory

The fifth of May is Cinco de Mayo, Mexican Independence Day. And in New Orleans it's another excuse for a party.

We had New Year's celebrations in January, Mardi Gras in February, St. Patrick's Day (and St. Joseph's Day for the Italians) in March, an Easter parade in April, and now Central American-themed festivities in May. Thus Big Rab turned up at the pub for the first Finn McCool's FC meeting wearing a poncho and a sombrero. Dave also arrived swathed in a multicolored blanket and wearing a hat, and when we praised his Mexican outfit, he looked confused and asked, "It's cinco de who day?"

Medhurst, the team's leader and organizer, had called the meeting and as well as the two desperadoes, invited Eric, Benji, Young Stephen, and me. Dave spent most of it slumped in a chair clutching a Corona with his head bowed and sombrero tipped down over his eyes. I think he was waiting for the church clock to strike noon, tumbleweed to blow across the floor, and a tall, dark stranger dressed in black to mosey into the saloon.

Medhurst, Big Rab, and Dave had been in from the start, Eric was in charge of training, and I was probably asked along because Medhurst thought he could exploit my eagerness, especially as I didn't have a job to interfere with tasks he'd delegate to me. Young Stephen was just glad to get out of the house. Stephen was busy behind the bar, humping crates and shuffling boxes about, but he stopped by to pledge moral and financial support.

Benji, who'd produced an amusing expletive-laden report of the first game and promised future articles offering "fair and balanced character assassinations," was there so he couldn't complain about not being involved. Frightened homeowners all over the city would invite him to Tupperware parties rather than risk an angry, abusive call the following week.

He calls himself the Mouth of the South, and rather than apologize for his outspokenness he'll shrug and tell you, "I'm a little guy with a big mouth and a lot to say." In South Africa he was jailed three times and his life threatened because of his vocal opposition to apartheid.

There had been tension between him and Medhurst from the beginning (Medhurst: "He'd call me a fat bastard and I'd call him a bald c−t and that was that"). At an early session Medhurst had fallen over, and Benji had gone over to him and mimed holding out a Mars bar, teasing, "Come on, Mars bar, get up and earn the Mars bar."

I think Benji has an innate distrust of authority figures in general, Englishmen in particular, and with a suspicious and pessimistic outlook is always searching for something to criticize. It was only natural that Medhurst, another strong personality who was trying to get a team off the ground, would get fed up with the carping and negativity. But it never amounted to more than a bit of bickering and they were like an old married couple. Who both supported Spurs.

Eric took notes and for three hours we talked about the team and took turns trying to keep Benji quiet. We quickly agreed the name would be Finn McCool's Football Club, which was a slice of luck as Medhurst happened to have brought along a bank card with that on it. We'd train every Thursday evening and once on the weekends, we'd ask for a one-hundred-dollar subscription, and we'd buy team uniforms from Eric's friend in the sportswear business. Medhurst said we should wait until the autumn to join the league, and I was concerned that September was a long way away and interest could die off by then. But we'd already moved onto the next topic, which was that Medhurst would be club captain, and this apparently also entitled him to take all throw-ins, free kicks, and penalties.

We devoted most time to two subjects we'd debate endlessly over the next four months: the need for a coach and whether good players should be picked ahead of pub regulars.

Medhurst said, "The team picks itself," but that wouldn't last forever, as new guys arrived and originals lost form, and we needed someone to choose the starting eleven on merit and call the shots during games. The obvious choice was Big Rab, but he was friends with everyone and Medhurst nixed the idea because he wouldn't be ruthless enough, or even at all.

So Big Rab became assistant coach, even though we didn't have a head coach, and Medhurst said he'd ask his colleague and fellow Englishman Steve Ebbs to consider the post (just what we needed, another Steve). Big Rab went off to get more Coronas and Dave briefly tilted his hat to smile at a passing gringo girl.

But what kind of team were we aiming for? Was this just a laugh with our mates or were we on the hunt for the best possible squad? It was a prickly pear wrapped in a cactus that had been eaten by a porcupine, and we'd stumble and bumble our way around this particular minefield for the next year.

Benji's considered view was: "Dude, f—k everybody else! This is our team for people like us who come to this pub. If there's a choice between some stranger and one of our crowd, then I'm going to go with our guy every time.

"I've played on good sides but walked away at the end of the season with no mates, and for me making friends is a big part of the team. I'm competitive and want to win but we should find a place for pub regulars if they train. The team was founded for the bar and the bar is the heart of the team. If you don't have heart then what's the point?"

But Medhurst cited Adrian: "I want him to play because he's a very entertaining personality and could be a decent footballer. But he's way overweight and can't be bothered to train, so how can we pick him over someone who turns up every week?" The one Sunday Adrian turned up for practice he had clapped his hands and asked, "Right then — who's up for a bender down the Quarter?" But he'd been involved from the start and was "one of the lads," so was it right to kick him out?

If being a pub regular was everything, where did that leave guys like Colin, a talented player who was always at training but never went to Finn's? By that criterion Captain Morgan, who was frequently in the bar but nowhere near as good as Colin, should start ahead of him.

I felt we should pick our best footballers, but enthusiastic pub regulars who showed up every week deserved to play as well. So eighteen-a-side then. We ended with a consensus we'd only pick blokes who trained, as it wasn't unreasonable to expect attendance at one of the twice-weekly sessions.

We toasted a successful powwow, Dave left to round up the donkeys and start the revolution, and Young Stephen said, "That was a very serious, proper meeting for a really poor pub football team who've only had a handful of training sessions and one match."

Two days later we had our second game on one of the

real pitches at the Fly. I had taped Chelsea's last home game of the season against Charlton, which kicked off at 6 A.M. our time, and said I didn't want to know the score so I could watch it later. "Do that if you want, but it was a bad match and you won with a last-minute penalty," replied Adrian ambiguously.

In the three weeks since our first match we'd solved our goalkeeping problem and recruited Mark Kirk, thirty-seven, an English recycling artist from Macclesfield who met his Scottish wife Heather MacFarlane while fighting over a rubber chicken. After living in Copenhagen and Prague, he tangled with Heather at Mardi Gras in 1999 when they argued over a rubber chicken thrown from a float. After a spell in New York he returned to the city and they got a place together. They still have the chicken.

It's an old cliché that all goalkeepers are crazy so I won't repeat it here, but Mark is . . . different. It was not atypical for him to wear sandals, pink trousers, a multicolored flowery shirt, and a flat tartan cap. And that was just to play in. I'm kidding, though he did wear flamboyant ensembles like this to the pub and often took to the field in different-colored socks.

He played in the city's Hispanic Islano league for four years and occasionally went to O'Flaherty's to watch games but mostly avoided it because, "If I wanted to be around a bunch of Brits, I'd have stayed at home." Medhurst knew he was a good keeper and told him we were starting a team, but Mark hadn't exactly been brimming with enthusiasm: "I wasn't into it and didn't want to play with a bunch of old farts, but that first training session was a pleasant surprise, as I wasn't expecting much. For a bunch of aging drunks there was actually some running." I didn't know if that was a compliment or not.

Mark oozed confidence, barked orders, and was the only person with more to say for himself than Benji, though while Benji would insult opponents and wind them up, Mark's comments were aimed at his own side. If he ever made a mistake the rest of us were too frightened of him to say a thing. Except for Benji.

The only time I ever saw him lost for words was when he shouted at Captain Morgan, "Just do the simple thing! Can you not remember what you did at school for Christ's sake?"

The Captain yelled back, "I never played football at school!" That shut him up.

Our team now sporting a goalkeeper, we faced the day's competition. With a name like Inner City Crew, our opponents sounded more like a rap band than a soccer team and had finished bottom of the league we were going to enter. We posed for another team shot (if nothing else the club's history was going to be well documented photographically) and prospect coach Steve Ebbs called the substitutions.

We led 2-0 at halftime thanks to a double from Colin, although they weren't screamers like mine in the previous game when I'd beaten seventeen men and shot from my own half. We were more composed than during the first match, but then hysterical teenage girls in the front row of the Beatles concert at Shea Stadium had been calmer than us in that game.

In the second half Mike Mac scored after great work by debutant Billy, then I whipped in a perfect cross (I'm sure I beat four men as well) that Billy headed home. It finished 4-0, but it could've been more and we dominated so much that Mark wandered out to watch from the halfway line.

The funniest moment was provided by the head bangers Young Stephen and Dave. All week Dave had been instructing Young Stephen to "pick up the bits," meaning it was his job to swoop on any loose balls in and around the penalty box. "Pick up the bits, play it in, and we'll stick it away," Dave had said for days as he drew diagrams on bar napkins and beer mats. Midway through the second half, Young Stephen "picked up the bits" from a corner and crossed the ball right onto Dave's head in the middle of the goal just six yards out—and Dave somehow contrived to head it over the bar.

Afterwards Inner City Crew's Nathanael Sprague, a quality midfielder and Finn's regular I'd spent the afternoon running after, said, "Dude, I went to one of your first practices and I can't believe how far you've come since then. You kicked our butts today."

I'd expect a tall young American with long blond hair and an earring to call me "dude." However, it sounded strange when used by our referee Stephen Kirk (yes I know, another Stephen), a short balding Scotsman from Glasgow. He'd awarded a foul against me on the edge of our penalty box.

"I never touched him, ref," I lied, standing over the ball to delay the kick.

"Dude, back away from the ball."

"Dude? Ref, you've been in America too long. But . . ." I stalled.

"Dude, keep going backwards, keep going, keep going."

"But I never . . ."

Adrian walked across as if he was going to calm me down and pulled me away, turning his back on the referee. "Great, Stevie! Get stuck in there, mate! Keep it up—carry on kicking these f—kers and don't let them away with anything!"

At Finn's our victory celebrations were tinged with

sadness because Young Stephen was returning to Belfast the following week. I was devastated. No longer would I be known as Big Stephen. We were strong-armed into standing on the pavement outside while Big Rab rated our individual performances. I got a generous seven out of ten, but I think it was only because Julie was there. And he'd had a few.

After this game you could smell the spreading scent of seriousness. Medhurst says, "We'd subbed in players who were nice guys but just not good enough. When everything is being thrown at you, then you want to see the commitment in their eyes and feel that they'll get stuck in and have no fear. That wasn't there with some of them."

We moved training from St. Patrick's to the Fly and Eric started keeping a list of everyone who showed up (I imagined it would only be a matter of time before we'd be waiting cross-legged on the ground and calling out, "Present, sir!"). I paid my last ten dollars of the season to watch the English FA Cup Final, so what with FSC, the radio, and the odd match I'd caught via Albania's Country & Western TV channel on the internet I'd spent just eighty dollars.

The next Saturday I was an impartial observer as a partisan crowd split in half for the exhibition game between the United States and England. The old country won 2-1 and Medhurst taunted, "Beating America wasn't as much fun as beating Northern Ireland."

At that moment I honestly think I could have killed him. And laughed while doing it.

CHAPTER 13

We Hit a Pothole

Only four of us turned up to train the first Sunday in June, and I emailed Young Stephen worried it was "the beginning of the end."

I was always extremely pessimistic about the Finn's team and scared it would crumble to pieces. I lived in perpetual fear it was too good to last and something was bound to go wrong. I still had my pickup games at the Fly, and I maybe knew enough players to get an indoor squad together, but Finn's had everything: I was comfortable with the style, there were no cliques and we'd pass to the best-placed players rather than to our friends, we'd wind each other up and talk about English teams, and afterwards we'd go to the pub together. I'd been in the States for a year and it was the single most enjoyable thing I did, so the slightest hint of trouble had me tossing and turning in bed for nights.

Thankfully, we were soon back to our usual crowd of between twelve and sixteen. Those summer practices at the Fly at 6 P.M. on Thursdays and 10 A.M. on Sundays are my favorite memories of Finn McCool's FC.

Dave, who already had a seventies porn-star moustache, had taken to wearing a chest-hugging white Lycra see-through training top. Every time he opened his bag we expected him to say, "I've come to fix the fridge" and a funky bass line to start up. Adrian called it his "Oz look," after a gay club on Bourbon Street, but then Dave announced his girlfriend, Brandi Bourgeois, was pregnant and added, "I've never been out with a barmaid before. I feel like a rock star."

Motor-mouth Benji would deliver a constant monologue as we jogged to warm up, and once when Dave shouted to "give it a rest," he shot back, "No way, dude. I do my talking off the pitch." Sean and I collapsed in hysterics at his inversion of the old sports cliché. Another time he arrived twenty minutes late and admitted, "I forgot all about training and I was at a barbeque and had two joints and six beers. I'm wasted, dude." You can judge our skill level by the fact that he was still one of the best players.

Mike Mac was the first to bring beer and after that we took turns buying a cooler of the cheapest booze we could find (or was that just me?). After an exhausting evening workout we'd lie on the grass for hours and talk about the team as the sultry heat finally simmered down and the setting sun perched on the lip of the levee.

Eric would stand with a towel wrapped around his waist swigging beer, Medhurst would fill us in on the latest developments, and we'd discuss guys who hadn't shown up (Adrian), the standard of the league, kickoff times, and how we were going to do. It would get so dark we couldn't see each other fighting off the mosquitoes lining up to dive-bomb us, and eventually, after the fiftieth thigh slap, someone would say they were going, someone else would ask who was headed to Finn's, and we'd slowly and reluctantly slope off to the cars.

We were taking on an international makeup with Dutchman Frank tackling harder in training than the rest of us did during games, and between apologies for hard challenges he'd complain about the backpackers at the hostel who'd date him but never give him "shex." With the casual attitude towards sex common in Continentals, after training one day he told us about a seventies edition of *Playboy* he'd found and went into graphic detail about the models — "Their boobs weren't fake and they had these tan lines and their bodies . . ." — not caring that beside us were Medhurst's visiting elderly parents.

He invited us to a party at India House but said it was a couple of bucks a head for alcohol. "That's not a party, that's a bar," said Medhurst.

"There'll be hot dogs and hamburgers as well," replied Frank defensively.

"Then that's a cafe," answered Medhurst.

Captain Morgan, meanwhile, brought along a bike-riding Frenchman he'd met in a coffee shop (a real one, not a Frank "coffee shop"). At just twenty-eight, lawyer Julien Meyer, in New Orleans on an eighteen-month contract, was the baby of the team who immediately took the predictable abuse about his nationality at his first session. When he failed to show the next week, we assumed he'd decided against joining our team of xenophobes, but he returned and became a vital defensive lynchpin.

In the past, no matter how friendly I got with anyone whose first language wasn't English, I always felt there was a barrier, even if they spoke it perfectly, but Frank and Julien crossed that cultural divide and picked up the inherent subtleties and inferences to slip seamlessly into our squad.

Julien had been rusty at first and we'd picked up new French swearwords as he loudly berated himself for stray passes, but soon he was winning the ball from a forward, shimmying past him, and laying it off while simultaneously fending off French insults, mostly from his own team. He loved playing with us and it made sense when he said he was a big *Monty Python* fan and that half the players at his club in Paris had been English.

"The first session was really hot and hard and I almost passed away [I think he meant passed out], so I went to rest and laid down on top of some ants which crawled all over me [Aha! I'm not the only one!]. I had come to Louisiana to improve my English but when everyone was talking afterwards all I could think about was that I was ruining it.

"But it was friendly and organized and Medhurst would take the time to call me and that made me feel wanted. I'd played a few other games here, but they were all so — what's the word? — anonymous."

Anonymous. Exactly. Trust a foreigner to accurately describe the city's pickup games in a single pithy word.

But we did have our first career-ending injury, which ironically wasn't due to a zealous tackle from Dave, Frank, or even mad Phil. Jonathan snapped his Achilles tendon and felt such a lightning-sharp instantaneous pain, he spun around to see who had kicked him in the back of the leg. He was hospitalized, on crutches for weeks, and his wife, Cathryn, forbade him from playing with us again. We cheered him up by commiserating that it could've been worse — she could've stopped him from drinking with us.

On June 9, Macca ran our practice at the Shell Shockers' field, Pan American Stadium in City Park. Despite the terrible state of the pitch, it was the best training session I'd ever had, and the good news was that two days later we would have a rematch against Inner City Crew in the five-thousand-seat venue.

For that practice, one of our Americans had brought along his friend Kirk, whose pink shorts were so outrageous that in comparison Mark appeared to have dressed for an appearance at the Supreme Court. Kirk had fallen over his own feet a few times but, sad to say, he wasn't too much out of his depth with us.

When Macca finished, Mark ordered me to set up shooting practice. I stood with my back to the goal, players hit the ball to me, I'd stop it, and they'd run up and try to score past Mark without being distracted by his crazy eyes or wild hair. Of course after twenty seconds most of the balls were in the bushes and I went on safari to retrieve them.

When I returned Dave said, "Did you see that new guy? He stormed off because he took a crap shot and Mark shouted, 'If you're going to kick like a girl then go off and play with girls.' He threw his hands in the air and said, 'I only need to hear that once. I'm outta here,' and stomped off in a sulk."

We laughed that if a bit of good-natured ribbing was so offensive he wouldn't have lasted long anyway, but his pal called him and told him not to take eccentric Mark's insults personally and persuaded him to give the team another go. So he showed up at Pan American at 5:30 P.M. on Saturday for the friendly, as did lots of other players. Enough for four teams in fact, as Pan American had been double-booked.

Kenny had promised the pitch in Finn's and Medhurst said, "He told me the booking was 99.99 percent certain. I'm a banker, I rounded that up." Adrian, whose company sponsored the Shell Shockers, was angrily stamping about trying to track down anyone connected with them on the phone.

While Adrian stomped, Benji turned up with a plaster on his nose and I asked what happened. "I walked into a chainsaw."

"Seriously, what did you do?" I said.

"It's true, dude. It was in the back of the truck and I didn't see it sticking out and I walked right into it."

"Well at least it wasn't on," I said, concerned that our striker whom we relied on to score from twenty yards hadn't seen a chainsaw an inch in front of his face.

A new field was found and we raced against the failing

light to a cross-town field, and as I had to pick up the goal netting on the way, I arrived with barely enough time to change and ran on as we kicked off. I was so rushed I hadn't removed the tag from the new jersey and played wearing two pairs of shorts, as I'd forgotten to take off the ones I already had on. I'd also missed the latest drama featuring poor Kirk.

The recently arrived uniforms were still sealed in the box and Eric sliced it open and everyone grabbed a jersey. But when Kirk reached over, Eric erupted, "What are you doing? You come to one training session and you think you can rummage in our kit? Oh no, I don't think so." A chastised Kirk slunk away and was never seen again.

Benji was delighted. "Eric, way to go dude, I'm right behind you. I don't care who he is, if he's not one of us he's not getting a shirt."

It was the day's only moment of levity, as the team we'd rolled over 4-0 five weeks before stuffed us 3-0. Both Mark and backup keeper Michael were out of town and we press-ganged an Algerian Finn's regular into nets. Within two minutes we were a goal down. He was absolutely hopeless. But we were all pretty hopeless.

Medhurst was injured after becoming Phil's latest victim the previous week. He resembles the English actor Bob Hoskins anyway, so when he sat in the back of Sean's car on the way to the game with Mike Mac in the passenger seat, he felt he was in the end scene of the famous British movie *The Long Good Friday*. He hobbled along the line and shouted advice, but I doubt even a coach with a long white beard, a flowing robe, and a staff could've helped us.

ICC put out a much-improved team and in the second half Colin and I had been substituted and he said to me, "Look, that's our problem right there: four defenders, a big gap, four midfielders, a big gap, two attackers." As we discussed it they scored two more soft goals within a minute. We were all grateful to reach the sanctuary of the pub.

The atmosphere was funereal. Billy was gutted he'd missed a chance to level the score at 1-0 down but he was even more upset some players had congratulated our keeper. "They said 'well done' and 'well played' to him and I hate that stuff. He was terrible—we shouldn't be applauding him for that. What's the point of playing if you think that performance deserves praise? He sabotaged us. I'm so angry. I hate getting beat."

Sean was equally suicidal. "Billy is almost mentally ill at the thought of losing and I never do anything I don't expect to be successful at. I paced the house all day because I was so excited about the match. We've a core who wants to succeed, but a few on the periphery are missing that desire. It's time to decide if this is just a bit of fun with our mates or are we entering the league to try and win it, because if it's no more than an excuse to get out of the house and have a laugh, then Billy will be off."

Billy had played for Olympiakos before and they wanted him back, and the threat of losing our best player had me make an impassioned but reasoned case why he should sign for us. I finished by saying I'd bet we were the only team in the city serious enough to be training twice a week more than three months before the season started.

Sean summed it up. "When we won 4-0 we weren't as good as we thought we were, and now we've lost 3-0 we're not as bad as we think we are." Then we all had a laugh about Eric shouting at Kirk.

Medhurst shrugged. "He wasn't up to much. It's no loss." I, on the other hand, would've bent over backwards to beg average (and that's being kind) players like him to join. I feared sooner or later we'd arrange a game, only eight of us would show, and the team would disintegrate, but Medhurst's determination to only sign anyone who improved us for the twenty-two-man league roster was proved right in the end.

That night in Finn's, Sean pointed out to me that the players were grouping together. Subconsciously we were drawn to each other and there was now an invisible barrier between us and our friends who were regulars but not on the team. He said, "It was very interesting how it developed so it was hard for others in the pub to break in. There were a few big lads like Rab and Mike Mac around us and it was as if without even realizing it we'd created an almost impenetrable half-circle."

Stephen had noticed it too when we arrived after training. "Even though I wasn't there, I could tell who'd been to practice, as ten or twelve of you would be grouped around one table, or maybe little pockets of three or four would stand in a circle at the bar. Boys who'd shown no previous interest in playing wanted to be part of it because you could tell you had a fantastic buzz, great camaraderie, and the fun was mighty."

Medhurst agreed. "You have a common bond because of your nationality and Finn's, but the footballers were growing closer as a group while other drinkers were not part of the conversation. Even those who didn't come to practice regularly were becoming alienated and didn't want to be left out."

I busted through the cordon long enough to speak to our referee Stephen "Dude" Kirk. I chatted with him and his wife, Siobhan, who told me about their teenage daughter's visit to Siobhan's brother in Glasgow. She had excitedly phoned with the news that her uncle had said he'd take her camping around Europe the following year and they'd be going to Spain, Portugal, and France.

Siobhan rang her brother to check and asked, "Is it true you're going to take my daughter off around the Continent next year?"

He replied, "Jesus, did I say that? I must have been friggin' steaming!"

I loved that: no hint of embarrassment or regret, just a simple explanation that he'd been really drunk and promised something while in an intoxicated state.

Stephen said he thought I'd been the best player on the pitch (strangely for a Scotsman, he was sober as he was Siobhan's designated driver) and I rushed to buy them drinks, eager to hear more.

That night, in an uncharacteristically restrained moment of clarity, Benji wrote in his match report: "Better organization is crucial to the future development of the team . . . Clearly we need more practice and to prepare for matches better." Then he returned to mercilessly ribbing the English players.

In Finn's on June 25, I got talking to a twenty-three-year-old Irish student from Dublin on a three-month visa who had played soccer as a kid. I invited him to training the next day and asked his name.

He stuck out his hand. "Pleased to meet you. I'm Stephen."

CHAPTER 14

Gringo Ken

One dark, stormy Thursday night at the Fly, I was grabbed by a shady-looking Central American with a big black bushy moustache and an accent straight out of *Scarface*. In broken, halting English he tried to ask a question and Nick, a thirty-eight-year-old half-Indian from Belize and one of the few regulars at the pickup games with whom I'd held a conversation beyond, "Pass the bloody ball!" offered to translate.

Nick and I had talked about the difficulty in breaking past the casual nodding stage with the others and he said, "That's why I always speak to you. I could tell you were feeling the same thing, but it's even worse for me because I don't look like anyone else and feel like even more of an outsider than you."

However, I didn't feel like an outsider, because after coming twice a week for a year I knew there was no inside to penetrate! Everybody turned up alone, played, went home. If my experience was typical, then I understood why so many city dwellers in America's highly transient population felt alienated and isolated, and it was no wonder online dating had exploded.

Nick said the swarthy character (Felix) wasn't recruiting old men to be drug mules but was recruiting old men to play on an over-thirty-five team in the Islano league. I thanked him and declined, but Felix persisted. Using a combination of sign language, snatches of garbled English, and with the help of a part-Mayan he made it clear he *really* wanted me to join his team. Eventually — just to get rid of him — I agreed to think about it. But still he kept on, worse than a Turkish rug salesman.

I took a registration form, stuck it in my pocket, and promised to ring him, but he latched onto my shoulder and said he needed an answer because the sign-up deadline was tomorrow. I wouldn't have to pay anything. I wouldn't have to play every game. I wouldn't have to train with them. I'm sure Nick was making half the translation up just so I'd sign the damn thing and we'd all get home before dawn. I relented, and Felix whipped out a Polaroid camera and took my photo, which is probably now on a Nicaraguan passport under the name Felipe Martinez.

A manager begging you to join his club is a great ego boost, especially because in the past I'd only ever been begged to, "Get off the field, you idiot!" Of course the fact that Felix was trawling parks and approaching complete strangers twelve hours before the registration deadline was a clue — a big clue — that he was desperate for players and would have signed the Royal Air Force's legless World War II pilot Douglas Bader if he'd been there feeding the ducks. When he left I checked if Nick had joined. "No way, I'm not interested. Play for that guy's team? Are you crazy?"

The phone calls started the next day.

Felix's wife spoke perfect English and rang with the time for Saturday's game and to make sure I would be there. I was caught off guard and hedged that I'd love to play but I might have to work. By "have to work" I meant "have to go to Finn's." She called back, but now I had her caller ID and didn't answer, so she left a message. Felix rang later and left one as well. They left another Saturday morning.

I threw my boots in the car and went to Finn's intending to watch one match and then leave in time for the 1 P.M. kickoff.

But I ended up talking to Sean and Paul and Medhurst and Dave and Big Rab and the next thing I knew it was 12:45 P.M.

Julie called to say, "I'm back from shopping and there are a load of messages on the answering machine from some strange Spanish-speaking man. I think he's asking where you are." I told her to ignore them, make herself a cup of hot soup, and wrap up warm, and if he called back tell him I'd been landed with a double shift. I went back to "work" thinking that would be the end of that.

But the following Friday when his wife left two messages with the game time, I felt guilty and tried to talk myself into going: it would increase my fitness level; I'd gain experience of the energy-sapping heat on a full-size pitch; I might be able to poach talented players for Finn's; it was a proper team so they wouldn't play in that selfish Latino hogging-the-ball style; there were bound to be other English speakers on the squad. So I went.

They played that ball-hogging way. And there were no other English speakers.

Actually, I was the only Caucasian in a two-mile radius. It's called the Islano league because games are held in a clearing on an island (*islano* means "island") in City Park, one of the ten biggest urban parks in the nation with more than 11 million annual visitors and the largest collection of mature live oaks in the world. I walked across a rickety wooden bridge, smiled at the middle-aged man holding a tin beside the bent metal fence, and thought an astral portal had transported me to a village fiesta in Honduras.

Many Hispanics either work illegally or for minimum wage and can't afford visits to upmarket restaurants or attractions like the aquarium, so this is their big day out when they down a few beers and catch up with friends while their children run around the park. A PA blasted salsa music, stalls sold soccer jerseys, chefs grilled on barbeques the size of cars, and leathery-skinned old men fanned their faces with tattered brown hats. There were players and coaches and referees and administrators and wives and girlfriends and fans and babies.

As I looked around, it hit me that not only had I met Felix just once (at night), but I didn't even know the name of my team. Hundreds of people swarmed around me, so I wandered aimlessly along the touchlines until finally a grinning clipboard-carrying man materialized out of the crowd. He waved and called, "Hi, Ken."

Foreigners having difficulty saying my name is a recurring theme in my life. Our Galapagos Islands guide pronounced "Stephen Rea" as "Stephanie Raz," and I never corrected him because I liked that it made me sound like a porn actor.

On our around-the-world jaunt, Julie and I took a nine-week cruise and there were two exits from the ship's restaurant. A Filipino waiter handed out mouth-freshening pieces of ginger (it was a posh liner) as we left, and I'd always say hello. After a few days he asked my name. I said "Steve," as non-English speakers find the shortened version easier.

"Jake?" he asked.

"No, Steve."

"Jake?"

"Stttteeeevvvveee."

"Jake?"

"Sure, why not, Jake."

From then on he'd call, "Hi, Jake!" whenever he saw me, but sometimes we left through the other door manned by a different ginger-on-cocktail-stick-dispensing crew member. He too asked my name and I replied that it was Steve.

"What?"

I suddenly realized if he called me Steve in front of his colleague who thought my name was Jake, it could all get very confusing. They'd think I was either an idiot or a liar. So like the lying idiot I am I said, "My name's Jake."

For the next two months every time either passed me in the corridor or served me afternoon tea or plumped my pillows they'd chirp, "Hi, Jake!" My fellow cruisers would shoot me a questioning look, convinced I was either mad or playing a twisted joke on the staff, and I'd shake my head and say, "Don't ask."

On my birthday the waiters brought out a cake and sang, "Happy birthday, dear Jake." I swear to God.

Anyway, Felix told me to choose one of the gaudy multicolored shirts laid out on the grass and asked, "Where you play, Ken?"

"How about midfield?"

"Hokay. Play middle, Ken."

Our goalkeeper either had had an incredibly hard life or was a sprightly seventy-year-old. He had long untamed gray hair and leaped around with the dramatic flair of a silent movie star. He was also mental. Twice he ran full pelt into the other half of the pitch to remonstrate loudly and gesticulate riotously at the referee, his flowing locks blowing in the wind like an epileptic kite.

At halftime it was scoreless and the medieval wizard look-alike continued to rant, mostly to himself it seemed. I'd done okay and received a couple of appreciative nods from teammates, and my lack of Spanish wasn't as problematic as I'd feared because the coach's tactical briefing consisted of everybody smoking and drinking beer. No doubt David Beckham had the same experience when he joined Spanish giants Real Madrid.

In the second half we scored and clung on to win 1-0. That meant celebrations, backslaps, and more drinking, and even if I'd been fluent in Spanish it wouldn't have mattered as I couldn't hear myself think over the pulsating beat pounding out from the increasingly loud sound system.

The league officials made me go to the car for my driver's license. I'd like to think it was to prove my age because I looked so young, but they have probably spent their lives being ordered around by Americans and thought here was a chance to throw a bit of authority the other way. Christ knows what they made of my name compared to whatever aberration Felix had come up with.

It had certainly been an experience, but not a completely enjoyable one. I'd played the full ninety minutes and it was hard work in the heat; when I checked at home it was 97 degrees. I sweated so much on the ride back home that for weeks it felt like you were squashing down into a swamp when you sat in the driver's seat. I could hardly move for two days. So much energy had been wasted; I'd burst a lung to get into the penalty box but, like at the Fly, the player would try to beat six men before releasing the ball.

I appreciated how organized Finn's was compared to this outfit who threw on substitutes willy-nilly without a passing mention of positions. After repeatedly bumping into teammates, I'd worked out that we had five in the attacking midfielder role and I'd asked, "Centro? Izquierda? Derecha?" After pointing and shouting and gesturing and looking at the coach, my teammates would shrug and stroll off towards the ball. I'd try to work out what position was lacking, a particularly taxing task as we employed a tactical system I'd describe as "a bunch of grown men running after the ball." I finished the game at left back in defense.

I'd started watching soccer in the seventies, decades

before the weekly live European Champions League matches nowadays, when it was still exciting to see British sides compete against the exotic and mysterious Europeans and South Americans. Even as a youngster I remember being skeptical when commentators and coaches talked about the suspect Latino temperament and their reputation for cheating, but this game nailed home to me the truth of the stereotype. Every time a ball ran out or a shot went wide, players would throw up their hands, pout or complain, and with my frequent stray passes I was thankful I couldn't understand half of what was said.

But more annoying was the constant diving and feigning injury, and if an opponent so much as glanced aggressively in their direction they'd roll over and over, clutching their leg and screaming until the referee either awarded a free kick or waved play on. Then without a hint of shame they'd jump up and run about as if nothing had happened.

Five minutes in I won the ball cleanly, but the guy I tackled went down like he'd been shot by a passing Cajun sportsman. Luckily the referee was right beside us and shook his head, and when I "gestured" to the player that he was a cheat, he smiled and shrugged. To him it was just a legitimate tactic, but after the umpteenth time someone collapsed and writhed around shrilling and yelping, I was sick of it.

Each Friday night the phone rang every few hours and Felix's wife left messages with the time of the next day's game along with a battery of phone numbers, any of which I could call to confirm my attendance. If Felix did it the message was simpler, something like, "Hokay, Ken. You play tomorrow, yes, Ken? Ken? Two o'clock. Yes, Ken? See you, Ken."

If I had a legitimate excuse I'd answer and say, "I've been

looking forward to the game all week but unfortunately I can't make it as . . ." I learned it had to be a watertight, cast-iron reason though because, as you're probably now gathering, Felix was pretty persistent and conversations would go like this:

"Hello, Felix."

"Ken? This Ken?"

"No, it's Steve, wait, yes, I mean Ken."

"Hi, Ken. Game two o'clock, Ken."

"Yes, I got the five messages you left earlier."

"You leave message, Ken? I no get message, Ken. Ken?"

"No, no, I got *your* message. About the game, that's why I'm calling."

"Yes, have game, Ken. Two o'clock. See you then, Ken."

"No, no, I'm calling because I can't play tomorrow."

"Yes, yes, play tomorrow, Ken. See you then, Ken."

"No, I can't play. I'm playing for my other team tomorrow."

"Yes, play other team tomorrow, Ken. Not same team as last week. We play other team. See you then, Ken."

"No, I'm playing for Finn McCool's, *my* other team. Not your team. I have a game at twelve tomorrow."

"No, no, no, Ken. Game at two, not twelve. See you then, Ken."

"No, I am playing for someone else at twelve. Listen—is your wife there?"

I'd repeat everything, she'd translate, and through her Felix would try to persuade me to come along after my noon match for Finn's, giving you an idea of how short of players he was. If I couldn't face getting entangled in this mangled dialogue and avoided speaking to them it didn't make the slightest bit of difference. Regular as clockwork the calls started up again the next Friday. Once more, guilt got the better of me and I went back for a second game.

However, as I was leaving the house I was attacked by a watermelon. I'd bought the gargantuan green beast for four dollars and in a possessed state of frenzied fruit euphoria that morning I'd chomped through half. I didn't know that much melon in one sitting could cause what in polite company you'd refer to as "a stomach upset." Imagine trying to squeeze the last of the detergent out of the bottle, only it's not filled with watery green soap but . . . I'm sure you get the picture.

I tried to leave five times — once making it as far as the porch — but every time I got near the front door I felt a terrible ominous grumbling in my guts and, not wanting to risk the stairs, I'd run to the first-floor toilet. Eventually the rumbling thunder passed and I arrived at City Park as we kicked off.

In the time it took to throw on the uniform, we conceded three goals and changed the goalkeeper twice. I lost count of how many we were beaten by, but it was well into double figures. This team argued and fought and apportioned blame when we won, so you can imagine what it was like when we were getting stuffed. A maelstrom of recrimination swirled about me as I ran around the midfield like I was playing on my own in the eye of a hurricane.

We had players sent off and others stormed away in a fit, while two simply gave up the ghost, walked to the side, changed, and headed to the parking lot. With a few minutes left and the score at 18-0 or something, a defender scythed me down from behind, and the next morning I had the Goodyear Blimp where my left calf used to be.

I clumped to Finn's practice anyway and from the sideline our lack of mobility was painfully evident, as despite training for five months we'd pass the ball then stop to get our breath back. It was glaringly obvious that in this heat we'd need a full squad and a regular switching of substitutes.

The sun was so strong that my newspaper had yellowed by the end of the session, and that there was any movement at all from our aging squad was a testament to their dedication. Even lying on the grass I felt like I was in an oven that had been placed in a sauna and I was wearing a wetsuit. I took two weeks off to let my leg heal.

Felix kept calling.

CHAPTER 15

An Eight-Goal Thriller

I returned to fitness just in time for our next test against a strengthened version of the Chalmette team we'd taken on in our first game. The match was under Friday night lights at Pan American and to ensure there were no cock-ups, this time we got Kenny to play and Macca to referee.

Watching was the biggest crowd I'd ever played in front of and on the bench were Adrian and four Southern Irishmen: Sean, Mike Mac, Kenny, and Stephen Burke, the student I'd met in Finn's and now known as "New Stephen." Mike Mac complained, "I thought this was supposed to be an Irish team! They just want us to serve the drink."

Our experimental 3-5-2 formation collapsed quicker than Big Rab's pledge to stop drinking. Billy put us one up but they equalized quickly and our midfield anchor Julien went off injured after ten minutes. They scored twice more and threatened to overrun us, and then finally I did something of consequence and released Benji, who made it 3-2 to them at halftime.

Big Rab was in charge of substitutions and was taking his role more seriously than in the first game and only drinking one beer at a time. He later revealed his decisions weren't entirely tactically motivated, as he'd put Adrian on in left midfield just to shut him up and get him as far away as possible. Kenny advised putting speed on the right wing, and as I was moved to that position, it tells you how slow the rest of the team were.

The match ended 4-4, although the Chalmette team hit the

post with a penalty and both Dave and I should have been sent off after committing last-ditch "professional" fouls to deny their forwards clean shots on goal.

Though our prematch plan and formation had disintegrated within minutes, there were positives to take away from the game. They were the best team we'd played (Wispy Hair from Lafreniere Park appeared and I'd almost broken my neck trying to put a crunching tackle in on him, but sadly the opportunity never arose) and we'd scored four against them. We'd been without Mark again and Michael had gone into goals for his first outdoor game ever, to become our fourth different goalkeeper in four games. Still recovering from a double hernia operation, he'd let in two soft, weak shots.

Also, diminutive English redhead Andy Smith had impressed in his first start. He'd come to New Orleans in 1999 to work for three years and met his Louisiana girlfriend Stacey, then after a spell in Aberdeen, Scotland, he requested a transfer back. A barmaid at Finn's told him about the team and he quickly became a regular fixture, both on the team and at the pub. His initial nickname was Rio, not due to his samba skills or his Brazilian-like trickery but because he once missed practice to go to a Duran Duran concert. It then evolved into the Ginger Whinger.

Billy had shown his class once more and notched a hat trick. My dad, who even closing in on sixty is still a better player than I'll ever be, was watching and his opinion was, "I wouldn't like to see the team without Billy, but the biggest thing I saw was that you need a coach."

Benji's report said: "We have clearly progressed in some areas but remain perplexingly hamstrung in others . . . a draw is like kissing your sister—strangely unsatisfying."

At training the next week Dave pulled me aside. "I have

to say sorry to you, mate; I've been worrying about it all weekend." Near the end of the match when I was playing in front of him on the right, I'd chased an attacker back, the ball broke free, and as I followed it Dave shouted, "Get out of the way or I'll break your leg!" He'd knocked the ball clear and then had a set-to with the opponent, who squared up to Dave for threatening him, convinced Dave would never yell like that at his own teammate. I laughed as I ran away because I knew it had been directed at me. I told him I accepted his apology and then spent the rest of the session trying to kick him.

On July 23, Finn's celebrated its third birthday, and three days later I met my friend Jason again to see Chelsea on their latest U.S. tour, this time in Washington, D.C., scarcely believing it had been a year since the guy in the bar talked about the "false friendliness" in New Orleans.

Due to a sense of loyalty to Felix and (more pertinently) because of the constant barrage of muddled phone calls, I returned to the Hispanic team whose name I didn't know and kept forgetting to ask. In my third appearance, the only time I'd ever been officiated by two referees with each covering half the pitch, we went 4-0 down and had a man sent off. Though we managed to get back to 4-3, I was fed up with running myself into the ground for nothing when most of the team were still not passing to me. I decided to play one more game to see if things improved.

The next Saturday we had seven players, one of whom was Felix. He reminded me of Argentina's greatest-ever player Diego Maradona—a testimonial-playing fat and bloated Diego ten years after retirement with a lurid psychedelic jersey stretched across his stomach like a second skin. As I lined up alongside five middle-aged players and a heavily perspiring coach in near-100-degree heat, I thought the league organizers could find themselves charged with a number of manslaughter counts, as dying from heatstroke seemed a very real possibility.

By halftime my legs were jelly and I wobbled to the sideline like Elvis with St. Vitus' dance. I had made my decision: I jacked it in to concentrate on Finn's. Goodbye Hispanic Ken and hello Irish Steve.

Shortly after my desertion of the Islano league, Finn's started a Monday night fitness session with jogging, sprinting, sit-ups, and push-ups. Balls were banned, and when Adrian turned up with one he ignored Medhurst, who was shouting at him to put it away, and played keepy-uppy as we ran around the pitch. A guy was standing in the middle of a field with a fishing rod practicing his casting and as we passed, Dave asked, "Catch anything, mate?" I said he looked really stupid and I'd a good mind to swim out and have a word with him.

I hadn't gone to these sessions the first few weeks, preferring to play my pickup game and arrogantly assuming I was fitter than nearly everyone anyway. When I did show up, I was a whisker away from becoming the first person in the squad to throw up (in my defense I'd been unwell), and the next day every muscle in the top half of my body ached.

When I whined about the soreness to Paul, he told me about a friend in his fifties who'd disappeared on a bachelor party. Paul went to his room the next morning to rouse him for the flight home and found him fully clothed on top of the bed with no idea where he'd been or what he'd done. He did, however, have a sharp pain in his chest, and when he lifted up his shirt he discovered he'd had his nipple pierced.

Medhurst said he'd never been on a squad dedicated

enough to train three times a week. Dave replied he'd never been on a team with such a collection of characters.

The big kickoff was five weeks away. It was time for another meeting.

On August 7 the team gathered. We watched Chelsea beat Arsenal in the Community Shield, an English season curtain raiser, and then crowded around the pool table to listen to Stephen and Medhurst talk about the soccer-watching club and its two-hundred-dollar annual fee. Medhurst urged us all to join so they'd have the funds to continue showing games. He was so passionate because when he lived in L.A., he'd been unable to see live matches and had really missed it.

Stephen explained Finn's didn't make money from the membership and said he felt embarrassed taking the cover charge. Setanta took 80 percent of the cash collected at the door and mandated a twenty-dollar fee for international games. The pub had once charged a visiting group from San Diego ten dollars a head, word had somehow reached Setanta, and they'd phoned Stephen to remind him it should've been twenty dollars. As it had been the Ireland and Israel World Cup qualifying game, there were the inevitable jokes about Jews and money.

Finally, Stephen told everyone to come kitted out in their colors. "There's no politics in this bar lads—we've never allowed it and never will. We've only ever had a problem with one guy, a mad Celtic fan who just couldn't accept that he had to sit and watch games with Rangers supporters. So come along and support your team with pride. Apart from you Chelsea bastards."

He didn't really say that last sentence, so I handed Medhurst my down payment. I'd occasionally gone to watch Rangers in Glasgow when I lived in Newcastle in Northern England, and I never would have imagined fifteen years later I'd be paying money to an organization called the New Orleans Celtic Supporters' Club after their bitter rivals.

We moved onto discussing the team and Stephen said he'd pay to have badges made when we came up with a club logo. Medhurst handed out sheets with the dates of the Sunday games and said that as the first was scheduled for September 11, he'd ordered black armbands. To this day I don't know if he was being serious.

Medhurst and Adrian had been to a meeting that week to sort out league regulations (The minutes on the SELASA Web site read: "We welcomed a new team called Finn McCool's. Adrian invited us all to drink there after games"). Benji marked the occasion with another abusive email masquerading as a news update: "There's been a lot of talk since our foundation, but the time has come to put up or shut up. Few would've predicted the increased fitness and general good vibe and credit is certainly due to our leaders—Medhurst in particular has led from the front and kept the team moving in a positive direction." Then he made fun of everyone.

Medhurst said he wanted a backseat role in the club and volunteered to be treasurer and nominated Jonathan for secretary. With the quest to find a coach ongoing, Medhurst cleverly proposed a three-player selection committee to pick the team in the meantime. We settled on Mark, Colin, and Benji, representing the defense, midfield, and attack. Mark and Benji were loudmouthed and didn't give a rat's arse what anyone else thought—exactly the kind of people you want to make difficult decisions—while Colin would be the quiet but knowledgeable arbitrator between them.

Medhurst had originally put me forward and I'd been flattered, as I was keen to get involved in team tactics and selection. I was initially disappointed not to be chosen, but upon later reflection I was delighted: there would've been hard choices to make, friends to disappoint, and I'd have fretted about picking myself. The more I thought about it the happier I was not to have made the cut.

By now our attention was wandering to the thought of downing a beer on this hot summer day, and Benji was jumping up and down like a spring-heeled jack making points and asking questions like, did anyone bloody well read his match reports and did we want him to keep doing them and who wanted a drink and when were we going to organize a team binge?

Jonathan closed the meeting by saying, "This time last year we lost a member of this pub. He was sick and didn't tell anyone and we all miss him. Don't let that ever happen again. Remember, we aren't just a social club but a support group as well, one which is here to help one another."

When he left, the ex-pats talked about the "touchy-feely" attitude in the States, and how Jonathan had thought nothing of saying that to a pub full of blokes but back home, he would have been laughed out of the room. Weeks later his sentiments were proved frighteningly prophetic.

The next day Jonathan launched into his club secretary role and compiled a list of email addresses, sending a message reading, "Training tonight at 6 P.M. The first match is September 11—you do the math." We had created a monster.

With email as our main method of communication, it meant poor Julien was now receiving cyber insults as well as taking stick at training, and he despairingly emailed me asking how many weeks the season lasted so he would know how long the baiting would go on. I replied that it would last longer than the French had against the Germans in World War II.

Not that he was the only object of abuse. Dave and

Medhurst referred to me as the Hobbit or Frodo, and Benji thoughtfully circulated an email rounding up everyone's nicknames. At least he was self-aware enough to put "wanker" beside his own . . .

Chapter 16

The Calm Before the Storm

August in Louisiana is hot and wet. It's a hard concept to grasp if you're from the U.K. In Belfast, summer is three weeks during which it might stop bucketing out of the heavens and be warm enough for shorts, but in New Orleans the rain arrives with the sun. Most of the year we played on baked-solid ground and patchy grass with the ball bobbling around on a surface like the cracked mud you see on Discovery Channel shows about famine in Africa. Now we reveled in the chance to splash through muddy fields, launch ourselves into lakes of water, and kick the ball so that it sent fountains of spray into the air.

One night I was the only person to turn up for a pickup game at the Fly, and the next week when I told one of the friendlier guys, he said, "Well, it looked a bit stormy out." Just the threat of a chance of a drop of rain was enough to stop these big strapping lads from daring to venture outdoors.

In contrast, I loved getting drenched, and as I scrubbed my boots in the kitchen sink it took me back to my school days, although my mum never shouted at me for making a mess as much as Julie did. She'd come home from work and yell at me for getting dirt on the cabinets, demand to know why I still couldn't work out how to use the dishwasher, and ask why there were Band-Aids where the oregano should be. Then she'd remove her snowsuit and light a fire.

We had a rematch against ICC on August 13, and as I was at Ray's daughter Hannah's fourth birthday party a few blocks away, I stuffed my face with cake and sweets and arrived early — to find most of the squad already there.

I asked Benji how the selection committee had worked out. "Dude, I was up half the night emailing Colin back and forth. Eventually we agreed upon the team and then we spoke to Mark and he changed it all." The trio went off to huddle underneath a tree.

The vibe for the warmup felt different, nervous even. No longer did "the team pick itself." Even though we were just aging, balding, out-of-shape blokes getting ready for a kick-about on what Benji called "a crappy cabbage patch," you could sense trepidation in the air. When Colin took me aside to say I was playing central midfield, I felt like kissing him, and not just because of his movie-star looks.

I started alongside Scotsman Graeme Shand, who was making his debut but whose life had been intertwined with Finn's and New Orleans for years. Graeme, from *Braveheart*'s William Wallace's hometown of Elderslie, had actually met Big Rab at Govan shipyard the day before Rab immigrated to the States and had followed him out here in 1994 for a seven-year spell broken by six months in Belfast of all places.

When he returned to the area in July after having lived in San Diego, I had met him at the Fly and invited him to training. He already knew many of the lads from O'Flaherty's so hadn't needed much persuasion to join, and we added another rugged, hard, full-blooded, tough-tackling player to our collection. We seemed to have a few. If we could find a Welshman, it would complete the British Isles set.

Our other debutant wasn't Welsh but had been born in New Orleans to El Salvadorian parents of Italian descent with relatives in Argentina. Erick Granados, twenty-seven, had recently moved back after three years in the navy and was recruited by Medhurst, who worked with his wife. The cleaning company owner had grown disillusioned by "the macho culture" in the Islano league. "I had to adapt to having less touches with your European-style setup, but I didn't find it hard to fit in because I'm the son of immigrants and have dealt with being an outsider all my life." The irony of a local-born player describing himself in his own city as an outsider was not lost on me.

I knew the ICC goalkeeper from our SOP indoor team and he came over to say hello. When he left I rushed to tell our forwards to shoot on sight because he was truly useless. It was nothing personal. It was just business.

By kickoff our opponents had only eight players, so we gave them Adrian, Kenny, and Macca. When another guy turned up fifteen minutes late he came on and the player he replaced ran to the sideline, collapsed in a heap, and vomited, so I'm guessing he wasn't exactly at his peak fitness level.

Injured committee members Colin and Benji took their new duty seriously and watched dispassionately from the bench and made notes. After just two minutes I shot from outside the penalty box and the ball squirmed through the goalkeeper's hands as I'd predicted. Eric and Billy scored, then I got my second from twenty yards and it was 4-0 at halftime.

After the break Andy scored, I notched a hat trick with another strike from distance, Kenny clawed one back, and we gave them Mark for the last twenty minutes. I hit my fourth and Billy his second to make the final result 8-1.

This time I won the man-of-the-match award, a can of warm beer Benji had left in the sun. As the rest of the team dived on the ice chest I realized I'd been rewarded with a prize less appealing than everyone else's drink. I went home to shower and told Julie I'd scored four. "Were the other team not very good then?" she asked. I thanked her for the ego boost, sneakily turned down the heating, and retired to the pub.

Later Benji revealed that he wasn't thrilled with his quasi-managerial role. "I'm happy to take responsibility as I'll treat everybody the same and don't have a problem speaking my mind and pissing people off. But I think it'll turn into a nightmare which will affect my own game during the season."

Dave said we still needed a coach. "A committee can pick the side but it's the setup on the field which sometimes lets us down. It's more important to have a game plan and someone on the touchline with the ability, for example, to spot a weakness in the opposition and exploit it."

Eric thought ICC hadn't used Macca enough, as he was "the best player on their team and *maybe* the best player on the pitch." Yep, *maybe* the ex-English Premiership star was a better player than any of our drunken halfwits!

Macca, meanwhile, only at quarter speed but still head and shoulders above everyone, was shocked how organized we'd become. "It has opened my eyes to just how serious your commitment level is and that you've gone beyond it being just a mess-around."

But Adrian said we'd been awful and with a decent goalkeeper they'd have won. During the match he'd cracked us up when he taunted Kenny, "I thought you said you'd played the game!" His lack of attendance at training was highlighted when Medhurst told him he'd be up against Julien and Adrian asked, "Who the hell's Julien?" even though the Frenchman had been with us for months.

Adrian spent the game bumping into our elegant center-half and goading him. "I learned as a kid to bounce off defenders and indulge in a bit of gamesmanship and I kept doing it to him until he got really riled up. Then I said to him, it was about time he got pissed off, and he was cool after that."

In four months we'd played five games, winning two, losing one, and tying two. We'd chalked up eighteen goals and conceded ten, and Billy and I were joint top scorers with six each, although I'd played one game more. Now the league loomed large.

"I'm excited" said Medhurst. "Are you all excited?"

"I'm excited" I replied.

"I'm excited. It's going to be great. I can't bloody wait," said Dave.

Medhurst asked if I was going to cut my hair for the league, and I promised to shave my head if we won the title, confident we'd face younger, fitter, and more talented teams. When I mentioned the pledge to Graeme he said, "I've played in that league. From what I've seen so far, we'll walk it."

Benji's match report had mutated from mere abuse about height and weight to a bizarre, sweeping epic encompassing bouts of poetry and a storyline based on the *Lord of the Rings* trilogy. It was obvious his literary abilities were expanding in direct proportion to the quality of weed he was smoking.

Julie, meantime, had come up with a great concept for our club badge. It was an Arctic explorer wrapped in a hat and scarf . . . only kidding. Julie suggested, and it made sense, to relate it to Finn McCool, the folkloristic Northern Irish giant the pub and the team were named after. But it's difficult to portray a giant on a badge, so she sketched part of the Giant's Causeway, a World Heritage Site of hexagonal volcanic rock formations in Antrim that legend says he created.

We started with seven columns representing the seven nationalities in the squad and added three stars in tribute to our adopted country's national flag, one for each of the continents from which players were drawn. We ringed it with red and white for the Cross of St. George, as we'd seven Englishmen on the roster, and topped it off with a shamrock. Two different graphic artist friends in Belfast worked on it and emailed logos.

Everybody hated them. Dave said the columns looked like cigarettes, while someone else thought they were coffins. Adrian wanted an emblem with two fingers showing a V sign to everyone else in the league. For some reason Captain Morgan drew a goat. I explained that it had been Julie's idea.

While things motored along nicely with Finn's, I also managed to make progress with my pickup games, as restaurateur Nanou, a Frenchman with the Polish surname De Rezinsky, asked me to join his indoor team. He may have invited me because he'd played with me for a year and knew I'd be the perfect addition to his team, but more likely he hadn't been able to rope in enough suckers to pay the sixty-six-dollar fee for the ten-week season. At least I was finally learning some names and I fantasized that one day soon I'd have real-life American friends outside of the pub. I was still the only person in the shower afterwards though.

When Finn's training finished on Thursday, August 25, we hung around even longer than normal, and not just because it took forever to figure out how to pack away the new collapsible goal Dave had bought. There was a lot to discuss.

We filled our last two squad places that night. Joe Ryan was thirty-eight but fitter than most players half his age.

He'd moved back home within the last year after living in Colorado for a decade, but twelve years ago he'd played with Sean and had coached at Billy's school fifteen years earlier. He'd been walking in the park one night and recognized Sean, who had immediately urged Medhurst to snap him up.

He was a superb player who sparkled all over the field and I dashed to warn him about Mark before he was scared away. He was quiet and with six-year-old twin boys to look after, he rarely went to bars; in fact, six months after he joined us he still thought the team name was pronounced "Finn McCull's." When I told him I'd had trouble making friends at pickup games he said, "Americans live a fast-paced life and squeeze everything in they can. So they squeeze soccer in as well and then have trouble relaxing afterwards." It was a good point.

Sebastian Villarreal was a twenty-nine-year-old Uruguayan anesthesiologist whose father had played professionally and who had turned out for the under-twenty-one national team. I'd cornered him when he showed up at the Fly and he shone like the North Star in the desert sky at the handful of sessions he'd made it to.

Dave said that he "fit in really well with us," which I took to mean he thought he was a dirty bastard. He'd lost his temper a few times and we all loved the idea of adding a hot-headed mercurial South American with Latin flair to our workman-like British team. He probably felt like Brazilian legend Pele signing for the small-town English club Barnsley. Or possibly Spurs.

Because I'd recruited Graeme and Sebastian, after he'd had a few pints and turned into the Ginger Whinger, Andy would moan, "Stephen, please don't bring any more players." I didn't know why he was worried, as he was the only left-footer we had, and if anyone was going to be forced out, it'd be me with my injury-prone, erratic form.

We also found out that Macca, in a moment of weakness (translation: inebriation) at Finn's, had agreed to coach us and pick the team for just five dollars per person per week. Dave had quickly and drunkenly scrawled out a contract on a paper napkin and made him sign it.

It was most likely a better option than the other candidate who'd expressed an interest in the position: Little Dave, an African-American midget who hung around Finn's and washed cars and cut grass. Medhurst wanted a dance off to choose between them, but Little Dave had failed the first question of his informal interview by saying he thought there were seven players on a soccer team.

Macca's deal was a bargain and Sean offered to fund the first week out of his own pocket. It was a typically generous offer by Sean and later Medhurst told me, "I probably shouldn't tell you this, but he sidled up to me one day and said he knew you didn't have much spare cash and wanted to pay your one-hundred-dollar team subscription." I was genuinely touched, but I had already paid the money, which I'd earned from a day's freelance consultancy stint for Sean's firm, which he'd arranged! I resolved to cut back on mentions of my unemployment, as thanks to Julie's hard work I wasn't a charity case just yet. And besides, I was still hopeful I'd convince her to take a second job delivering pizzas.

Lastly, we considered Sunday's match against Olympiakos, which had been arranged just days before. Big Rab explained the circumstances. "Like everything else with this team it started off with a drunken conversation when Dave was completely off his head. He met one of their players in the pub, and the more wasted he got the more outrageous his claims became, until he decided we should play them and the guy called their coach and organized the game."

I couldn't decide if it was a good idea or not. Both our goalkeepers were away, and as Olympiakos had been the city's top team for years, they could give us a hiding that might be psychologically damaging right before the league kicked off. On the other hand, Kenny had promised us one of the Shell Shockers' goalkeepers (it was 99.99 percent certain apparently) and it would be a chance to test ourselves against the best team in the first division.

The next day, Friday, August 26, 2005, Julie came home from work and said the staff had received a Severe Weather Alert email from the company that afternoon. Nobody in her office was taking it too seriously, but apparently there was an outside chance we could get brushed by a hurricane this weekend.

"Really? What's its name?" I asked.

"Katrina."

"Oh, we'll be fine then. Katrina is an eighties pop singer, not a deadly storm. Can you imagine being killed by something named Katrina? It'd be as bad as getting hit by a hurricane called Britney." I laughed and helped remove her snow pants.

CHAPTER 17

Landfall

I got home from Finn's in the early afternoon of Saturday, August 27, to find two messages from Felix's wife. The first said that day's game kicked off at 6 P.M., the second message eighty minutes later said it'd been canceled due to the hurricane.

I checked the English soccer results on the internet, tidied the house, and then called my friend Blair Harvey, whom I hadn't spoken to in months. We chatted for more than an hour and at one stage an emergency broadcast test signal flashed across the TV screen and I told him about Katrina. I said we weren't evacuating after our experience with Ivan last year and he enquired as to what Julie thought. I replied she couldn't be too bothered, as she was out shopping.

At 4:48 P.M., New Stephen rang from his job in an upmarket teashop. The owners had told him to shut the café early and go, and he asked if we were leaving. His employers had urged him to flee the city and even offered to take him with them. I told him not to worry and to come over to our house later for a drink.

Julie called an hour later to tell me she was having a fabulous shopping day. There were no crowds and the stores were empty. She was now in T.J. Maxx and could see that Wal-Mart across the way was boarding up its windows. T.J. Maxx never did charge her credit card and we still have the receipt for the purchase made at 6:01 P.M. Unfortunately she hadn't gone on a mad shopping spree splashing out hundreds of dollars but had only paid $5.43 for a bowl. She phoned again at 7:49 P.M. to ask if I wanted anything from Taco Bell. Ray had called her to make sure we were out of harm's way and was amazed she was calmly eating in a fast-food joint.

New Stephen arrived at 9 P.M. and we switched on the news. Julie wanted to at least consider leaving. I told her none of the lads from Finn's were evacuating and she was acting like an excitable American drama queen. I'd build a wee fort out of sofa cushions to protect us.

Every New Orleanian will tell you the same story: the women wanted to leave and the men insisted on staying. There is probably a Darwinian basis for this, something hard-wired into our genetics about male determination to fight and defend the cave, while the female predisposition is to run and protect her family. Nevertheless, I have the utmost respect for nature's awesome, destructive power.

In Australia, Julie and I visited Northern Queensland's Daintree Rainforest and a sudden tropical downpour swelled the river, flooding a stone bridge and stopping us from leaving the area. Hulking great SUVs and trucks ploughed breezily through the water, but we'd hired the cheapest, smallest (and therefore lowest-lying) car we'd found and were trapped.

As we stood looking at the blocked crossing, two young English tourist couples in the same predicament and with similar-sized vehicles parked beside us. Both men wanted to chance it. They argued with their partners and asked my opinion, presuming the agreement of an old man like me would reassure the girls.

But it just so happened that the previous night we'd watched a terrifying documentary about how dangerous a flood of even a few feet can be if you are in a car. Because a car is full of air it floats and is quickly and easily swept downstream, becoming a buoyant, uncontrollable coffin spelling certain death. Victims featured had lost their clothes and even their skin as they'd been churned around amongst stones and rocks that had found their way into the car and turned the vehicle into a deadly giant washing machine.

If this scenario wasn't scary enough, signs warned against standing too close to the river because of the aggressive, dangerous crocodiles. We'd heard about these fearsome reptiles for weeks in Australia. So if we did get swept off the bridge, our choice would be either to stay in the car and get the skin ripped from our bodies or to swim for it and fight off one of the greatest predators evolution has ever produced.

After a terse summary of the salient facts from the TV show, the others swallowed hard and followed me to a pub where we waited a few hours for the level to drop.

So when I say I had no intention of evacuating, it wasn't because of some misplaced macho belief that I could battle and defeat the elements. I just couldn't be bothered. I simply didn't see the point. Our house had withstood more than a century of everything Mother Nature had thrown at it. I was sure everything would turn out fine. New Stephen cycled home and we went to bed.

Our phone rang at 7 A.M.

When you are called at that time on a Sunday, it can't be good news. The only other occasion I was phoned so early on a weekend was in 1991 when my mate Dave Feldstein contacted me to say the newspaper we worked for was folding.

New Stephen was panicking. His landlord had rapped him up at 6:30 A.M. to grab some things from the apartment. He told him he was skedaddling and begged him to leave as well. I said I'd call him back.

We went downstairs and turned on the TV. It didn't look good. A swirling white mass was spinning around and obliterating the blues and greens on the weather map graphics. Local programs had been canceled as the networks concentrated on the hurricane sweeping up the Gulf of Mexico and barreling down on New Orleans. It had strengthened to a Category Five overnight.

Julie looked at me and said, "Dear?" I tried to argue for a minute but my heart wasn't in it. I called New Stephen and said I'd come to pick him up in a couple of hours.

Julie's parents rang to make sure we were evacuating. Soon after, they phoned back again. Then they called to see if we'd left yet. When you're frantically trying to make your house hurricane-proof at the last minute, things get tense, nerves get frazzled, tempers get shortened. If you ever find yourself in this situation, take the phone off the hook. Having to deal with incredulous relatives asking why you're still there doesn't help matters, believe me.

We piled the TV and a few breakables into the downstairs bathroom then nailed shut the storm shutters on our front upstairs windows. My pal from home, Richard, who also married an American, called and invited us to their home in Atlanta. We said okay; at this stage we hadn't even begun to think about where we were actually going to head.

His wife, Leslie, whose brother used to live in New Orleans, said, "Stephen, my parents just rang asking about you. They said, 'Do your friends realize how serious this thing is? They are leaving okay, aren't they'?" I reassured her that yes indeed, we were now fully aware we'd be well advised to be on our way.

I drove along St. Charles to get New Stephen. Normally the wide, regal boulevard is bustling with joggers and rickety streetcars. But New Orleans was a ghost town. It reminded me of the opening scene in the film *28 Days Later*. There was no one around. No people, no streetcars, no buses, no cars. It finally dawned on me that everyone else had left. For the only time in my life, I actually felt the hairs stand up on the back of my neck. It was eerie, portentous.

The rock radio station was no longer playing rock but hurricane evacuation information. As I arrived at New Stephen's, the radio station went live to a press conference and for the first time in history the mayor ordered a mandatory evacuation of the city.

New Stephen jumped into the car and said the teashop owners had told him to empty the cash register and take the food because they didn't expect it to be standing when they returned. We stopped off and grabbed dozens of brownies, orange-and-cranberry muffins, and slices of coffee cake.

Back at the house, I packed. I thought I'd be away two days, three at the most. Into my sports bag I put one tee-shirt, one pair of shorts, one pair of socks, and two pairs of boxers. And three books, because I'm always paranoid about having nothing to read. I didn't bring practical articles like a razor, sentimental stuff such as my wedding ring, or "for God's sake, what were you thinking?" items like a copy of the novel I'd spent a year writing. Julie worried Georgia could be cool in August and loaded up with six sweaters just in case.

I checked my email and our game with Olympiakos was definitely scrapped. At 6 P.M. on Saturday, Medhurst had sent a message reading: "Let's call the game off for Sunday. I'm out of here. See ya. Just got gas at Shell close to Finn's and witnessed a full-scale brawl. Tensions are running high."

Mike Mac had replied, "Hey wait—if we show up to play and they don't then we get the win, right?"

And just a few minutes before, a one-word email had arrived from Billy: "Cowards."

That message and Saturday's conversation with Benji when he said he'd be staying haunted me again and again in the coming weeks.

The last thing I did before walking out the door was try and contact my parents to tell them we were evacuating, but I couldn't get through to either. As we left, our next-door neighbor was helping the elderly black couple across the street board up, and they declined our offer of assistance, as they'd almost finished. They were all staying and were confident there wouldn't be enough rain to flood our street.

We avoided the interstate and picked our way east along secondary roads. Judging by the traffic, everybody was avoiding the interstate. Our map ended at St. Bernard Parish and we had to bleed into the interstate. We literally inched forward, crawling along painstakingly slowly. The roadside was littered with broken-down and parked vehicles. The occupants either sat forlornly waiting for help or watched their kids and pets on a break from the tedium of the car-clogged highway.

Our spirits were pretty high though. We'd been through all this before and could put up with a few days' disruption. I couldn't stop singing the Scorpions song "Rock You Like a Hurricane."

After three hours we ground to a halt when we hit a police roadblock near the state line. Someone said there was a bridge out. It was now late afternoon. Atlanta is a seven-hour drive when the roads are clear; at this rate it would take days to get there. The wind started to pick up.

Then out of the blue we got an offer to stay with a relative of a friend of a friend of Julie's who lived in the small

Mississippi town Philadelphia. I couldn't remember why the name rang a bell with me, but later I discovered that two months earlier it had been the location of the murder trial of eighty-year-old preacher Edgar Ray Killen. He was sentenced to sixty years for masterminding the brutal slaying in 1964 of three civil rights workers, which was dramatized in the film *Mississippi Burning*.

New Stephen got excited when we told him we'd be making the four-hour drive to Philadelphia and said he'd always wanted to see the Liberty Bell. He was crushed when we explained that was housed in Pennsylvania's Philadelphia, twelve hundred miles away, which was a four-hour trip only if you were piloting a jet.

We turned off the interstate and edged north through rural Mississippi, still in Katrina's projected path but far enough inland to hopefully be safe. We arrived exhausted but relieved late on Sunday.

The next morning our host said the house had a hurricane shelter but "it was very, very small," adding, "You guys need to get on the road as early as you can." So taking the hint we borrowed a map, ate muffins, and tried to come up with a plan. Memphis was a possibility (New Stephen was keen as long as it was the same Memphis that Elvis came from and not another Memphis he didn't know about), but we didn't really want to be that far from home.

Instead we would head west back into Louisiana, spend the day sitting out Katrina in the northern part of the state, then dart south back to New Orleans before the world and his wife got on the road. As we walked outside, the wind whipped across the fields and the rain was unrelenting. Still, we weren't taking the storm seriously as we got in the car to drive through the outer bands of one of the most powerful hurricanes ever to hit the United States.

The ride through the back roads of the south was harrowing and draining. Belatedly we realized what we were up against. We were repeatedly buffeted by crazy winds and fought to dodge broken branches skimming along the ground like flat stones across a pond.

We broke for the interstate to try and outrun the weather and tuned into the emergency radio frequency. Tornadoes were spinning off from Katrina and popping up all over the county. Announcers pleaded with drivers to get off the roads. The highway was empty. The only vehicles around were police cars and massive eighteen-wheeler trucks. The sky was a blanket of black. It was the most frightening car journey of my life.

We limped into Vicksburg on the Louisiana/Mississippi border, parked, and polished off more muffins. Conditions were undoubtedly atrocious, but we thought it would be less dangerous to continue west, away from Katrina. We pushed on. The wind and rain eased. By early evening we'd traveled another eighty miles and pulled into a bar in Monroe for something to eat.

That's when we saw the first TV pictures from New Orleans.

The shock was unbelievable and indescribable. Newscasters said Lake Pontchartrain was pouring into the city. There were major breeches in the Industrial Canal and the 17th Street Canal levees. We didn't know where those canals were.

We'd heard radio reports of storm surge and levees overtopping. We anticipated smashed windows, missing roof tiles, and fallen trees. Never, ever, ever, in our worst nightmares did we expect to see water crashing through holes hundreds of feet wide.

We shuffled out of the bar and studied the map for an

hour in the parking lot weighing our options. New Stephen checked with a couple of nearby motels but they gave him photocopied hand-written sheets with a list of available accommodations. There wasn't a room to be had in the entire state. The nearest were in Dallas, a five-hour drive away. We got back on the road and made for Texas.

Even now we hadn't really grasped the true enormity of the situation and the scale of the disaster. We were still cracking jokes and refusing to accept what we'd just seen with our own eyes. Our cell phone with its New Orleans area code stopped working. Darkness fell and we kept driving.

It was after midnight when we eventually arrived in Dallas. The motel clerk said a downtown hotel had a discounted rate for New Orleans evacuees and cut his price to match it. We were exhausted and emotionally drained after traveling all day in trying conditions.

The news was that New Orleans was filling up like a soup bowl. Residents might not get back this year. But I couldn't accept it was really that bad. Things like that didn't happen. It didn't seem real.

We collapsed into bed.

CHAPTER 18

Katrina By the Numbers

0.3	number of inches New Orleans sinks annually
2	number of more powerful storms ever to have made landfall in the U.S.
5	amount of storm names retired after the 2005 hurricane season—the most ever (Katrina, Rita, Dennis, Stan, and Wilma)
11	number of people killed in Florida after the first landfall while Katrina was still a Category One hurricane
22	number of pumping stations built to drain New Orleans
28	number of named storms in the 2005 hurricane season—so many that scientists ran out of letters and were forced to use the Greek alphabet (The twenty-eighth was confirmed on April 12, 2006, when a review of records found a storm in October near the Azores had reached 52 mph.)
35	height in feet of waves in the Gulf of Mexico, the highest figure ever recorded
80	approximate percentage of New Orleans flooded
90	percentage of hurricane victims who are killed by storm surge
118	square miles of coastline lost during Katrina and Rita—five years' worth of erosion
200	amount in yards of Louisiana's wetlands lost to coastal erosion every hour of every day
200	recorded wind speed in mph of Katrina at 3 A.M. on Monday, four hours before landfall

350	length in miles of levees protecting New Orleans
900	length in feet of the Industrial Canal levee breach
10,000	amount of rubble in tons needed to fill the hole in the 17th Street Canal levee
87,000	total of square miles of debris (roughly the size of Great Britain) Katrina left behind in Louisiana, Alabama, Arkansas, Texas, Mississippi, and Florida, according to the Army Corps of Engineers
108,731	number of homes drowned by more than four feet of water
58 billion	gallons of water (3 percent of Lake Pontchartrain's volume) that flooded New Orleans and a small section of east Jefferson
150 billion	estimate in dollars of Katrina's economic impact in Louisiana and Mississippi, according to Marshall University
250 billion	total number of gallons of water that poured into New Orleans after Katrina and Rita
Unknown	height of storm surge in Lake Pontchartrain (Katrina knocked out the measuring equipment)

Some More Numbers . . .

8	months the Finn's team had spent training for our season
13	days until kickoff

But to Put Things in Perspective . . .

1,833	total confirmed deaths. In a matter of hours Katrina killed more than half the number of people who died in three decades of the Troubles in Northern Ireland.

CHAPTER 19

The End of the World as We Know It

At 8 A.M. on Tuesday, August 30, the lobby was packed. Dozens of displaced New Orleanians milled around the breakfast buffet hungry for information. What have you heard? What areas are under water? When can we get home?

We swapped evacuation stories by the pool. Our escape had been a piece of cake compared to most. An extended black family had driven for twenty hours straight with small children and pets to get here. It had taken another family thirty hours. But everyone was just grateful to be safe and were praying their relatives made it out okay.

I wandered over to where New Stephen was talking with a white evacuee who was going to visit her brother in Austin. She told me, "I might move to Texas 'cus the Mexicans seem a lot nicer than those people we have at home. You know who I mean, don't-cha?" She nodded towards the black grandmother I'd been chatting with in case it wasn't crystal clear. Even though we were all in the same boat, hundreds of miles from home and worried about our friends and property, racism was still casual and assumed.

Back in the room we watched the news. The water was still rising. They were finding more holes in the levees. Most neighborhoods were submerged. The world's most famous low-lying city was drowning. Estimates of when we could return ranged from thirty days to four months. We weren't going home anytime soon and we couldn't afford to stay in a hotel forever.

Julie wanted to see her parents in North Carolina. I called Gordon Sheals, a school friend from Belfast now an American Airlines pilot, and he said New Stephen and I should fly out to visit him in Carlsbad near San Diego. He used his buddy passes to book the three of us flights; we ate the last of our muffins and jumped in a taxi to the airport.

It may seem strange that at a time of crisis and uncertainty Julie and I opted for opposite ends of the country, but it made sense to us. I've known Gordon thirty years and he's the closest thing I have to family in the States. He has been in the U.S. since 1992 but I'd hadn't seen him in two years and in fact visited him more frequently when I lived in Belfast. He and his wife, Dawn, were flying to Northern Ireland on Friday to see the World Cup qualifying games against Azerbaijan and England, and New Stephen and I could look after their dog and save them kennel fees.

We also didn't want to abandon New Stephen. Julie's mum had offered to put him up, but Gastonia wasn't the most suitable destination for a young, homeless, clothesless Irishman who couldn't even drive. We didn't know how long we were going to be displaced, and having Gordon's to ourselves for a week appeared a better option than living on top of Julie's family indefinitely.

At the airport Julie got through to our next-door neighbor. He had the same big old black rotary phone as Finn's, and unlike cell phones they continued to function, as they weren't linked to the decimated underground digital exchange network. He said our house had a damaged roof and broken windows, but the street hadn't flooded.

I was euphoric. I punched the air and whooped like a lunatic. On the plane to San Diego, I felt grateful that without even knowing it we'd bought in a high part of the city. When Gordon came home from work that night New

Stephen and I were sitting in the neighbor's garden wearing his sweatshirts and drinking his wine.

But if I thought things were looking up, I was sadly mistaken. Wednesday and Thursday were two of the worst days of my life. The mayor announced they'd been unable to sandbag the levee and the water level was still rising. Maybe I'd celebrated too soon. The news from New Orleans kept spiraling downwards. It was horrendous.

Looking back, I can clearly plot my moods as reactions to what was unfolding on live TV. At the start I'd been blissfully unaware of the hurricane's cataclysmic power, and when it ripped through the region I entered a state of denial bolstered by our neighbor's first-hand report our home hadn't flooded. Next, relief mixed with a tingle of excitement. But then came despair and helplessness as the city ripped itself apart on around-the-clock TV.

I spent the days either on the phone or glued to the news. Friends and family had tracked me down and I spoke with them for hours. Initially it really helped me deal with the emotion of it all, but after discussing the same things and going around and around the what-ifs and the maybes, I couldn't handle it anymore. I stopped answering calls. It was all just too much to take.

I was the most depressed I have ever been in my life. Even now I'm at a bit of a loss to understand why it affected me so much. I think there were a few factors, not least the sheer scale of the disaster. It was clearly a catastrophe. It was obvious the death toll would be high. But many more died in the tsunami of 2004 and on September 11 and those didn't resonate as much with me.

Was it because I was personally involved? Sure. You can read all the words you want about human suffering, but you only appreciate the true impact when it directly affects you. We had homeowners' insurance but no contents cover, and if our home was destroyed then we'd receive no compensation for losing all our worldly possessions. Thousands of photographs, daft knick-knacks, holiday mementos, my three-hundred-page book, all could be lost.

I'm sure I was feeling sorry for myself; we'd moved to Louisiana to start afresh and I feared our new life had already been snuffed out in just over a year. But part of it was that after fourteen months I'd fallen in love with vibrant, intoxicating New Orleans. It was outrageous and elegant, languid and raucous, and it felt like home. Watching it self-destruct on TV was breaking my heart.

Occasionally, for a fleeting moment, I'd mourn the possible loss of my 1982 World Cup vinyl single or Chelsea English FA Cup Final ticket, but it wouldn't last long. I knew the pensioners I watched wading in chest-high water with a plastic bag weren't carrying their lunch but everything they now owned. When I saw helicopter rescue teams axe their way through the roof to pluck a toddler from the attic, I couldn't get worked up about the CD collection I'd left behind. How could I wallow in self-pity for long when critically ill patients waited on a flooded hospital's rooftop to be airlifted to safety? Images like a blanket casually thrown over a dead woman in a wheelchair at the Convention Center kept my experience relative.

The places on TV were places I knew. I lived there. It was my city, my neighborhood, my block. The stores being looted were shops I bought food in, the streets being flooded were roads I drove along, the residents dying were my neighbors. Ignorance then denial then relief then despair and now anger.

Some blame Mayor Nagin for the shambolic response to the aftermath, others Governor Blanco; many say it was

President Bush's fault. Personally, I think there is plenty of blame to go around. Every level of government screwed up. Time and again you come back to the same question: why?

Why are there tens of thousands of people trapped on the streets of a major American metropolis? Why can't we get them out? Why can't we rescue them? If CNN and bloody Wal-Mart trucks can find their way into the city, why can't the federal forces? Why can Third World drought-ravaged countries in Asia and Africa provide better relief to their citizens than the richest, most powerful country on Earth?

The friends and family who had visited us knew what a poverty-stricken place it was, but others were confused by the TV pictures and asked why the (mostly black) trapped inhabitants hadn't evacuated. I explained that two-fifths of Orleans Parish residents live below the poverty line and the vast majority of those who had remained had done so because they had been unable to leave. They had no cars to drive, no credit cards to book flights, and no money for hotel rooms. This disadvantaged underclass propping up the American Dream didn't ride out the hurricane for a laugh. They stayed because they had no choice.

Watching the news was killing me, but I couldn't tear myself away. I channel-surfed obsessively and ravenously devoured every studio bulletin and live broadcast. As an ex-journalist I knew it was inevitable some half-truths and exaggerations would be reported as fact, but the stories were so horrifying that if they were even partly true I feared everything I knew before was gone. I'm a child of the global TV news age, hardened by everything from Ethiopian famine to Middle Eastern beheadings, but it's only when you're personally involved that you appreciate the effect of such a tragedy on your well-being. I couldn't sleep and felt swamped, overwhelmed, and physically sick.

It was one apocalyptic tale after another. The hurricane had wrecked buildings. The lake flooded the city. Raw sewage was spreading disease. Standing fetid water had bred mosquitoes. Downed power lines were electrocuting people. There were snakes in the water. There were alligators in the water. Then armed gangs of looters. Babies being raped. The sick and elderly dying on the streets. Gas leaks. Chemical plants exploding. Fires sweeping the city. Civilization had collapsed. It felt like the end of the world.

The camera zoomed in on two men plodding through five feet of water, and I was able to read the street sign at the intersection. I pulled out my New Orleans map and counted the blocks to our house. We were ten away. I was sure five feet of water wouldn't disappear in ten blocks and resigned myself to the fact that we'd taken water.

One positive I clung to through bouts of depression was that Julie's job should be safe. She worked on the twenty-ninth floor of the Canal Place tower block, and though Canal Street had flooded we knew the water obviously hadn't reached her office. I switched on the news on Friday morning to hear, "Fire rages through the downtown Canal Place mall!"

"Jesus Christ! Just give us a break here, please!" I yelled at the screen.

I'm not overdramatizing my feelings or trying to make out that I suffered heroically through unbelievable hardship. I know I had it easy, watching TV in Carlsbad, but for the first time I understood what psychologists mean by "survivor's guilt." Even if our home was destroyed by water, fire, or looters, we still had insurance, and the worst that could happen was we'd receive a big fat check. I ached inside seeing storm victims battle to stay alive.

Julie was faring much better. Her cousins donated a

suitcase full of clothes, her company quickly relocated to Houston, and she flew there on Friday. Having a job to focus on and being with colleagues experiencing the same thing who could support each other undoubtedly helped her cope. She wasn't moping about all day like me.

She said, "Stephen, if we've lost everything and have to start over again, then we'll do it. We've been through it once already. We moved to New Orleans with next to nothing." She was right. Stuff is just stuff. Things are just things.

On Thursday, New Stephen went to San Diego for a few days, and that Friday morning I drove Gordon to the airport. He wanted me to come to Belfast and offered me a ticket for the match against England. I did think about it because I wouldn't be moving back to New Orleans in the foreseeable future. Nagin had given the order to abandon the city and the military was going door to door kicking out residents. But the situation was so unprecedented, unpredictable, and fluid (literally) that it was changing everyday, and I didn't think it would be a good idea to take off to Northern Ireland right now.

He asked me if I was going to be okay on my own. I think he thought I might slit my wrists. Dawn's parents phoned me every day she and Gordon were away, just to check in. I felt like I'd been placed on suicide watch, although I appreciated the concern.

On Friday the National Guard arrived in New Orleans and it finally felt like headway was being made. People were being evacuated and order was being restored. The cavalry had arrived.

CHAPTER 20

You Need Friends

Listless but also increasingly restless, I roamed Gordon's house on Friday, September 2. I drifted aimlessly from room to room, vegetated in front of the TV, checked emails. I still have those sent to me after Katrina, and even today it's heartwarming reading the messages of support and offers of help we received. When you go through an experience like that you find out who your friends are.

People I hadn't heard from in years got in touch. Relatives offered to cash in savings bonds for us. Friends said they'd lend us money and to just pay it back when we could. My schoolmate Jackson Collins, whom I hadn't seen in more than fifteen years, got hold of my number and called asking how he could help. Bill and Karin Hamilton, a couple we'd met on our cruise, sent the key to their holiday home and told us to live there as long as we wanted. My friend Kenny McClure volunteered his laptop computer so I could keep writing. Kevin Palmer, a journalist I'd worked with in the eighties, insisted on sending me tee-shirts.

It was unbelievably touching that people were thinking about us and wanted to help, and reading the messages made me even more emotional. I emailed that Julie and I were fine, but so many friends asked for Gordon's address to mail stuff I had to send another clarifying that we didn't need anything. I did accept the laptop though. Well, Kenny said he had two.

You could track the U.K. news coverage of the hurricane. At the start of the week mates had sent flippant, light-hearted emails with subjects like, "Got your water wings on?" and "Hope my holiday villa doesn't get damaged!"

On Tuesday, Trevor McCormick, the graphic designer who'd worked on the Finn's badge, had sent me the logo spun into a whirlwind adding, "It's current . . . it's dynamic." The next day he apologized: "Sorry about yesterday's funny — didn't realize it was such serious s — t." Months later I sent it to the rest of the squad and everyone preferred it to the original.

Mark was the first person from the team to get in touch. He'd left the Friday before the storm for a wedding in Memphis and as cell phones were down he started a list of landlines to make sure everyone was safe. Julien posted his number in Baton Rouge and I called him even though it was the wee hours.

He was as upset as me. He'd evacuated on Saturday night to a Belgian friend's house in Baton Rouge but left on Sunday as they'd heard Katrina was heading that way. They'd spent all day in Lafayette trying to find a hotel, then in the late afternoon a policeman in McDonald's advised them to go to Breaux Bridge, where a veterans' home had been turned into a shelter. There were three people in a large room with no furniture or beds and they went to Wal-Mart and bought sleeping bags. When they returned the place had filled with around one hundred worried evacuees.

I went to bed close to 4 A.M. I was having difficulty sleeping. That night I dreamed I was being chased by a monster. If I was being tortured like this with a practically trauma-free escape, I could only imagine the nightmares of those seriously impacted.

The next day Andy texted (text messaging worked more or less throughout the hurricane and its aftermath) that he and Stacey where with her parents in Monroe, the town where we'd stopped and seen the first TV pictures from New Orleans. They had evacuated late Sunday morning, taking twelve hours to drive three hundred miles. He said there were more guns in Stacey's parents' house than in Iraq.

But I really wanted to chat with my teammates and re-dialed constantly, attempting to contact those with a New Orleans area code cell phone. Eventually I got through to Paul. It was lunchtime for him in Houston, but he was already tanked as he'd started drinking at 8 A.M. He said watching the England versus Wales World Cup qualifying match in a pub full of strangers brought home how much he missed Finn's and he told me about his evacuation.

"On Saturday afternoon I hadn't been able to come up with a single reason to stay. I'd friends visiting from Aberdeen and we headed out, but the roads were just choc-a-block and after not moving for twenty minutes we thought, 'To hell with this,' and turned around. I'd never been through a hurricane before and wanted to see what it was like, so we went to Home Depot and bought supplies and flashlights.

"In the Quarter that night only the crazies were out. It was weird. There weren't that many people and those that were around just sat in bars watching CNN. One of my friends has always been a worrier anyway and he just kept asking, 'Why are we still here?' We walked to Frenchmen Street and it was deserted and that's when I got worried.

"So we left around 9 A.M. on Sunday and it took fifteen hours to get to Houston. I went into our office there on Monday and the news wasn't too bad at first, but then we saw the collapse of the 17th Street Canal levee and one of the workers said, 'You see that house three in from the breech? That's mine.'"

I also got hold of Medhurst, who was holed up with his girlfriend, Kim Miller, at her parents' place in Sarasota, Florida. Last Saturday he'd passed out drunk after coming home from Finn's, and Kim, who was in Florida for the weekend, had called and ordered him to go to friends in Shreveport.

"I'd never left for a hurricane before, but this was mad. There was no gas anywhere. At a petrol station near Finn's there was arguing and pushing and this geezer in his seventies started swinging punches at a young guy. You could tell something bad was happening. I got into Shreveport about 4 A.M. and was falling asleep at the wheel and slapping my face to stay awake.

"After two days I drove to Sarasota and was really nervous I'd run out of gas, as there were half-mile queues at stations on the way. I got on the internet at a bank branch and someone had sent photos of my neighborhood in Lakeview, and a grocery store two blocks away had taken ten feet of water. I knew then I was f—ked."

I asked if he'd heard from Billy or Benji and he said, "No. I'm worried about Benji. It's not like him to be so quiet." I was worried too.

Other players checked in with emails. Graeme was in Lafourche Parish in rural Louisiana and wrote: "I couldn't believe the state of my trailer when I returned—Katrina improved it enormously! But I'm concerned about Macca, Billy, and Benji if they did stay. I heard about some folks who did and it's a real bad story."

Colin had flown to Los Angeles while Sean and Mike Mac were in Covington, north of New Orleans, and asked when the next game was. Captain Morgan replied there was water polo training at Pan American over the weekend. He'd actually been on holiday in England when Katrina hit and had been relocated to Little Rock in Arkansas by work.

We weren't the only ones who had evacuated haphazardly and lurched from one town to another. Kenny was in Ireland after stays in towns in Louisiana and North Carolina. Big Rab had spent Saturday night at Finn's and met barmaid Shannon's new roommate, who'd arrived on what would be the last commercial flight into the city for weeks. He evacuated Sunday morning and was now in San Antonio, Texas, via Monroe; Jackson, Mississippi; Lafayette and Baton Rouge, Louisiana; and Beaumont, Texas.

Finn's owner Stevie had gone home in July to see his dying father while Stephen and Pauline were in Crowley near the Texas/Louisiana border. Joy emailed from Tyler, Texas, that barmaid Toni Weick had seen water up to the doorknob of the pub before she left.

I also spoke at length to Ray in Arkansas, and as he and his wife both owned small businesses relying on conventions and tourists, he was understandably worried about the future. But he also made a positive point that I hadn't considered: maybe some evacuees had been given the chance of a better life and a new start. Tens of thousands of poor and ill-educated New Orleanians, the overwhelming majority black, had been trapped in a net of poverty and joblessness. The city hadn't been able to afford even mediocre schooling and the economy couldn't provide decent-paying work to help them break out of the cycle of depravation. Now much of that disadvantaged population might end up with a higher standard of living, distributed throughout America with housing and employment help to begin afresh. In fact the U.S. Post Office reported New Orleans evacuees filled in change-of-address cards forwarding mail to every state in the nation.

Even though I was watching horrendous images of

death and destruction and civilized society disintegrating, little things that make up the humdrum minutia of daily life would pop into my head. What would happen to the money I'd paid to Finn's? What about the shirt Medhurst lent me which I'd left at the dry-cleaners? How about the letter I posted on Saturday night? I wasn't more worried about a thirty-seven cent stamp than the people trapped in the city; it was a realization that every single facet of day-to-day living was going to be affected. This wasn't a death in the family or a fire in the living room which, although painful, would only matter to a handful of people. Katrina was going to permeate every aspect of life on every level for a long time.

I walked Gordon's dog near the beach amongst surfers and joggers and walkers and swimmers in the late-summer Californian sun. It sounds idyllic, the kind of ocean-side suburban Saturday afternoon the middle-class earn the right to enjoy after working hard all week. But I was miserable. Carlsbad seemed pretty and clean but sterile and dull. I missed my home. New Orleans is like a scruffy scamp of a dog. It may be a dirty mongrel, but you wouldn't trade it for the purest-bred poodle.

I called New Stephen and we arranged to leave the next morning on a road trip into the desert. I had to get away before I became more depressed.

CHAPTER 21

The Healing Power of Soccer

I wouldn't advise going on vacation while suffering emotional upheaval. I'm sure there are doctors and psychologists who extol the therapeutic benefits of getting away from your worries for a while in the midst of a draining and traumatic experience, but it didn't work for me.

What I would recommend instead is watching Northern Ireland beat England at soccer.

I can pinpoint the upturn in my mood to an exact time and place: 1:55 P.M. Pacific Time, Wednesday, September 7, the Crown & Anchor Bar, Las Vegas, Nevada. The instant the final whistle blew of that World Cup qualifying game in Belfast, I began to feel better, no question. Like Churchill's "the end of the beginning."

It had taken me nine days to run through the full gamut of emotions, but as I left Las Vegas that afternoon I felt ready to pull myself together and get on with my life. Christ knows how long it would have taken if we'd been crushed. Perhaps I'd still be a wreck today.

I had thought it would rejuvenate me to get out into the wilderness away from pictures of our dying city and reports of wide-scale lawlessness, so New Stephen and I spent four days in Arizona and Nevada. But it didn't work. The wide empty spaces of the West only offered more time to brood on what was happening. We passed our days incessantly discussing the variables, the what-happens-nows and the where-do-we-go-nexts. Maybe it would have been different if I'd canoed down the Orinoco or taken an adventure that occupied my mind and had me focus on a task. Instead, the endless barren wasteland stretching in front of us only exacerbated my gloom.

On Sunday, September 4, in a motel in the resort of Page on Lake Mead we met the man whose face will one day—mark my words—stare out from the front page of the nation's newspapers underneath the headline "Crazed Killer Goes Berserk in Wal-Mart." The Irish editions will add, "Ulsterman caught in crossfire as he returns item 89 days after purchase."

The motel's desk clerk was a paranoid conspiracy theorist of the highest order who initially appeared weird but harmless. When he saw my New Orleans driver's license at check-in he exhibited compassion and concern. The first red flag signaling something was slightly off kilter was raised when after ten seconds of talking about Katrina, he suddenly slammed his fist onto the table and yelled, "Man, in the past I just wanted to kill President Bush. Get it over with quick and easy. Now I'll make sure the f—ker suffers! I'll torture him, slowly and painfully, know what I mean? He's not getting off so lightly. That bastard! Know what I mean?"

New Stephen and I nodded earnestly in harmony, murmured agreement, and exchanged quick, nervous glances. But our friend didn't notice and was off and running. He railed against everyone and everything in Washington but reserved a special hatred for Bush, and his diatribe against the government was only interrupted by the occasional four-letter interjection about his ex-wife because—I'm guessing here—he'd been scarred by a particularly bitter divorce.

He informed us there were already plans afoot to turn New Orleans into the Las Vegas of the south. He knew this because someone had heard two people in a restaurant talk about it and had posted the conversation on the internet.

Once he discovered I was an ex-journalist, he rather worryingly assumed I was familiar with a wide variety of conspiracy theory Web sites and peppered me with questions like, "Have you checked out theworldisrunbygiantaliens.com? Do you ever post on howtomaimapolitician.com?" He was genuinely surprised I didn't spend my days surfing them, and if I was a betting man I'd gamble he didn't get out much.

He kept repeating, "I know the truth because I get the *real* news, not the censored version," and said the Bush family was responsible for importing all the drugs into America. Amongst other things. He also told us the government controlled the weather, which was something I had never realized until then.

He couldn't recommend a pub that served food because he was no longer allowed into most bars in the town. That was a shock. He said he spent his evenings drinking whiskey, and then when he got loaded he'd sit up until the early hours posting "rants" on the internet. "Rants," as opposed to the reasoned, informed arguments he was expostulating at the minute. We just knew he had an assault rifle he polished every night and a stack of militiamen bank notes under the floorboards.

Right when we thought we'd finally managed to get away, and as we edged out of the office with our backs to the wall like escaping POWs, he said, "Hey, wait a minute! What was I thinking? You guys don't need to pay for a room—I have a spare room at my place! You can both come and stay with me! We'll drink some booze and have a ball!" I thanked him but said I was tired from driving all day, adding I was sure New Stephen would love to take him up on his offer of a drink later.

Everywhere we hit in California, Nevada, and Arizona, people were shocked and saddened by what had happened in New Orleans. In a bar in Flagstaff a brewery promotions girl gave us free tee-shirts and drinks. She wanted us to come with her to a Katrina benefit at a pub around the corner, but she was so earnest and sympathetic we had visions of being paraded on stage and her holding a fund-raiser for us or something, so we promised to meet her there and then fled.

Signs advertised yard sales to raise money for victims, kids sold cookies for hurricane relief at the malls, and the Navajo Nation traffic policeman slashed my fine when I was stopped for speeding on tribal land. We found the Americans supportive, warm-hearted, and generous. Then there was the staff at the Crown & Anchor British Pub in Las Vegas.

We stayed in Las Vegas and I discovered that the remote ex-pat outpost near the airport and miles from the glitzy Strip was showing the Northern Ireland match the next day. I knew it'd be packed so got there an hour before kickoff at 11 A.M., but already there were a fleet of taxis crammed with tourists in front of me and it was so busy staff were directing traffic away from the congestion. The cover charge was twenty dollars cash. I had twenty-one dollars in my wallet.

After our experience with the condoling Americans, and as I'd signed up for the two-hundred-dollar Setanta season pass at Finn's, I hoped my fellow Brits may have been minded to waive the entrance fee. The place was crammed and I thought the bloke at the door collecting money hand over fist might let me slip in for free when I explained the situation.

He said no but double-checked with an English girl grilling burgers outside, and she almost gleefully confirmed, like it was a prized company policy, they were charging New

Orleans evacuees. As I handed him the money he suggested emailing Setanta for a twenty-dollar refund when I returned home. I thought I'd put that on my to-do list, right below "check house is still standing."

The last time I'd seen Medhurst he told me he'd booked today off work so we could watch the game live together. A pile of other English regulars would also have been at Finn's, and although I fully expected we'd lose, I had been looking forward to the banter. My dad had sent me a special 125th anniversary Irish Football Association commemorative jersey I hadn't even worn, as I'd been waiting for this game to christen it; instead, I was engulfed by an XXL tee-shirt donated by Gordon, a six-foot, six-inch giant, and I was marooned eighteen hundred miles away in a sea of vacationers.

Inside was a heaving mass of English red and white. Conference attendees from Liverpool, gamblers from Bristol, and families from Sunderland mobbed the bar and shouted orders at the swamped barmaid. I corkscrewed my way though a three-hundred-strong crowd to a spot in front of the big screen. With just a dollar to my name and smarting from paying the cover charge I'd no intention of fighting to get served. The Londoner on my right asked me to watch his Prada carrier bag while he went to the bathroom. I heard a supporter from Birmingham on my left say, "I don't know any of their team. We'll murder this lot. Easy." The first chant of "Inger-lund" started up.

The first half finished scoreless and we'd done okay, but I wasn't getting carried away as it had been that way in the game in Manchester six months earlier and fifteen minutes later we'd conceded four. I spotted a guy in a Northern Ireland shirt elbow his way to the bar, and Sam Gunnion, a twenty-two-year-old forklift driver from Newtownards, just a few miles from my hometown, saw me waving and twirled through the throng towards me.

He'd lived in Vegas four years and was full of youthful exuberance as the second half kicked off, saying, "We're doing great, mate. We could nick this, you know." I gave him the patronizing smile his misplaced confidence deserved. I said we'd tire and then the English quality would show. But we didn't crumble. I started to believe we could snatch a draw. And then in the seventy-fourth minute the unthinkable happened.

Samuel had just told me how well Steven Davis was playing for his club team Aston Villa every week. Seconds later Davis got the ball, swiveled, and lobbed an inch-perfect pass to David Healy, running through the defense in the right channel.

I still see it clearly today. I can picture exactly how it happened. Even writing about it gives me a chill. My first instinct is that he's offside. I see English defender Ashley Cole raise his arm, appealing. Crucially, the assistant referee is in the TV frame also. I see him running, pointing downwards. Healy's run is good, timed to perfection. Healy strikes the ball. The net bulges. We've scored against England. We're leading one-nil.

For a heartbeat the bar fell silent. You would've heard David Beckham's diamond earring drop. Then Sam and I went nuts. Real, honest-to-goodness, jumping-up-and-punching-the-air, stepping-on-people's-toes, careen-ing-into-everyone-while-yelling-at-the-top-of-our-voices, and hugging- each-other-as-we-screamed-hysterically nuts. I have watched soccer for more than thirty years and on all six inhabited continents. Never have I had such an outpour-ing of emotion after a goal.

"You see! You see! Whadda tell you about Davis?

Whadda I say, eh? I told you, I told you," laughed Sam as they replayed the goal and we shook each other by the shoulders. By the time we stopped yelling, the game had restarted. There was fifteen minutes to go.

My head spun like a roulette wheel. The atmosphere around us darkened from mild anxiety to deep frustration. Englishmen kicked the ground and slammed down pints. The TV showed their countrymen at the match in Belfast sullen and silent. I remember one guy in a ridiculous yellow sweater jumping up and flashing the rude "fingers" gesture to the home fans as they taunted, "Are you Scotland in disguise?"

The clock ground down in slow motion. With five minutes remaining, Sam said he couldn't stand the tension and needed a drink. I didn't want him to go in case he missed anything and because I was keen not to be left alone. Thankfully he was back quickly as space opened up around us. England supporters melted away, either because they thought there'd soon be glasses flying through the air in our direction or because they didn't want to stand beside the only people in the packed pub cheering on the Irish.

When the board appeared signaling four minutes of injury time we roared insults at the screen, but they were lost in the increasingly desperate howling of the English. But finally, beautifully, it was all over. Some of our recent results—a tie with Liechtenstein and a home defeat to ten-man Canada—had been enough to bring tears to the eyes of Northern Ireland supporters. But the victory against host nation Spain in the 1982 World Cup Finals was the last time I'd been so proud of a performance it made me cry.

My first thought was for Gordon who'd done so much for me and now his last-minute twelve-thousand-mile return-trip dash was all worthwhile. Sometimes good things do happen to good people. The English patrons who approached were all gracious in defeat. One grabbed my upper arm in a vicelike grip, looked me dead in the eye, and said, "Well done. Northern Ireland deserved it." And we did.

It was time to go. I was overwrought. It had been a hell of a week. Sam and I hugged and I told him to come and visit when they rebuild New Orleans. We were two exiled, outnumbered Ulstermen who came together on the edge of the Nevada desert and will forever share the memory of the day we defeated England.

I blinked my way into the blazing sun and 110-degree heat. Four days in the hot, arid climate after humid Louisiana had left my lips cracked and bleeding. My head was throbbing from the excitement. My throat was hoarse from a mixture of the desert wind and shouting during the match. But I looked at the sullen faces of the pasty-skinned English fans in the taxi queue snaking its red-and-white way around the bar, and for the first time since Katrina hit I felt good. Really good.

Gordon got through on the cell phone he'd lent me as I waited for New Stephen in a casino on the Strip. We talked for ages and dissected every aspect of the match again and again. He said he never cried, but I'm sure he did.

We left behind the gaudiness and razzmatazz of Sin City and drove headlong into the blinding setting sun beaming through the windshield like a prison searchlight above a no-man's land of scrubland. I tried to explain to New Stephen what the victory meant.

In a soccer sense it meant nothing. England still won the qualifying group and made it to the World Cup finals. We still finished fourth out of six and didn't. But we'd triumphed over our big brother, the country that dominates

Britain, the elder sibling whose shadow we live in 365 days a year. A team of jobbing professionals and lower-league journeymen humbled a glittering array of world-famous superstars. It's happened before. It will happen again. In fact it happens all the time.

But make no mistake, this was a stratospheric win. I'd never seen us beat England, even though growing up the match was an annual fixture. And never before had we played them with such a disparity in our respective world rankings—109 to be precise—as we were 116th and they were 7th. We were rated below Lebanon, Congo, and Rwanda, while they were supposedly better than France, Germany, and Italy. At times in the nineties there had been just eighteen places between us.

We stopped at a diner in Baker where a sign read, "Home of the world's largest thermometer," not a boast you hear everyday. Gordon called again. It was 2 A.M. in Belfast and he couldn't sleep. He'd just watched the game on video. We talked about it some more. He said, "You know what I was thinking, Steve? We'll always have this. This result against England, it's ours for ever. And no English person we'll ever meet can take it away."

In the restaurant—I couldn't believe my luck—we were seated next to a table with three middle-aged English couples. I leaned over and said, "Hello there. Did you hear the score of the match today?"

One of the men shook his head. "We've no interest in football, I'm afraid. But by any chance do you know what's happening with the cricket?"

"No idea. But let me tell you all about the football . . ." No bloody way I was going to let them get away that easy.

I would've loved to have been there. I had the chance to go and a guaranteed ticket. The three greatest words in the

English language are "I was there." But part of me is happy things worked out the way they did. Stumbling upon a strange bar in a strange city and making a new friend in a sea of strangers after the strangest week of my life seems fitting somehow. I think the incredible raw emotions and heightened sensations I experienced wouldn't have been the same either surrounded by thousands of other Ulstermen at the game or sitting with friends in Finn's.

I'll take to the grave my memory of being in Valencia the night we defeated Spain in 1982 for the greatest result in our history. But I'll also always remember being in Las Vegas the morning we beat England in 2005.

CHAPTER 22

Think You've Got It Bad?

While I had been feeling sorry for myself as I swanned around the West, walking on the beach and sipping wine at sunset, Macca's ordeal hadn't ended when he was plucked from the roof.

After being whipped to safety by the Coast Guard, he was dropped on the interstate at the rescue staging post near Causeway Boulevard in Metairie. Medics treated his cuts and gashes and gave him water and rehydration tablets. At dusk he edged unsteadily out of the first-aid tent into a scene reminiscent of a medieval battlefield.

"It was like a war zone. Complete chaos. There were thousands of people there, all sorts of people from everywhere. I just sat on the road all night and didn't know who was around me. I was scared s—tless. Nobody had a clue what was happening.

"There was nowhere to hide from the sun when it came up. We were milling about, being shepherded around like sheep, and you were frightened of going anywhere in case you missed your turn to get evacuated. I got on a bus about lunchtime and sat for around thirty minutes—it was baking hot, there was no air conditioning—then a guy got on and told the driver to take us to the Superdome. But we were all shouting that we didn't want that because we'd heard reports and rumors from TV crews that things were bad in there.

"So we argued back and forth and he said they'd send us to Nicholls State University sixty miles away in Thibodaux and we yelled, 'Why the hell are you taking us there? How are we going to get anywhere if we're stranded in the middle of nowhere?' They could have dumped us somewhere where we could've got a bus or a train or a plane, but we lost the fight and that was that.

"We were shoved into a basketball court in the gym. There must have been five hundred or six hundred of us in a space fit for fifty. There was no power, no lights, no air conditioning. People were fighting and robbing each other in the darkness. It stank. It was horrible. Man, it was frightening.

"I was there for two and a half days. Outside, the sun was brutal, but it was roasting inside as well with so many people and no air conditioning. Every day you got one dry sandwich and a couple of cups of water they doled out at certain times; if you missed the slot, that was it. Oh, and a packet of crisps [chips], which made you even more thirsty!

"I was talking with a guy at the entrance when a woman pulled up in her car to donate clothes. We pleaded with her to take us to Baton Rouge. We offered her one hundred dollars each. She was wary of us but we just kept on for ages. We were desperate. Man, we were like beggars. I had the tee-shirt and shorts I had on. I didn't even have shoes. When she eventually agreed, I just thought, 'Yes! Happy days!'"

Macca called Big Rab, who picked him up and dropped him with his friend Stacey Schexnayder in Beaumont, Texas. He stopped there a night, then flew to stay with another friend in Atlanta, and finally, six days after being swept into the street by Katrina, he was able to call his frantic parents in Scotland to say he was safe.

Meanwhile, Frank, after two days in the lap of luxury

in Baton Rouge, was picked up by a friend and spent two nights in Little Rock. Then they'd driven to Flagstaff, where he got a job at a hostel on the recommendation of India House owner Mark, and he'd actually been there when New Stephen and I passed through. But his visa ran out in mid-November, and after a couple of weeks, when it was obvious India House wasn't going to be opening for months, he flew home to live in his mother's attic in Holland.

Eric, who had grown up in North Carolina and learned that "you don't fool around with Cat Four and Fives," had cleared out on Saturday afternoon to his girlfriend Grace's mother's house in Daytona, Florida. A fortnight later he'd gone to his cousin's beach house on the Outer Banks in North Carolina, only to have to evacuate again to his mum's in Virginia when Hurricane Ophelia headed their way. He'd met up with the friend who had sold us our uniforms and who had started an organization donating soccer gear and boots to kids in Cameroon. The Africans had been in touch wanting to send jerseys to hurricane victims in the States!

Eric's friends Jason and Angel stayed for the storm and after a couple of days went hunting for supplies. "They hit Wal-Mart to loot for the whole neighborhood and were snagging things like dog food and chain pulleys. There were cops in there, but it was mayhem. They couldn't keep their footing because there were all kinds of stuff like wine and mayonnaise spilled on the floor.

"Two dudes ran up waving guns and tried to grab their cart from them, but Jason and John had six weapons between them and pulled out theirs and said, 'You ain't getting this stuff, I promise you that. If you kill me, he'll kill you.' It was a real Mexican standoff for a bit but the others eventually backed away.

"They stayed all the way through until the following

Saturday and then they loaded up their truck and drove to the Convention Center and started handing out food and stuff. Then this guy told them they needed to get out of there because someone with a gun was on his way to hijack their vehicle."

The team's other Erick had left with eight family members in two cars early on Sunday. "Having grown up here, I know that for hurricanes you leave for a couple of days and it's a little vacation and you come back and everything is okay. Often they come straight for us and then steer away." After four nights in a town on the Georgia/Florida border, they spent a month in the house of his wife's aunt in Miami, and the supportive locals, frequently battered by storms themselves, had brought groceries to the family.

Indeed, it was ironic how many people had evacuated *to* Florida, the state most associated with residents evacuating *from* hurricanes. Adrian was there in Sandestin with his girlfriend at her family's condo. He had stayed up late on Saturday trying vainly to book a hotel room and had awakened at 5 A.M. on his sofa. After two days in a CBD hotel he'd cadged a ride to meet her in Biloxi, Mississippi, and they'd gone to the beach. "They have a fake Bourbon Street in the resort and I went out for a binge on it, which was a bit surreal. But there were ten of us and I had to share a room with an alcoholic uncle so I wanted to leave, and I went to Louisville, Kentucky, to stay with a mate who owns a restaurant there."

New Orleans native Joe and his family had left for the first time in the twenty-eight years he'd lived in the city. They evacuated Saturday morning and after a few days with his aunt and uncle in Alexandria, Louisiana, they'd moved to his brother's place in Austin, Texas, and enrolled the boys in school. Joe and the kids stayed there for two months and he played for his brother's over-thirty team. The traitor.

Stephen and Pauline left early Sunday and managed to book a hotel room in Monroe, but by the time they got there it had been given away. Like us, they'd been told Dallas was the nearest available accommodation and they'd headed west, but on the way they were offered a spot at a friend's mother's home in Crowley.

Stephen says, "Watching the news we had the same emotional roller-coaster as everybody else, as the water wasn't going down but up. We were thinking: this is bad, this is really, really bad, f−k me it's getting worse. We were frantically trying to get in touch with people and a load of texts would arrive at once in the middle of the night. We assumed the bar had flooded, but we were thinking it was only a few inches.

"Our barmaid Toni Weick had stayed in the second floor of an old dairy up the street and her friends canoed down and said the water was up above the bar. We were both in tears and said, 'That's it, we're done.' We thought that our livelihood was gone as we'd no loss-of-use insurance and everything was lost. I called Stevie and told him the whole city was f−ked and I didn't think he'd get back before Christmas."

Stevie was in Donegal and had been due to fly back on September 4. "A friend told me there was a hurricane which was going to flatten New Orleans. I was completely oblivious and didn't even watch TV [reports about the impending storm] because you become very flippant living in this city. My brother had cable and in his house [after the storm hit] I was going through every channel and when the levees broke I knew it was bad, really bad, just awful. I knew the pub was f−ked."

Dave got through to me on the drive back to Gordon's

from Las Vegas and we talked about the Northern Ireland game. He and Brandi were also out West on a back-to-nature camping trip that seemed to be a mixture of a spiritual journey of enlightenment and high-altitude training. He told me their story.

"When I got home from work on Sunday and saw the daunting, awesome mass of wind and rain heading straight for us, I got my important documents and went to a mate's who'd turned his home into Fortress Harahan. He had a week's supply of Chunky Chicken, a gas burner, ten thousand beers, and enough pot to keep Frank in business for a year. He boarded up his house and cut a hole so he could stare out, and he'd stocked up on hallucinogenic drugs and was planning to trip his way through the hurricane.

"But Brandi kept calling and because she was pregnant I finally agreed to meet her on the North Shore [of Lake Pontchartrain]. The front had arrived and I was getting sprayed by warm water coming in horizontally through the back of my Jeep. We couldn't find a hotel and went due north to Little Rock, and then at Wal-Mart we bought a tent and sleeping bags and headed to Hot Springs, Arkansas. When the levees broke we decided to go west and set up camp on a riverbank in the wilderness.

"Brandi's mother had multiple sclerosis and died with the strain of the evacuation, so we wanted to separate ourselves from the whole situation and get away from everything. We're trying to relax because we know as soon as we get back to New Orleans the s—t's gonna hit the fan. But wait and see, even though the team has been scattered around the States, going through this will bring all of us closer together." He had texted Big Rab, "Get yourself a tent and come and meet me," but Big Rab replied, "I'm a refugee not a gypsy!"

Back at Gordon's there was an email from Julien. Two days earlier, just a week after Katrina had hit, he and his boss had been allowed past the security cordon into the city. They'd driven for miles before encountering anyone, and eventually on St. Charles they'd met two soldiers with M-16s driving a golf cart they'd commandeered from the nearby golf club.

Julien said there was a lot of wind damage in our area but no flooding. He had tried to drive to our house, but the surrounding roads were blocked by fallen trees. But it was good news that the water, which had now leveled, hadn't made it as far as us. What damage the storm, looters, and fires had done was another thing.

Graeme had also made it back into the city. His resolve not to drink on his birthday had collapsed like a New Orleans levee after I'd left Finn's. "The lads insisted on buying me drinks and we moved on to all kinds of crazy shots and it went downhill fast. I got torn up, hatched a plan to sit out the hurricane at Big Rab's place, and was in the pub until midnight.

"On Sunday, I went back expecting it to be open for the Manchester United versus Newcastle game but it was closed. I thought, 'What's going on here?' The seriousness of the situation started to sink in and I went back to my mate's house and he was cracking up. It really dawned on me while watching TV, there's a pretty good chance we all could die.

"He left and kicked me out so I couldn't stay there. I called Big Rab, but he'd left as well, so the idea to sit it out at his place was out the window and there was nowhere else to go. I ended up at a friend's concrete house in Thibodaux, but he was totally freaking out and he's a nutty guy anyway who wasn't dealing with the whole situation very well. We lost electric but I stayed there until Wednesday, when I went back to my trailer in Lafourche, and within a week of the storm coming through I returned to work.

"I drove back to New Orleans about ten days after Katrina. Mid-City was really bad, but it didn't look like there'd been much looting. At the projects every single car had been broken into and around Broad Street it was like a nuclear bomb had gone off. There were still flooded places you couldn't drive through and on the street outside Finn's the water level mark was above my head."

Despite the news, in the four days New Stephen and I had been on our road trip, the mood in cyber space had definitely lightened. Michael had compiled a spoof report of the canceled Olympiakos game played by "Finn McCool's Beach Club" reading: "You bunch of pussies! I took them on all by myself! I would expect Julien to flee, but no one else has an excuse . . . Julien, the team's Frenchman, was seen later that night apparently collaborating with the storm." It would take more than an unprecedented devastating natural disaster to stop the French baiting.

Michael had intended to evacuate but drank in Finn's "later than I should have," and so left on Sunday at lunchtime instead. It took him seventeen hours to get to his wife and son in Houston, but their three hotel suites were costing one thousand dollars a night, so his family flew and he drove to one of his mother-in-law's two vacation homes in Seaside, Florida.

"Just two days after the storm I was driving right through where it had gone. I traveled for fifteen hours and didn't see a single street light, house light, nothing. I got all the way to Alabama and had a quarter tank of gas and thought I'd end up as a refugee on the side of the road, and then the radio said Brookhaven in Mississippi had some and I turned right around and drove an hour back.

"I'd left Houston at noon on Tuesday and got into Seaside twenty-three hours later. I stayed there five days and then came back to check on our lake house on the North Shore, and the whole underneath had been taken out by the tidal surge and there was no running water or power." He'd set up his office in Baton Rouge, but the huge influx of evacuees had swelled the city so much the streets were permanently blocked with traffic and it took hours to go anywhere, so he moved to Slidell, thirty miles from New Orleans.

Medhurst emailed that he'd spoken to Dave, who was "going on a twelve-mile pilgrimage in sandals and purifying his body with water as a way of getting the hurricane demons out." Having spoken to Dave, I knew he wasn't joking.

He continued: "We were saying how much we're looking forward to meeting up with everyone at Finn's when we have all moved back and have survived and become stronger characters. So Pauline and Stephen, please don't sell the pub! Just thinking about it puts a smile on my face, which is something I definitely need right now. Has anyone heard from Benji?" He was still unaccounted for and his silence was deafening.

Jonathan wrote, "I just want to let you all know that at the risk of sounding gay, I miss everyone a lot."

Captain Morgan replied: "We all miss each other a lot. It's just that you were the first to have the balls to say it."

Adrian emailed, "Jonathan, you bummer. Get a grip!" But he added, "I miss you all too and can't wait for a group drinking session. F—king England."

Ah yes, England. Gordon returned weighed down like a Himalayan Sherpa with Thursday's edition of every British and Irish newspaper he could find, and for two days all I did was read about the game. He and Dawn had also doubled my collection of shirts, as they'd brought me back a Chelsea top and a Northern Ireland jersey. They shrugged off my gratitude.

"You would've done the same for me," said Gordon, and that made me feel better because I knew he was right. I would have done. Probably.

New Stephen and I took them out for dinner to thank them for everything. During our meal, Gordon wondered what I thought about life in the States sixteen months after immigrating. I said that until Katrina, I was happy: I was in a city I loved; I wore shorts in February; I played soccer four times a week; I watched games with knowledgeable, committed fans; and I'd a happy social life with a bunch of new mates.

He said, "But have you made any American friends?" When I considered it, I hadn't. I was close to a few American teammates, such as Eric and Billy, but they acted more European than some of the Europeans, and I couldn't count Ray, as we'd first met ten years ago. I had to admit that despite my best intentions I'd fallen headfirst into the very trap I'd been determined to avoid and was immersed in a cocooned world of ex-pats.

He asked what would happen now. I said I didn't know. He asked if any publisher would touch my novel, as it was a comedy set in New Orleans. I hadn't even considered that. A girl selling raffle tickets to raise money for hurricane victims found out I lived in New Orleans and came over to hug and kiss me. She asked if my home was badly damaged. I didn't know that either. On Monday, September 12, a fortnight after Katrina hit, I flew to Houston to meet up with Julie and find some answers.

CHAPTER 23

JouRney to the City
of the Dead

Our new home was on Space Center Boulevard in Clear Lake, southeast Houston. Although I'd been to the city at least six times, I was shocked how big it was: it sprawled for miles and was interlaced with highway after highway up to twelve lanes wide. On the way to the apartment from Bush Intercontinental Airport, a radio D.J. complained about New Orleans evacuees driving too slowly and choking the roads. Thanks for your empathy, pal. And it's just swell to be in Texas.

We set up home in a tiny studio with nothing but a few clothes to our name. But there was no self-pity, only gratitude at how lucky we'd been. I only ever wore tee-shirts and shorts anyway. Julie still had her job with Westway Terminal and was earning money. Some of her colleagues had it much tougher. For instance her coworker Roxanne Montgomery was crammed into a small two-bedroom apartment with her husband David, children Alexis and Sam, her elderly in-laws, and a dog. Seven-year-old Sam had nightmares, waking up screaming that he wanted to be back in his own bed.

Children had to be enrolled in new schools, make new friends, learn new subjects. Katrina had whirled into our lives, ripped us from our routines, and flung us hundreds of miles away. The difference between this and other recent tragedies like September 11 and the Oklahoma bombing was the people affected by those could still go home at night. But everything in life is relative, and I never once heard any of Julie's coworkers laboring to cope with their new circumstances complain about their lot.

Early one morning I drove to the Red Cross/FEMA center near the Astrodome and eventually found a space on the farthest boundary of the vast parking lot patrolled by mounted police. From the road it looked like there were a lot of evacuees lined up outside, but as I walked towards the entrance I realized the queue curled around and around the crash barriers, weaved back and forth along the parking lot, then doubled backed on itself and wrapped around the building. It was like the line for the Space Mountain ride in Disney World Hell. Tens of thousands of people needed help. It was a sobering thought that the four jerseys I had were probably three more than many of these desperate refugees.

Twice a day I'd go down to the management office in the apartment complex and ask to use the internet. The staff were always polite and accommodating despite the obvious stress and heavy workload of the 100 percent occupancy; like every other housing agency in Houston, they'd been swamped by hundreds of thousands of internal American refugees descending on the city.

The day I arrived in Houston, Stephen emailed two photos he'd been sent of the pub, adding, "We are grateful to finally see what we had feared." Finn McCool's was a mess.

In the first picture of the exterior, taken from a boat, the water was nearer the roof than the ground. The top of a car drifted close to the front door and the floodwater was dark and dirty in the bright sunlight. A ring of mud showed the level had actually been higher before the shot was taken.

Because the interior photo was darker with less contrast it didn't appear too bad at first glance. However, when I looked closer I realized the stools, tables, and chairs weren't lying on the floor but were floating on the water, which almost reached the top of the bar. The place was ruined.

The TV news was still grim. If anything, FEMA was becoming even more incompetent. FEMA workers had put 180 evacuees on a chartered plane and told Charleston in South Carolina to prepare for their arrival. Then they flew them to Charleston, West Virginia. This happened twice. You couldn't make it up.

Meanwhile, in Belfast thieves used a forklift truck to steal an ATM machine during a night of rioting. As outraged politicians condemned the looting in New Orleans, it was comforting to think my opportunistic countrymen didn't need to wait for the aftermath of a catastrophic disaster to go on a thieving rampage.

I got hold of Sean and Mike Mac billeted in a makeshift Irish commune at a large pillared house near Covington, on the North Shore. They were holed up with twenty-two adults, five kids, four dogs, and a pot-bellied pig. And Mike Mac's wife, Marian, was eight and a half months pregnant.

Sean said, "We evacuated Sunday and that night I was on a blow-up bed at the top of this high house with an incredible howling wind. The place was shaking, and rain came in through the windows and ran down the walls.

"The power went, then the back-up generators failed, and we desperately tried to get them going. As we were on the wrap-around porch a tornado touched down not fifty feet away and a whole clatter of trees went over one after another. We were fools when you think about it.

"I hadn't said the rosary since I was fourteen, but three nights running we all said it together. It was like civilization had been rolled back: the women washed clothes by hand and hung them all around the place to dry and the men kept occupied and worked with no tops on.

"After a week a neighbor and his four big strapping sons used chainsaws to cut a path through the fallen trees, which were five feet high, and a couple of days later we drove into Metairie. At the intersection of Causeway and Airline we saw all this water and thought, 'What's going on here?' We tried a different way and there were a ton of boats on Veterans Boulevard. You could see water everywhere.

"I met the guy who'd installed our office phones and his house had come though the hurricane okay, but then he watched as the canal poured in through the hole in the levee and he'd nine feet of water in his home in just thirty-five minutes."

Mike Mac told me, "We were very blasé about the whole thing and even brought the kids out onto the balcony to watch the winds go by, which was very stupid really. One of the guys was stuck to the radio morning, noon, and night, but without a shadow of a doubt we were better off not seeing the TV pictures and didn't know how bad it was.

"When the family got through on the phone they were freaking out and telling us to just get in the car and leave, and my brother in New York said he'd drive down and meet us halfway. But we were content and there was a bit of a purging for us in a perverse way. The only worry was that the driveway was blocked, so there was no way an ambulance would get in or we could get out and my wife was due any day.

"After ten days we moved into a friend's house in Mandeville for two weeks when they went back to England and I'll never forget that first hot shower. That's when I realized what I'd missed." The house in Covington was without power for six weeks.

Like Julie and I, Paul and his girlfriend, Jamie Mathews, had relocated to Houston, and two days after I arrived they stuck a dodgy business permit on the dashboard of Paul's monster truck and drove back to New Orleans. That night he emailed: "I was hopeful my house had escaped as it was dry just two blocks away but it was flooded by about three feet. I had to kick the door in to get inside and there was no sound apart from the odd helicopter. I felt like I was looting my own home.

"The water pretty much destroyed everything on the ground, while everything higher was covered in thick mold and fungus. But that's the way things go sometimes. We got some personal things out though, like photos, so it wasn't a completely wasted journey.

"There is not a lot of hassle to get into Orleans Parish. There are checkpoints but nobody questions you and you can go straight through."

The email made up my mind to try and get back into the city. We were pretty confident our place hadn't flooded, but there were still plenty of other bullets to dodge. On the internet we saw a house just three doors down that had been destroyed, and there'd been a fire on Camp Street two blocks away. Our neighbor had told us we'd lost at least one window, and if our home had been exposed to the elements for weeks, then who knew what damage had been done by the wind and rain.

Then there was the looting. Touro Hospital, a few hundred yards away, had shut down due to civil unrest, while the local paper, which published daily on the Web, showed ransacked shops around the corner. I couldn't relax while uncertain about our home's condition, and that combined with an increasing feeling of impotence and confinement as I sat in the small room watching TV made me determined to set out on the four-hundred-mile drive.

New Orleans was officially a no-go area. The city had

been abandoned and the National Guard was sweeping door to door telling people to leave. The military was in control and checkpoints encircling the city ensured only vital workers were granted entry. Nevertheless, there were conflicting forum postings about how effective the ban was and what guidelines were being used by those manning the roadblocks.

Some drivers had done no more than say they wanted to retrieve a pet and had been waved through. Another bought army fatigues, hired a large white truck, and simply hadn't stopped. A student found a line of utility vehicles and maneuvered amongst them, while a barman wrote the earlier you went, the better your chance of success, as some barricades weren't manned at dawn. He also advised bringing cans of soft drinks as a "gift" for the police.

But one resident drove for eleven hours only to be refused entry, and when he tried a different route later he was turned away again. A restaurant owner had also failed to talk his way in despite a sob story guaranteed to tug the most rigid heartstrings. However, when the mayor announced he'd open downtown for the day so business owners could retrieve essential records and computer equipment we decided to risk it.

We got up at 4 A.M. on Saturday, September 17, and skirted the edge of the east Texas oilfields through an infernal landscape where flames from the refineries licked at the sky. Crossing into Louisiana, we passed convoy after convoy of electricity trucks, vans with power crews, and lorries stacked with portable toilets. Streaming away from the disaster zone on the other side of the highway were dozens of army vehicles fresh from Iraq painted in desert camouflage. Near the airport, about fifteen miles from home, the first taste of Katrina's devastation shocked us into silence.

Single-story homes and buildings were flattened like pancakes. Office buildings had row upon row of windows smashed, curtains and blinds flapping in the breeze. Roadside billboards towering eighty feet in the air had been bent backwards to touch the ground like straws twisted by a giant child. One car dealership's massive advertising sign had been doubled over to crush a row of new SUVs.

The dazzling gleam from the Superdome dominating the skyline like a spaceship was dulled by the patches of brown now visible on its damaged roof. A storage facility had been literally torn in half and all kinds of personal effects — shoes, magazines, clothes — were squalling around the wrecked shell. Almost a mile away a sofa littered the roadway like a discarded fast-food wrapper.

We turned off the interstate and at the checkpoint on the Jefferson/Orleans Parish border joined the queue of cars. Julie showed the female police officer her work ID and told her she needed to get payroll records. The cop asked to see our permit. We said, "What permit?"

"The entry permit of course," she replied. No permit, no entry. Simple as that. I started to speak, but she was having none of it. She immediately cut me off and said the city was a secure, restricted area. She shouted to another patrolwoman fifty yards away that she was turning us around.

We U-turned and looped in front of the second officer, and I stopped and tried a different tactic. I claimed to be a journalist who'd traveled over from the U.K. to write a post-Katrina piece. As proof I showed her a Belfast newspaper my mum had sent me, which had published a story I'd written about the hurricane. She enquired why we didn't have press passes and I said our paper had been unable to contact the authorities. I begged her to let us in because the editor was counting on us for a piece. She studied me for an eternity as Julie surreptitiously hid our New Orleans licenses.

"What did the other officer say?" she asked.

"That it was up to you," I lied.

"Okay, I'll let you in. But make sure you're out by six." She signaled to her colleague to allow us access. My Northern Irish accent had got us through the ring of steel built by the largest military machine on the planet.

We were in.

It was the most surreal experience of my life. We zigzagged around storm debris towards our neighborhood. One moment we were in a post-apocalyptic film as we drove past destroyed homes, between tangled trees, and across snapped power lines on empty roads. The next instant we were zapped to the middle of a war zone, a place swarming with the National Guard, where we had to pull over as colossal troop carriers barreled down the middle of quiet suburban streets. I grew up with soldiers patrolling the sidewalks and police checkpoints on the roads, but I never imagined I'd have a similar experience in modern-day America.

Pockets of power workers feverishly repaired electricity lines. A knot of shop owners chatted and surveyed ravaged storefronts on Magazine Street. Enormous downed trees lay everywhere. Audubon Park had been turned into a makeshift military camp and our training pitch was now a helicopter landing pad surrounded by an ocean of canvas.

We turned onto our street not knowing what to expect; I squeezed Julie's arm and smiled. The car was loaded down with tarpaulins, plastic sheets, and all kinds of DIY materials. After twenty long days fretting and worrying and guessing and wondering, we'd finally get to see our house with our own eyes. We braced ourselves for the worst.

But our nineteenth-century home had survived one of the most ferocious storms on record and its aftermath surprisingly intact. Our spare-room window had been smashed, but the hole was just three inches wide and the interior was unscathed. In the attic, daylight poked through the roof in places, but the gaps were only a few inches across.

As I covered up the broken glass in the bedroom and plugged the holes in the roof, I felt like the skin was melting off my body. The sweltering summer heat combined with three weeks without air conditioning and the hot air rising to the top of the house left me lashed in perspiration. Slathered in sweat and stripped to my boxer shorts and shoes, I prowled the loft like a serial killer, looking for damage.

We shoved huge globs of Vicks Vaporub up our noses, took a deep breath to steel ourselves, and opened the fridge-freezer doors. Soaring humid temperatures had turned our food into a putrid decomposing mass. Maggots wriggled across plates, flies buzzed between the shelves, and blood and melted cheese pooled together in a disgusting liquid mess at the bottom in the fruit tray. We grabbed a trash bag each and shoveled in the complete contents. A can of biscuits had exploded and goo dripped everywhere. Creepy-crawlies were dropping off ledges all around us.

Julie suddenly remembered she had important packing to do upstairs, and I dismantled the unit and wiped the parts with bottled water and disinfectant. Sporadically her head appeared at the top of the stairs and she'd ask how I was getting on. She finished—strangely enough—just as I put it back together and closed the door.

She boxed up the computer and important documents while I tackled our small backyard. It resembled the floor of the Amazon rainforest with a two-foot deep carpet of tree branches interwoven with hundreds of shingles and pieces of glass that glinted like jewels in the sunlight.

I dragged twelve-foot-long limbs out to the sidewalk until I was forced indoors by insecticide raining on me from helicopters spraying to kill mosquitoes before they spread the West Nile virus. They droned overhead constantly, sweeping back and forth above the city, sometimes flying so low the whole house shook and rattled.

By early evening the choppers had gone and so had the electricity crew who'd been inching along our street checking the supply. The atmosphere changed. All day we'd scrubbed, worked, and packed up to a buzzing soundtrack of cleanup teams. Now it fell frighteningly still, deathly, deathly silent. No birds singing, no music floating by from a distant radio, no far-off sounds from cars on suburban highways. Welcome to New Orleans, the City of the Dead.

It was already 6 P.M., but we risked a quick walk. The next-door neighbor's front door had been kicked in and a message in luminous yellow paint splattered across the front of the house. We later learned he'd been mistakenly reported missing and the National Guard had broken in fearing he lay dead. We nipped two blocks down to check on the Maison Perrier, a gorgeous bed and breakfast owned by our friends Tom and Patricia Schoenbrun, and apart from some broken windows it was in good shape.

Julie photographed the messages homeowners had daubed on their fences threatening looters. "We are home and armed," warned one. "So are we," wrote his neighbor. When Gordon saw the pictures, he said I should've painted, "Northern Ireland 1, England 0."

An undelivered pile of Sunday newspapers dated August 28 lay yellowing in the gutter with the headline, "Katrina takes aim." Cozy Creole cottages had been slammed by toppled trees and telegraph poles. Occasionally we passed a building and a smell made us gag.

The decimated house we'd seen on the Web—no more than 20 yards away—looked worse in real life. The whole upstairs front had been sheered off and lay like a bonfire in the garden. Possessions blew about in the breeze, and you could see right into their dining room.

We fed tuna to a wandering hungry family of cats then drove out along St. Charles. It too was dry, though the floodwaters had lapped right to the doors of the multi-million-dollar mansions before receding.

Our home had survived the hurricane, the floodwaters, the fires, and the looters. We had escaped by the skin of our teeth. We had been very lucky. The luck of the Irish.

CHAPTER 24

Texas (Will) Hold 'Em

We stayed the night with Medhurst sixty miles away in Gonzalez. Just in case we didn't know already, stopping with him hammered home how lucky we'd been. He hadn't made it to Lakeview but was sure he'd lost everything. Take a minute to imagine precisely what that means.

It's not an overflowing bathtub soaking into your living room and ruining your baby pictures. It's not an airline losing your suitcase and your precious holiday purchases. It's not coming back to find your dozy roommate mistakenly threw out your CD collection. Fleeing with little or no time to evacuate means losing everything. Everything you own. All your possessions in the world. It happened to tens of thousands of New Orleanians, and as I stood in Medhurst's rented apartment with its empty closets and cupboards, I appreciated how devastating it was. I felt even guiltier we'd escaped so lightly.

He was still shell-shocked, but it was great to see him again. It had been exactly three weeks since that last Chelsea/Spurs match at the pub and we discussed Katrina and the ramifications for hours. He had no clothes and had been sent to a shop by Kim's father, who paid for everything. That had made him cry.

He'd watched the Northern Ireland game in a Florida bar and the ex-pats there hadn't even bought him a drink and charged thirty dollars for one of their jerseys. He said, "Can you imagine if we'd been in Finn's and a hurricane victim had turned up? He wouldn't have put his hand in his pocket all day."

We were both worried about Benji, and when we said goodbye on Sunday, he promised he'd drive to a mutual friend's in Baton Rouge to see if he knew anything. He emailed the next day: "Our loveable little African-American friend Benji has apparently been holed up in Baton Rouge and has now moved back to Jefferson. Expect some nasty emails coming your way soon."

Sure enough an email appeared. "The Mouth of the South is back baby! News of my untimely demise has been greatly exaggerated. Though I spent all day at Finn's on Saturday getting drunk I managed to get to Baton Rouge safely.

"I had no internet access and am sorry I didn't check in. I've been reading my 2,000 emails all night! I'm now back at my undamaged home and working like there's no tomorrow, because maybe there isn't. I miss everybody and even miss practice!"

We'd spent three weeks fretting about him and the bastard had evacuated before any of us!

When I did speak to him, his twelve hours of drinking that Saturday meant his recollection was somewhat hazy. "I stayed at the pub until about 8 P.M. and was completely smashed. I remember Stephen saying that the storm wasn't coming and they were going to stay open and I went home and passed out on the couch.

"Shawn was in a panic and phoned to say she was flying back from San Diego and told me to pack my dumb butt because she was coming to pick me up. I'd refused to watch TV all day and was in denial and was also totally loaded. If it wasn't for her I'd definitely have stayed, as I was way too drunk to do anything.

"So I packed, but because I was so drunk I just threw stupid, retarded stuff into the suitcase to fill it up and didn't have any socks or toothbrushes or anything useful. Thank

God she checked it and did it again and we left for her sister's in Baton Rouge around midnight.

"When the levees broke I thought, 'There goes nothing. We're screwed.' I thought New Orleans was done, as I'm a negative person by nature and always presume the worst.

"After two nights I didn't want to talk to anybody and had to get away, and luckily a mate in Baton Rouge went home to England and we moved into his place. I used to live in the city and knew where I could get a job, which was good because I didn't have time to dwell on the consequences— Shawn spent her days watching the news and would be in floods of tears. Mentally she was messed up and needed to get back to work, so she volunteered to work in Houston."

So like Julie and I, they split up and he returned home. He had gone to the library to use a computer to email but there was a seven-hour wait, and he was sure all the Finn's lads would be safe anyway. "I always assumed they'd be okay because they were white and middle class. I knew exactly who got screwed in New Orleans—the same people who always get screwed here."

On Monday, September 19, Julie's company bought pizzas and beer and hired out the apartment building's "party room" for the NFL game between the Saints and the New York Giants. It had been scheduled for the Superdome, and even though it was switched to the Big Apple it was still considered a Saints home game and Giants Stadium had been repainted with the Saints logo. It was a Katrina fund-raiser and during the commercial breaks Giants players wearing Saints jerseys appealed for donations to the Red Cross.

At that time I had no interest in American football and couldn't care less about the Saints. I think it's a disgrace "franchises" can be sold and moved from city to city. I agree with the Argentines: you can change your wife but you can't change your mother or your football team.

I also resented Louisiana's signing a ten-year contract to use our taxes to pay the franchise more than $186 million. About $359,000 a *week*, which could be used to improve education and clean up the city. That's my money (well, it's the wife's money, but let's not get technical) and as far as I was concerned the sooner they cleared off the better.

But watching the contest I found myself rooting for the boys in black and gold. If a disaster had wiped out Northern Ireland, what a shot in the arm the victory over England would have been. It would've offered a sliver of silver in a jumbo doom-laden black cloud, and a win against the Giants would give displaced fans a night of celebration during an otherwise awful time.

The Saints got pummeled by the way.

And two days later we evacuated from our evacuation.

We hadn't even unpacked from the trip to New Orleans when once more we were on the run from another Category Five storm. While we'd been in Louisiana, Hurricane Rita surged into the Gulf of Mexico and targeted the coastal city of Galveston, just twenty-six miles from our Houston apartment. We were in Texas Flood Zone B, and a mandatory evacuation order was slipped under our door and the police instructed us to leave.

Not that we'd planned on staying anyway. Julie had decided. My role as an equal partner in marriage ended forever on Monday, August 29, when Katrina hit. I will never win another argument with my wife in my life. Now whenever we have a discussion, debate, or disagreement she says, "Yes, Stephen, but you didn't want to evacuate for Katrina."

How can I argue? It's the ultimate trump card. Sometimes I'll stutter, "Yes, darling, but in this particular instance . . ."

She'll interrupt, "Now, dear, we know how suspect your judgment is. You were the one who said we only needed to build a wee fort . . ." and at this point I hold my hands up and admit defeat. We do what she says. I know when I'm beat. And I'll be beat for the rest of my married life.

Actually, this evacuation knocked the stuffing out of Julie and hit her hard. My psychologist friend Sharon Miles had warned she might not have dealt with the trauma of Katrina properly and those unresolved emotions could pack a more powerful punch later. Many of her colleagues also had crushed demeanors at becoming double evacuees, and a resigned gloom settled over the whole complex. A quarter of a million Louisiana evacuees were estimated to have descended upon Houston and most got ready to leave again.

It was extremely rare for a tropical storm to spin this far west and the locals weren't used to dealing with them. I assumed the air of an amused old-timer as I potted about on Wednesday afternoon with grocery store customers pushing, shoving, and panic buying like they'd be caught present-less at 4:50 P.M. on Christmas Eve. In the drugstore checkout queue the overweight cashier was having a panic attack and kept repeating to herself, "I need to get home to pack; I need to get home; calm down, Betty; calm down." The gas station on the corner called the police when fights broke out as dozens of cars crammed around the pumps. It sounded a touch familiar.

This time we methodically loaded the car in a near-empty parking lot, the few remaining vehicles owned by demoralized New Orleanians wearily taking their time to pack up yet again. Many were heading back to Louisiana and we planned to return to Medhurst's in Gonzalez, but the interstates were choc-a-block—one driver on CNN had traveled forty miles in thirteen hours—and when Julie's

company offered a rented house in The Woodlands to anyone who needed it, we were spared a nightmare journey.

Even though we were now experienced evacuees and
tried to stick to back roads, it still took four hours to drive
fifty miles north as five million people strangled the road
system of the nation's fourth-largest city. With Katrina still
fresh in the memory it seemed no one was prepared to ride
out the storm.

When we couldn't avoid the interstate, the drive was
hideous. A record heat wave meant temperature in the
nineties at 11 P.M. Cars overheated or ran out of gas and
drivers attempted to push them across six lanes to the hard
shoulder. Orange traffic cones were forced apart as impatient
motorists weaved through road works. Emergency vehicles,
sirens screaming, floundered in the jams.

Six of us bunkered down in The Woodlands with enough
food to feed an army, while a neighbor siphoned his gas
tank and ferried fuel to increasingly frantic stranded
motorists fearing they'd be left exposed and vulnerable by
the roadside. We secured all the potential projectiles in the
garden and dropped the wrought-iron patio furniture into
the swimming pool.

Rita would make landfall in the early hours and at
midnight I walked outside. It was spooky. The wind
whipped through the trees, turning and twirling branches,
and clouds silently raced across the sky like a sped-up scene
from a horror movie. For the second time in less than four
weeks I had the same sense of foreboding.

But overnight the hurricane jogged east and crashed
ashore on the Texas/Louisiana border, devastating the cities
of Beaumont and Lake Charles, and again we watched New
Orleans drown as the patched-up levees crumbled. I'd have

preferred it to have hit us in Houston. For weeks workers had shored up New Orleans' floodwalls and now they were slammed back to square one. However, others in the house reckoned that as New Orleans had already been smacked, it may as well take another pounding rather than have Houston suffer. As it happened we didn't even lose power and beat the traffic to speed back to Clear Lake in an hour.

The storm spared Houston, but with a cruel sense of irony it washed out a planned Finn's reunion. Months earlier a load of regulars had organized a trip to the city for a feast of English AOR—Coldplay on Friday night and Oasis on Saturday—as it was a free weekend in our league schedule. The jaunt was scheduled as planned even after Katrina and I'd been looking forward to meeting up with everyone again, but with Rita closing in both gigs were pulled.

Hurricane season still had ten weeks to run, but thankfully Rita was the last serious scare. The deadly 2005 spell shattered all sorts of records: 28 named storms, which beat the previous record of 21 set in 1993; 15 hurricanes bettering the 12 in 1969; and 4 Category Fives, one more than the highest number recorded in 1961. There weren't enough letters in the alphabet to name them and scientists had to dip into the Greek alphabet.

But at least Benji was back. He invited us to a hurricane party for Rita and followed that up with a get-together for Monday Night Football. Billy showed up and it turned out the other player we'd all been really worried about had also evacuated before any of us.

"When you watch hurricanes and you live in New Orleans, you want to get off work, so you want them to point at you and then veer away so you get two days off work and get to go drink and go to Finn's. That Saturday afternoon I went home from the pub and this one scared me because it was coming straight for us. I thought, 'This hurricane is going to mess us up badly.'"

He'd sent his "cowards" email that Sunday from his grandmother's on the North Shore. After a few days there, he'd gone to a friend's in Memphis for a couple of weeks, ditching his car in Jackson, Mississippi, when it ran out of gas. He was now back home after spells with family in Baton Rouge and Florida.

He added, "Watching the TV, I thought I was looking at Rwanda and felt ashamed that this is what the whole nation and the world were seeing from New Orleans. I love our city but it was bad and embarrassing."

After his get-together, Benji emailed "minutes" featuring a plan to rebuild Finn's in a giant cooler so if the city flooded again we could stay afloat and carry on drinking. It was a tentative nudge back to the camaraderie we'd had before the storm, and though it was only a gesture designed to give us a chuckle, it was a sign the Finn's fellowship was still hanging in there.

His third invite in a week urged everyone to go around to watch Spurs play another mediocre London club, Charlton Athletic. Hadn't we suffered enough?

CHAPTER 25

I Like to Watch: Part Two

My search for a soccer-friendly pub was back at square one. In fact I was losing 1-0 with seconds to go, stuck behind the eightball, way behind at the bottom of the ninth, and all the other out-of-luck sporting clichés you can think of. In New Orleans, I had just started calling bars in the city, but in this mighty metropolis I didn't even know which of the five phone books in the apartment to trawl through.

It was oh so easy to start with. The day I arrived I spotted a sports bar less than three miles away. Chelsea was playing Liverpool on ESPN2 in the European Champions League on September 28 and I rang to confirm they had the channel and they'd put it on for me.

At 1:30 P.M. I squeaked open the dirty glass door in a nondescript suburb and entered the spacious watering hole pulsating with neon beer signs. Two drinkers in Stetsons sat on one side of the large square bar and a middle-aged guy was perched opposite. The barmaid, called something like Fifi, was blond and bubbly and petite and cheery with a halter top tied high above her belly. I'm guessing she did well on tips.

Conjuring up every ounce of my Irish charm, I asked her to put the soccer game on any of the eight TVs, one of which was showing a program called *Extreme Bulls*. I could tell I'd bowled her over, as she stuck it on a small set wedged in the corner with no sound.

Despite the unfortunate location of the TV, I was comforted to discover that the beacon hovering over my head that is only visible to crazies and acts as a lure was still flashing. As I talked to Fifi, the solitary, middle-aged patron, Chuck, "normaled" his way into a conversation.

To "normal" is the act of drawing you into believing you are talking to a reasonable, adjusted person. A nutter will engage you in a discussion and "normal" their way through the start of discourse. You think you are communicating with a rational, normal human being then realize they are in fact a raving lunatic. It may dawn on you relatively slowly during the conversation. Other times it comes completely out of the blue and in the middle of an otherwise sane sentence, they'll suddenly interject, "Of course I only have one kidney."

Hence, "Alright, mate. How did your date go?"

"Awful. She normaled her way through the first hour, but then she said she was a witch in a previous life and liked to get men to . . ."

Chuck tapped me on the shoulder and asked, "Who's playing?"

"Chelsea and Liverpool."

"Ah, London and Liverpool, the Beatles and the Stones."

I was impressed. His grasp of both British geography and musical history was better than the typical Texan's, and I laughed and scurried off to watch my game silently play out. But I was now Chuck's friend and he followed me to my corner.

The match was a boring, scoreless tie. The only thing more boring than watching a noiseless boring game in a boring bar in a boring city on a boring Wednesday afternoon was sitting beside Chuck. Turned out he was a big music fan, specifically seventies English rock music. I spent the whole game listening to Chuck's record of every single concert he'd seen in the last thirty years. He normaled his

way through the first ten minutes by talking about artists like
The Who and Eric Clapton. I'd ask a question or try to enter
into a gig-related dialogue about Deep Purple at Knebworth
in 1985, but he had no interest in shows I'd been to and ignored queries about specific concerts. Instead, he recounted
a chronological list of his gig-going life. In great detail.

"Caught Uriah Heep in 1976 in Austin. It were pr'ty good.
They played these songs . . ." And so on. Ad infinitum.
Three decades' worth of classic rock mentally catalogued
by year, genre, length of set, and entertainment value rated
out of ten. By midway through the second half, I'm sure he
went back to the beginning, as I distinctly remember 1974
following 2005. I was a captive one-man audience.

Rather than tell him to clear off and let me watch my
game, I'm such a sucker I even bought him a beer at halftime.
The instant the final whistle blew — and in the middle of the
great Pink Floyd tale of 1979 — I jumped up, but he grasped
my shirt and asked when the next match was. I said I'd be
back the following Wednesday, but I was so scarred I never
set foot in that bar again.

On Sunday, Chelsea and Liverpool played again, this time
in the English Premiership, and I drove forty-three miles to
an English pub called the Richmond Arms to meet Paul and
Scully, other than Medhurst the first Finn's regulars I'd seen
since Katrina five weeks before. Paul told me about a Finn's
kickball hurricane party — a posting on the kickball forum
read, "Anyone who doesn't come is a pussy!" — which had
turned into a twenty-first century *Lord of the Flies.*

When the levees broke the sixteen partygoers had been
forced higher and higher up the building, a converted
dairy, but had been able to follow the unfolding drama
and horror stories emanating from the city via a generator-
powered TV. They hadn't stocked any supplies and after

vicious arguments they finally agreed to send out a pair of volunteers with two canoes and a shotgun to go looting.

However, the duo had a different agenda than the hungry group waiting in the flooded-converted dairy. When they rowed back onto the street towing five large coolers roped together, the starving pack cheered and hungrily ripped open the lid . . . to find it packed with alcohol. The second was also full of wine and beer. As was the third. And the fourth. Buried at the bottom of the fifth — underneath more booze — was a big round slab of cheese.

"What were you thinking?" wailed one of the girls. "We're famished."

"Yes, but this wine is really expensive, ninety dollars a bottle. Let's save it for dinner."

"What do you care, you just stole it!" she replied (presumably adding, "And we don't have anything for dinner!").

The pillaging duo had floated into a partly ransacked grocery store and found two smiling looters serving behind the counter, playing "shop."

"Yes sir, what can I get you?" asked one.

"Ah, I guess that cheese up there would be great."

"Certainly. Eddie, fetch these dudes that cheese," said the pretend store owner, and his mate swam across, scooped the food off the shelf, and handed it over with a smile. The kickball players thanked them graciously and paddled out.

The pair had also rowed into Finn's, and even though the pub was underwater, the draft pumps were still partially working and they'd sat at the bar, water lapping at their waists, and poured themselves pints. Some people had their priorities straight.

The following Saturday was a day of international soccer

action including the big Northern Ireland versus Wales game, and as it was two British countries I thought it might be on a pay-per-view channel. I was so desperate to see it I even rang the Chuck-frequented sports bar.

Perky Fifi briefly raised my hopes. "Oh yes, we got a fax about soccer games tomorrow. Hang on a minute." She rustled about and I'm sure I heard the names Judas Priest and Wings in the background. She came back on the line and—I kid you not—she said, "We have, wait, is this right? Never Land and Macadamia?"

"I think that's Netherlands against Macedonia," I offered, certain that a contest between Peter Pan and the Lost Boys and a packet of nuts was too ridiculous even for an American sports channel. I hung up to a faint soundtrack of a description of Cozy Powell's drum solo at a 1979 Rainbow concert.

I listened to the Radio Ulster broadcast over the internet, then after our latest defeat got to the Richmond Arms in time to pay twenty dollars for the second half of the England versus Poland game. More importantly it was a mini Finn's reunion: Paul, Scully, Scully's wife Rachel and daughter Mia, Joy, and Benji and Shawn.

As soon as I walked into the dark, busy bar I saw the loud mouth's bush hat silhouetted against the big screen, and despite its being 10 A.M., Shawn was already drunk. We hugged and kissed and slapped each other's backs and met later to reminisce over dinner. It was as if Finn McCool was a real person we'd just buried and now we were cathartically raking over our fondest memories. I've been to funerals with less mourning.

I was still smarting from paying twenty dollars to watch forty-five minutes of England, and Joy compared it to what was offered at a recent international day at Finn's: "First, you got three games. Then Eric's dog made a lunge for Oban and was hanging off his neck and we had to scramble around and grapple them apart. Next, Daithi and his girlfriend Michelle [an ex-Finn's barmaid] somehow or other ended up on the pool table simulating sex. After that Kieran—do you know Kieran the singer? [I shook my head.] Well, he stood up and belted out a few songs. So you got the matches, a dog fight, a live sex show, and a musical performance, all for twenty bucks." That's value for money right there.

Paul said, "The ex-pat scene in Houston is so anonymous, but in New Orleans I feel like I'm part of the community, and after a few weeks here you appreciate what you had before." We hoped Joy was wrong when she told us she'd heard rumors Finn's wouldn't be rebuilt.

Afterwards our Louisiana licenses got us free entrance to a fund-raising concert that presumably was organized by a New Orleanian, as the banner read, "Katrina benifit." It had been great to see everyone again, but there was no time to dwell on the warm, fuzzy feeling of rekindled friendship. I had to find a way to follow Northern Ireland's vital game against Austria because if we won we'd finish third in the group. Vital indeed.

It wasn't on Radio Ulster or the Web and after thousands of phone calls, Gordon and I settled on a plan. The showdown was on live at home so our mate Conrad in Belfast would position his webcam in front of the TV and Gordon would hook up his camera to a neighbor's broadband computer. We'd have an open phone line and he'd give me a running commentary.

Then, incredibly, just twenty-four hours before the game, FSC announced they would be showing a delayed broadcast of the entire match at 8 P.M.! What the hell prompted this was anybody's guess, but we didn't care and rejoiced as if we'd won the World Cup. I'd avoid the score all day then drive to the Richmond Arms and watch Northern Ireland on American soil for only the third time ever. The pub was even listing it as a featured game on its Web site.

Unfortunately, the fact that the Houston Astros baseball team was marching relentlessly towards the first World Series in its history had completely passed me by. So when I arrived the place was packed, and there were no other Northern Irishmen in evidence.

Three English lads worked weekends, but behind the bar tonight was a tall ponytailed local in an Astros jersey. When I enquired which screen would be showing the soccer, he looked at me as if I'd asked permission to shag his granny.

"It's not on," he said, managing to sound simultaneously authoritative and uninterested. I pointed to a small poster on my side of the bar advertising the game. He craned his neck around, rolled his eyes, huffed and puffed, then said, "Well, it'll have to be that screen." He waved dismissively and walked off. I assumed he meant the tiny corner TV in the restaurant area. There seemed to be a pattern developing.

I elbowed into a table of businessmen and their wives tucking into pie and chips. The TV was screening baseball. I waited, patiently. It crept closer to 8 P.M. Still there was baseball. I went back to the bar, coughed politely, and asked about the match. "Yes, yes, we're sorting it out," said the charm-school graduate.

I returned to the table and squeezed in again. Still baseball. I waited exactly two minutes then lunged at a waitress on her way to the kitchen. "Excuse me; they were going to put the soccer on for me and . . ."

"Yes, yes, they're sorting it out," she replied and carried on walking.

I waited. One minute past eight. Wry amusement tinged with mild frustration had long ago turned to angry disbelief. I grabbed another waitress. "Can you please see if they'll put on the soccer? The game's already started."

"Really? I'll ask behind the bar for you." She walked into the kitchen.

"They're sorting it out," I heard the first waitress shout.

I felt like Sisyphus. I couldn't believe I was being denied after getting so close. I was about to throw a fit when *boom*, the game flicked on! Fantastic! Then we were back to the baseball.

This happened twice more: brief, tantalizing glimpses of a cold autumnal night in Vienna suddenly swapped for a balmy Texan fall. Six minutes in they did indeed finally sort it out. I relaxed, smiled broadly, and gave the thumbs up to Smiler behind the bar. I decided to turn up the sound and stood on my chair to reach the volume button. I pressed the switch . . . and we returned to the baseball.

Could I get back to the match? The hell I could. For ages I balanced on that seat, jabbing and poking every knob, button, and switch on the set and in the general vicinity evermore frantically. I didn't dare ask the staff for help as I'd have to confess to messing with the controls. I think the lights in the pub dimmed twice.

My string of obscenities drove away my dining companions until mercifully I eventually found the game and collapsed sweat drenched into my chair. I'd watch it in silence. At least I didn't have to endure the walking progressive rock encyclopedia, Chuck.

After an hour or so, as the rest of the bar oohed and ahhed along to the baseball, I noticed a tall blond-haired drinker behind my right shoulder. I quickly turned my attention back to the soccer in case he started reciting ELO lineups of the eighties, but I was too late and he'd seen me looking. He cleared his throat and asked in accented English who was playing.

"Northern Ireland and Austria."

"Is that Steve Staunton at left back?"

I sighed. "No, it's not. Steve Staunton played for the Republic of Ireland, not Northern Ireland," I explained quickly and rudely.

"Oh yes, of course." He sipped his beer. "You have the forward from Spurs, don't you?"

"You're thinking of Robbie Keane. He plays for the Republic as well. This is Northern Ireland. *Northern* Ireland," I spat in reiteration and scowled at him. We were on our way to another defeat and I was in a bad mood.

When the game finished I felt guilty. The poor bloke was only being friendly and I'd chewed his nose off. I turned to chat and found out he was a Norwegian soccer fan named Jon. In a ham-fisted attempt to ease my conscience, I said I was a Chelsea supporter and we'd had some of his countrymen turn out for us, Jesper Gronkjaer for instance.

"He is Danish, not Norwegian," he replied.

"Oh right. Well Bjarne Goldbaek had . . ."

"He too was Danish."

What a twat. I was doing the very thing I'd got so annoyed at him for doing. At least he'd got the right island.

He was meeting a dozen fellow Norwegians (or was it Danes?) to watch their match against Belarus, which the bar had taped for them that afternoon. Apparently the staff were more accommodating to the Scandinavians than the Irish, although they had to mob the same corner TV. As they arrived and squished around us he introduced me to his pals, most of whom worked in the oil drilling industry; two had even been temporarily based at the shipyard in Belfast.

And so at midnight I found myself in a Northern Ireland

shirt sitting with Norwegians watching their country play Belarus in an English bar in Texas. But things were to get even stranger.

CHAPTER 26

Benji to the Rescue

At the start of October, Benji sent me an email. "The spirit is back, baby! I reckon the team will emerge stronger than ever."

He produced another elaborate set of "FEMA McCool's" minutes from the latest shindig at his house and it spurred him into organizing a training session. On Thursday, October 6, exactly six weeks since our last practice, the club took its first tottering, teetering baby steps back towards normality. Seven people showed up: Big Rab, Benji, Dave, Eric, Andy, Captain Morgan, and Kenny, which was particularly surprising as he hadn't made it to any sessions since the inaugural one nine months previously.

"Training" consisted of taking a couple of pictures and then going to a pub (Andy was worried because he'd downed a few beers beforehand but discovered on arrival he was one of the more sober participants), and Benji released a match report claiming victory over the Red Cross and Salvation Army. On seeing Dave's *Wild Man of Borneo* beard I joked we'd signed Father Christmas with dyed whiskers, while Julien reckoned we'd recruited Jesus.

Despite the levity, fear stalked the city. When Big Rab returned to the shipyard his security pass was checked by new guards wearing body armor and wielding M-16s, while Eric went home "with three shotguns and three handguns dripping off me."

Captain Morgan's concern about his property had been balanced by the adrenaline rush of coming back. As he was never a huge soccer fan and only a bit player, he'd always felt slightly awkward, but now he sensed he was truly involved in the group. "Katrina was a big turning point and it was neat the way people started banding together and I started feeling part of the community. I busied myself during the day as there was all sorts of stuff to do, and in the evenings I'd hang out at the bar and swap stories and flirt with women from the police and National Guard."

Dave had hoped his raised house close to Finn's had escaped the flooding, but just eight inches of water was enough to destroy everything on the floor. The rampant mold had taken care of the rest. "Brandi was pregnant, her mother had died, and I'd lost my home and my job, so between us we got proper f—ked." He hadn't even begun to deal with it emotionally and after a fortnight with Medhurst, he'd moved into Benji's, though even life in the relatively unscathed Jefferson Parish wasn't a walk in the park.

Benji said, "We'd no power for a week and it was as hot as Hell. My den was the coolest place in the house and I lived and slept there. Every night for three weeks I had to scrounge between curfew to find something to eat. The area was a lot worse than I'd imagined and you had to drive around for ages to find anywhere open, and when you saw something you were delighted, even if you had to wait an hour to get served."

The city had finally been pumped dry and Dave, Benji, and Big Rab went to Finn's and took photos of each other drinking on the doorstep. The brown water mark was six feet high and ruined cars covered in a layer of muck and dirt lay in the street.

"It breaks my heart," wrote Jonathan, and he sent photos of his home, which had taken even more water than the pub.

Ironically, after his speech at the team meeting exhorting us to stick together and support each other, a mixture of Churchillian rhetoric and Oprah Winfrey-style compassion, he was off to live in New Jersey!

Medhurst also sent pictures of his house. Like Jonathan's, it was totally destroyed and open to the elements, as parts had been swept or ripped away. I called to offer the use of our home and he was really down, saying, "I just wish I could turn back the clock six weeks and get my life back."

For a month his place in Gonzalez acted as a staging post for Finn's regulars sneaking into the city and he said, "The look on the faces of the people who stayed with me when we met up after Katrina is something I'll never forget." He'd now moved to Kenner and he told me about his visit to Lakeview.

"I got to the house and had to break down the back door with an axe. The fridge was embedded in the wall on its side. I got my passport, credit cards, green card, and Kim's jewelry and left. We went back the following week and pulled out all her clothes and started cleaning up. We needed a sledgehammer to get the fridge out.

"I was totally unprepared. It was devastating. I'd never seen anything like it in my life. It seemed completely hopeless. I thought, 'What am I going to do?' Everything was ruined and there was stuff everywhere. I felt angry and bitter when friends came back and they'd lost nothing or when people told me how blessed they'd been, and I wanted to be surrounded by mates like Dave who were going through the same thing.

"The first day back at work everyone was in tears but it was great being around other employees and knowing we'd all made it through. But I was losing my temper when customers said, 'I had two feet of water.' Well f—k you! I had six feet! I'd get into arguments and be more than happy to get back in their face and tell them not to treat my staff like s — t.

"An employee lost her baby through stress and my assistant's brother-in-law drowned trying to save his son caught in the undertow. I was annoyed I not only had to deal with my own stuff but comfort the staff as well, and it was very, very hard with everyone coming and complaining to me.

"Benji came back into town on a guilt trip because there was nothing wrong with his house and he was a good support person. He said, 'I feel for you guys; what do you need?' and we really bonded with him at that point. But I wasn't ready for football. I was dazed. Everything in my life had been turned upside down."

Medhurst was full of negativity, even emailing the day before training to point out that Orleans Parish had a curfew. "He's walking around like a freakin' zombie, dude," said Benji, who stepped in and took control.

Most of us had employment or property ties to New Orleans and we'd probably have filtered back in dribs and drabs and reignited the team. It would be a stretch to say Benji single-handedly saved Finn McCool's FC, but he undoubtedly held it together in that traumatic and dramatic post-Katrina period. He was the lifeline between us exiled players and home.

In October he was upbeat and proactive. He tried to arrange games, organized Sunday practices, and composed *The Finn's Fellowship,* a spoof screenplay taking in multiple locations, complete with stage directions.

"Communication was down and I needed to get it going again, but as the bad news continued it was important to not just communicate but communicate positively. We had a cool team going before the storm and we needed to get it back. There was also a selfish element in that I thought, 'My life is going to suck if my mates don't come back.'

"You do whatever you have to do to distract people from what is going on. Our lives would be changed forever so you have to concentrate on what keeps people together. When your lives are fractured like this it's easy to get disconnected and I felt a huge weight of responsibility to keep the club going and inspire the others to return."

On a lighter note the storm spawned new nicknames. Kenny became Coach Claimer because FEMA was sending him handouts left and right, while Captain Morgan had morphed into Captain Catfish. He was salvaging flood-damaged items ranging from fridges to football jerseys, and "Catfish" was coined after Medhurst called him a bottom feeder for scrabbling through Kenny's dumpster. He reveled in his new reputation and sent explicit directions about the best districts to trawl and how to clean flooded white goods. In fact he'd "liberated" a dumped fridge the night before that merely had "mold in the food box and some fly eggs." And to think people were just throwing it away . . .

By the end of the month little green shoots of hope poked through the crud-encrusted dead landscape. The lads formed the A Team, volunteers who gutted flooded homes of Finn's regulars on weekends and literally ripped out the inside, leaving only the structure's outer shell. They did Medhurst's house, Benji wrote more minutes, and Stephen and Pauline arrived with food and the news that Finn's was holding a party next month.

In fact Stephen sent me an email that day reading, "See ya in the new Finn's soon." Straight from the horse's mouth, the bar was coming back. But the rumor we'd heard from Joy that they'd considered jacking it all in had been true.

According to Stephen, "For the first couple of weeks we couldn't see any sort of hope at all and didn't want to rebuild. The place was wrecked. The doors were wide open, lots of booze had been looted — so had the cigarette and poker machines — and many of the things we spent years collecting were covered in mold and had to be chucked away.

"The street was caked in mud, there was dirt everywhere, and everything was dead and gray. It was a ghost town; the weirdest thing was driving for five or six minutes on the interstate with absolutely nobody about. It was like the end of the world.

"It was bad news after bad news after bad news and we actively looked at moving to other cities. I called Stevie in Northern Ireland and told him, 'Don't come back; it's done, it's finished.' But once we made up our minds to do it we got stuck in."

Stevie added, "I thought that we'd done it before and we could do it again. We spent three years building it up and what else were we going to do? We had great support from everyone asking us what we needed and how they could help, and the experience will be something that's part of the rest of our lives."

But Benji's optimism had turned to pessimism by the end of the month as he grew annoyed by the lackluster response to his emails and the sparse attendance at training. He emailed: "Frankly things need to change if we are to keep this team viable. I welcome further suggestions . . . Please could the rest of you respond!"

He told me, "I was angry that dudes who were in town didn't show and was thinking, 'I know you're here so why didn't you come?' I felt it was a crisis situation and they were turning their backs on the team, and I was angry with

Medhurst even though I understood why he didn't want to know."

I understood his frustration, but he was being too critical too soon. Some guys were still getting their lives back and coming to terms with the costliest natural disaster the country had ever experienced. Giving feedback about soccer wasn't uppermost in their minds right now. Others like me would've loved to have played but were shipwrecked hundreds of miles away.

His new housemate, Dave, moved to calm him. "I told him he was the catalyst for the rejuvenation of the club and he should think about the symbolism of that first session. He was getting upset, but I said he was doing a great job and if it wasn't for him nothing would be happening. He had to be patient and appreciate the circumstances, that people were shocked and devastated and that football was the last thing on their minds."

Slowly the flotsam and jetsam of our team were drifting back to the New Orleans shore. Graeme traveled in for training from the bayou, desperate to escape his Groundhog Day existence. "Down there it's really depressing, and I was functioning, not living. There are no outlets at all, but I hadn't got it too bad compared to someone like my roommate who'd lost everything. I just had to keep my head down, get through it, and hope life would be back to normal at the end of the year."

Michael paid a teenager in a flatboat to row him to his home in Old Metairie. "He took me to the house and I fell on my butt into the slop trying to get onto the roof. My kayak was floating around the garage, and of all the things we could have saved, my son had stored his paintball gun in it.

"I retrieved some jewelry and then canoed to my office,

which had also taken about four feet of water. The day before the storm I'd lifted the computer servers onto the desktops, but the water had flooded six inches above the tables. Our records were gone, our data was gone, and those six inches cost us about $150,000."

He was a "second floor guy" now, someone who couldn't cook at home because the first floor and kitchen had been ruined. "Oscars is the only local place serving food in the neighborhood, and wealthy guys in Mercedes and BMWs will be ordering burgers and fries to go. You look at each other across the bar and acknowledge, yep, another second floor guy."

Joe was back as well. "When I came home the last thing I expected was to run into our team, but I was walking in the park and saw some guys playing and sure enough it was Finn's." His return was great news for the club. But not for me personally. Now I was bound to be dropped . . .

CHAPTER 27

Through the Looking Glass

Hard as it is to believe, my soccer-watching life in Houston grew even more bizarre.

Chelsea against Spanish club Real Betis in the European Champions League was on ESPN Deportes and I found a sports bar thirty-five miles away (a Texan dander) called Big John's. I spoke to a guy named Rudy who said they had the channel and would show it for me.

It was a sprawling glass-fronted behemoth in a strip mall with about seventy TVs, each with a black and gold number stuck above it. There were so many corridors, nooks, and crannies it reminded me of an out-of-season haunted house, and as I tried to get my bearings I half expected a dust-covered ghost train to come hurtling past.

A gaggle of English Liverpool supporters were watching their game, which had just kicked off, but I didn't see the Chelsea match on anywhere. An old Lilliputian Latino woman suddenly materialized out of thin air two inches in front of me and asked why I was there.

"Chelsea versus Betis—it's on ESPN Deportes."

"There's a ten-dollar cover charge," she said, so close I had to shuffle back to prevent treading on her feet. The cash disappeared into her clothes and she stood looking at me as she shouted, "Rudy, Rudy."

"What?" a voice answered from somewhere out back.

"Put on ESPN Deportes."

"Okay, I'm coming."

Toe to toe, she remained transfixed, staring up into my

251

face. I coughed. She said, "He's going to get you fixed up in a second."

"That's fine." There was an uncomfortable pause.

"Just here in a second."

"Right you are."

"Just give him a minute."

I walked to the bar to get away, but she followed and stood right beside me again. I was beginning to feel like an exhibit in a creepy Hispanic zoo. Thankfully, Rudy, a small fat man with a massive unlit cigar clenched between his teeth, popped up at the end of the bar and I made a dash to freedom. When I glanced back, the money collector had vanished as quickly as she'd appeared and I never saw her again.

I thought it funny that with so many sets to choose from he put my game on at the back in a corner sandwiched between the Liverpool fans and the men's toilets. Then I worked out he'd done it to have someone to talk to. I don't know if he remembered me from our brief phone conversation or if I just had that "poor lonely bastard with no friends" look about me, but whatever the reason Rudy took me under his wing. Three TVs were stacked in a column and he put the match on the top screen.

"Do you want another game on these other sets?" he asked.

"No thanks, I'm fine with this one."

"Are you sure?"

"Absolutely. But thanks anyway."

"It's no trouble. What else would you like? Rangers? Liverpool?"

He waited beside me expectantly, though farther away than the phantom granny, and I realized I didn't have a choice if I wanted to watch Chelsea in peace.

"Sure, that would be great."

He dived behind the wires and plugs and cables, switching and tinkering until I was watching Valencia and Marseille or something. I said nothing and nodded my thanks, but if I thought now I'd be left to follow the match unbothered I was sadly mistaken.

Every few minutes he'd come over and say, "The Greeks are 2-1 down. Rangers are 0-0. The Turks are winning . . ." Whether he provided this service to all of his customers as a kind of roving reporter, or whether he thought I was an obsessive fan who needed constant updates on every game, I'm not really sure. Then, near the end of the first half, he dragged over a thirty-something blond and stood with his arm around her, chomping on his cigar.

"Here, kid, meet our barmaid. You ever heard of coyote ugly? Well look at this."

I didn't know what to say. She had teeth that screamed trailer park and a laugh suggesting she was no loss to NASA, but as a friend says, "I've had worse and boasted about it the next day."

"Hello there," I said, a bit frightened.

"Imagine waking up next to this, eh? I'm thinking of darkening the lights in here so she doesn't scare the customers." The barmaid giggled.

Thankfully the halftime whistle blew and I smiled, slid off my stool, and bolted for the restroom. Two minutes later I peered out to make sure they'd gone, and satisfied the coast was clear I explored the rest of the pub, briefly contemplating leaving a trail of peanuts to find my way back. At the opposite end a section was blocked off by a sliding plastic screen—it only occurred to me later it was a private area—and I pulled it back and marched in. In an Alice in Wonderland moment, I had to wonder if I had walked into some alternate reality.

I felt as if I'd been transplanted back to Belfast's Protestant Shankill Road. The walls were awash with red, white, and blue, with British Union Jack flags, photos of the queen, pictures of Rangers players and Rangers jerseys, scarves, and memorabilia. And a huge Texas flag, also red, white, and blue. I hadn't known Big John's was the headquarters of the Houston Rangers Supporters' Club, and around thirty fans were watching them play the Slovakian team Artmedia. I laughed when I spotted an Ulster flag and a gray-haired bloke beside me asked what was wrong.

"I don't think I've ever seen an Ulster flag flying in America," I told him. It was so incongruous to walk into a bar in Houston on a boiling Texas day and see a Northern Irish flag. The ubiquitous Irish Tricolor flutters from shops, hotels, and bars dotted around the globe, but it's very rare to see an Ulster flag outside of home.

Another middle-aged drinker overheard me and said, "Aye, it's rare enough, laddie—and the bastards arrested my son last year and all he was doing was trying to fly that flag."

"You can get arrested for flying an Ulster flag?" I asked, incredulous. I couldn't believe this antiseptic part of Houston was rife with antagonistic religious goading; indeed, I'd find it hard to dream up a setting less likely to be cursed with sectarian strife.

"Honestly, son, it's true. All he did was climb up the flagpole at the Alamo, take down the Texas flag, and try to stick up the Ulster one instead. And they arrested him for that! Bloody disgrace, that's what it is."

I shook my head in sympathy and murmured something about the police state we live in. To lighten the morose silence that had settled over us I airily asked a third supporter who'd wandered over, "Do any Celtic fans come here so you can all watch the games together and have a bit of a laugh?"

"Some used to. 'Til I put a stop to it," said the newcomer.

"Really? Was there trouble?"

"No, but they were coming here and wanting to wear their tops and sing their songs and what have you. No way, I wasn't having that." I got the impression he ran the club.

"In New Orleans, Rangers and Celtic fans watch matches side by side and have a bit of banter," I said.

"Yeah? Well not in this pub. Everton played here and we organized a bus from the bar to the match. Some of them turned up and wanted to get on the bus, but I wasn't having it. I'm getting old now and I'm all finished with that fighting lark, but believe me, I was ready to jump off and get in amongst them, I can tell ye."

"Well, I'm off for the second half of the Chelsea game. Nice meeting you," and I went back through the looking glass.

Once I would have found it inspiring and comforting that in a faraway land committed friends of Northern Ireland, proudly flying our province's flag, were so dedicated to Unionism they were offended by the very sight of the Irish Tricolor. Unionists often get a bad press (admittedly, much is self-inflicted) and need all the support they can get. I've sat beneath Tricolors in hundreds of places all over the world — Finn's included, obviously — and here for once was my own flag. I'm proud of my country. I will defend our right to have the union with Britain for the rest of my life. There are at least two Celtic supporters' clubs in Houston and it wouldn't surprise me if their members are equally virulent. Maybe as it's such a huge city fans come and go all the time and it's unrealistic to expect any sort of good-natured rivalry to develop between the most bitterly entrenched enemies in British soccer.

But when I called to tell Protestant friends back home about this interlude, it was because I'd found it funny and a touch sad. In the middle of a sunny afternoon it was amusing to have this type of encounter about a tiny country on a different continent thousands of miles away. And I felt sorry for these immigrants who were missing out on the chance to forge new friendships and unexpected alliances. The way they were acting was more typical of somewhere like the tiny Ulster town Tandragee than Texas. In New Orleans, Rangers and Celtic supporters sit together and buy each other drinks, and the political abuse is plentiful but good-humored. As I made the long trek back to my seat, I missed the intimacy and familiarity of Finn's.

Back at my chair a larger-than-life Texan caricature was eating chicken wings and blocking the view of all three TVs. He was tall and broad, wore jeans and cowboy boots, and had a Stetson pushed back on his head at a jaunty angle. While I worked up the courage to ask him to move, my friend Rudy appeared. He reached across the bar, lifted a hot-sauce-lathered wing from the plate, wrapped it in a napkin, and handed it to me.

"Here, take this," he said.

"Umm," I hesitated.

"Oh it's alright, this guy's butt is too big as it is," he explained.

"Okay. Thank you."

"Hey, where're you from?" asked the big-butted Texan in a stereotypical booming voice.

"Northern Ireland."

"Hell, I worked in Aberdeen for years. Crazy damn people

played golf in the damn snow! Met a lotta good guys, Irish and Scottish. Not so mad about the English though. Those dumb bastards are so stupid they still think they rule the world."

I laughed so hard I spat out my drink all over his chicken. I apologized while simultaneously looking over my shoulder to check if the English Liverpool fans were forming a posse.

"No matter, I'm done anyway. Take them. Gotta go. Good talking to ya, buddy." He tipped his hat and deafened the bar with a shouted good-bye to Rudy.

I picked at the sodden wings and had a short spell alone before Rudy reappeared with the latest scores. Ten minutes later he came back again and slapped down another plate of chicken.

"Eat these."

"Em, sure. Thanks."

He grabbed one himself. "Yeah, we've just got a new cook. Doesn't speak a damn word of English. No matter what you tell him the bastard makes chicken wings. This is the third order he's screwed up today. But he works hard, and I get to eat all the things he makes a mess of."

As we ate, the chortling blond barmaid manifested beside us. I was beginning to think the place was full of trapdoors.

"Hey ugly, is that waitress on tonight?" asked Rudy.

"Which one?"

"The one that used to be a stripper. The European."

"Oh, where's she from?" I wondered, purely out of geographical interest. And I might have enquired what time her shift started, I can't remember.

She said, "Ooooh, somewhere real exotic, like Sweden or Australia."

"Probably Sweden," I offered.

"There's a good story about her." Rudy told the blond to get lost in no uncertain terms and she walked away, tittering.

"I got a barman here, he's as old as dirt, completely useless, and nobody else in town will give him a job, so I said he could work for me. He's driving along the highway a while back and he picks up this chick hitchhiker. They get talking and he's like me — he just says what's on his mind — and he asks her would she give him a sexual favor if he pays her.

"She says okay, they settle on a price, and he pulls off and she does the business. He comes into work a few days later and he's straight into my office to tell me about it. Then I take him to the bar to introduce him to the new waitress and guess what? It's her!

"Anyway, I'm still hungry. I have some Halloween candy around here somewhere. I bought it for the kids, but to hell with 'em. You want some candy?" He ducked down, rummaged around, and then thrust a big Tupperware box of chocolates into my face. Suddenly the factory-wrapped sweets were more appealing then the meat prepared by the staff of this truly peculiar establishment.

He took off again then returned as the match ended and I felt I should make an effort to chat, what with him having fed me for free and everything. That night it was the Astros against St. Louis in the fifth game of the National League Championship Series, and I enquired if he was expecting a big crowd.

"Oh yeah, we'll be packed. Monday night's game was crazy. I thought I was going to get lynched. We had two bar staff on, one who is pregnant and as slow as anything and another who's dumb as a post. You couldn't move in here, and then the air conditioning gave out halfway through the game. There was sweat dripping off the walls. I had so many people shouting at me that in the end I ran out the back door."

I asked if he was showing Chelsea's next Champions League match and he said to follow him to his office and he'd check. "This is where I count the money, out the back here. One time a guy tried to rob me and pulled a gun on me. He didn't know I had one as well and I shot him. Killed him, right there and then. I keep a gun on me at all times now. So what am I looking up here?"

It had felt strange watching Belarus and Norway with a bunch of Scandinavians in Houston, but that afternoon topped it for sporting spectatorial surrealism. I went back to Big John's once more to meet Paul the day before Thanksgiving. We never saw the Rangers supporters, the chuckling blond barmaid, or Rudy. Sometimes I think I imagined the whole thing.

CHAPTER 28

Trip(s) Home

Away from the diversion of freakish visits to bars populated by a spectrum of Victorian grotesques, my loathing for Houston grew. I missed my home, friends, and FSC, and it drove me mad that I couldn't walk anywhere without dodging iceberg-sized trucks hurtling alongside the practically nonexistent sidewalk.

We were thankful Julie's work had found us an apartment to live in (and we'll always be grateful for everything they did after Katrina) but the unit opposite was now inhabited by a family who made the characters from *The Beverly Hillbillies* look sophisticated. This dysfunctional collection featured a mother, her son, and his wife or girlfriend (I hope it wasn't his sister), and I'd bet they were Louisiana evacuees. During the day they sat on the balcony drinking beer, yelling, and screaming at each other until the son lost his temper. Then he'd bang doors, clomp downstairs, and shout up at his mother before storming off, returning at night with a bunch of loud drunken mates. At one stage the police were called and told us the guy had threatened his partner with a gun.

However, it wasn't the pistol-wielding neighbor that made me desperate to get back to New Orleans but an inability to watch Chelsea play against Bolton Wanderers. I was driving to the Richmond Arms for the match when the car spluttered and juddered and I limped into a mechanic's a mile from home. It was a relatively minor engine problem, but as it was a Saturday morning they were backed up and it would be hours before they could work on it.

I morosely trudged back to the apartment, but on the way I passed a large bar and grill and called in on the off chance they had FSC. There were maybe twenty customers and the hostess went to find out and then came back.

She said, "Yes, we have it, but we can't put it on for you because we need all our screens for the Astros game." I counted sixteen TVs, less than two people to every set. How many screens did these bastards need? I was so hot and bothered I couldn't even work up the energy to plead my case.

Three days later I went for a drink with Andy, who'd been transferred to Houston, and amazingly for such an urban jungle he was in a hotel a few hundred yards away. Billy had also moved to a distant part of the city, so with us and Paul we now had four Finn's "hobbits" who according to Benji had "fled to higher ground." Houston became known as the Shire.

Andy and I spent the whole night talking about Finn McCool's FC. The life-altering storm invaded our conversation from time to time, but basically we examined players, lineups, and tactics for hours. He said, "I'm gutted. I was so looking forward to that league, and I have to keep telling myself there are people who lost all kinds of stuff and I'm worried about football." I saw him and Finn's regular Scully again that Sunday at the Richmond Arms, and Andy looked rough as he'd slept in his car after a Saturday night on the lash.

The next morning, eight weeks to the day since Katrina, I took another trip to New Orleans. I needed to pick up warmer clothes (and fourteen sweaters for Julie), and I wanted to inspect our hurried emergency patchwork job on the house and ensure it was even still standing as there were daily reports of unattended fires in our neighborhood.

If all was well then Dave and Brandi would move in, giving Benji back his home and alleviating some of our survivor's guilt.

On my way, I passed through the hurricane-devastated town of Orange, one hundred miles from Houston and just west of the Louisiana border. This damage had been done by Rita, the fourth-most intense Atlantic storm on record, which had roared ashore near here on September 24. Unlike New Orleans with its National Guard troops and electricity workmen, there was nothing going on in this small community. Roofs had been ripped off restaurants and diners, and the battered interiors were ruined after a month without protection from the weather. A strip mall had been leveled, three gas stations had lost roofs, and an overturned truck by the roadside looked like a child's abandoned Tonka truck. Farther out an ambulance had been picked up and flung into a metal shed, buckling the walls and leaving the structure in tatters. I parked and listened. The only sound was the heavy-duty black plastic sheets that had been nailed to shops and stores flapping in the wind.

I walked around a wiped-out rest area at the bottom of a sloping grass verge on the edge of a little lake. The water had rushed up and drenched the building, leaving a decaying, washed-up shell. Aluminum trash cans outside had been bent and contorted by Rita's force.

People lived in trailers for miles. Although Lake Charles, thirty-five miles closer to New Orleans, had been spared the worst of the initial impact, it was clear Rita had packed one hell of a punch. At the bridge across the lake boats of all shapes and sizes had been swept up from the water and dropped onto the highway. There was still severe wind damage ninety miles east of the state line.

The outskirts of New Orleans looked better than on

my visit thirty-seven days before. But not much. I drove through devastation after devastation after devastation: homes ruined, businesses wrecked, fences destroyed, trees down, a sea of blue roof tarpaulins. Some buildings, like the Metairie Motel 6, had not been touched since the storm and curtains blew in the wind from holes that had once been windows. Others, such as the storage facility I'd seen last time, had been boarded up and secured.

In the evening I wandered out to find an open store to buy milk. It was eerie. And very spooky. Not eerie and spooky in a someone-calling-you-when-you-were-about-to-call-them way. No, eerie and spooky in a frightening, bone-chilling, horror-film-type way. As I walked around, I expected to hear a throaty, atmospheric voice-over whispering, "Exactly one hundred years ago Stephen Rea's ancestors hacked to death a group of unfriendly soccer players. Tonight they return to exact their gory revenge . . . "

Hurricane Wilma (were these storms ever going to stop?) was lashing the Florida coast and New Orleans was getting hit with the tail winds. There were no street lights. No one was back, so the area was deserted and there were no burning house or porch lights. Wind chimes tinkled, damaged tree branches thrashed about, and debris tumbled along the sidewalk. I did not see or hear another living soul in our neighborhood all night.

I finally located an open gas station on St. Charles and talked to the employee for ages, glad of the company and psyching myself up for the Halloween-like trip back. I power-walked home faster than a frightened teenager in a slasher movie being stalked on her midnight shortcut through the graveyard.

The next day I cleaned the fridge again then drove around the new New Orleans. It was unrecognizable as the city I'd been living in two months before. There were Help Wanted signs everywhere, and I mean everywhere. Think of a business — any business — and they needed staff. The neutral ground on St. Charles was blanketed in tangled notices practically begging for workers. Burger King had doubled wages and was offering a six-thousand-dollar sign-on bonus.

All traffic signals were out and hastily erected stop signs turned every junction into a four-way stop. What with pausing at the intersections, streets still blocked off, and power workers scurrying all over the roads, it took forever to get anywhere. Every time I got to St. Charles, I stopped from force of habit at the streetcar tracks even though I knew the trolleys would be offline for years.

A nearby community center and a school had both been turned into FEMA Relief Centers with military vehicles outside and soldiers and citizens milling around the buildings. Dozens of trees had been stripped bare. Debris was piled everywhere: on the road, on the street, in gardens, in blown-out shops. There were bags of trash, parts of roofs, desks, sofas, clothes (why is there only ever one shoe, never a pair, amongst ruined or discarded clothes?). It was as if all the city's residents had turned into lunatics overnight and were holding yard sales on the same day.

And a fridge outside every home. Some lay open attracting flies, others were toppled on their side, most were wrapped in reams of duct tape and had been kicked or rolled onto the sidewalk. A neighbor two doors down had dumped three such maggot magnets at our front door rather than foul his own porch air.

I cruised Magazine Street but hardly anything was open, though a tattoo parlor was doing a brisk trade in (I assume) Katrina commemoration tattoos as it had an army Humvee outside and was packed with uniformed personnel. A massive corner warehouse with a ground-floor florist had imploded like a ruined soufflé. Mark was still in Memphis and his shop was closed, though he'd emailed that he'd be producing hurricane-inspired items and asked us to remember him for holiday gifts. Every cloud has a silver lining and all that.

A few doors away I laughed at the Aiden Gill for Men storefront. Dublin barber Aiden already had an Irish Tricolor above the door, but alongside it was now a defiant sign reading, "No Surrender!" That slogan has been the rallying cry of Ulster Loyalism for decades, and to see it blazoned on a poster juxtaposed beside the Tricolor would have raised a chuckle from anyone from Northern Ireland. All we needed was a "Troops Out!" banner for the National Guard and it would've been like home.

Strangely enough Convention Center Boulevard, where the previous month there had been human suffering on a scale unimaginable in a developed country, was the cleanest part of the whole city. There'd obviously been a concerted effort to clean it up and wipe away the visual, if not the mental, reminders of death and despair. The Quarter was empty, abandoned. I'd never seen it like that.

On the I-10 Interstate the brown high-water mark ringed the mammoth pumping station, which had been almost completely submerged, while the line climbed fifteen feet above the dipping Metairie Road off-ramp. I took West End Boulevard to Lakeview, the district where Medhurst and Jonathan lived, which had still been under water on my last visit.

The exit rises from the interstate, crests, and at the top you can see all the way down into the low-lying neighborhood. Two rows of homes on either side are separated by a large patch of grass, what the locals call a neutral ground, in the middle. That initial sight took my breath away. It's a soaring pyre. For a split second it looks like rubble. Then I realize it is belongings from people's houses. It's children's toys; it's rugs; it's bedroom furniture; it's shower fittings. It's all the clothes in your wardrobe. It's all your photographs. It's lifetimes of memories. It's heartbreaking.

It was a thirty-foot testament to the power of nature and a physical symbol of the psychological anguish the people who lost everything had to face. I'd never seen anything like it in my life. The closest firsthand experience I could compare it to was viewing the towers of skulls in the Cambodian Killing Fields. It was like a scene from *Schindler's List*. Groups of people were taking photos, but it was very depressing and I had to go home.

Back at the house, Sebastian's number was still on the phone's memory from a call before the hurricane, but the line was dead when I rang. The registration paperwork with his address had been washed away from Medhurst's place, and as he'd only shown up weeks before Katrina, nobody had his contact details. We had no idea where he'd gone or what had happened to him.

In the afternoon Dave arrived with a tiny rucksack and a pair of boots. That was him moving house with everything he had. My dad used a bigger bag for his shoe-polishing gear. I was whining about our wooden floor, which had been scratched by selfish and mental houseguests we'd had the misfortune of hosting just prior to the storm, and he said, "It looks a lot better than my floor." That shut me up.

I strolled through the darkness to a local bar to meet some Finn's regulars. Everyone had a story and had a friend with an even better story. If someone who lost their home said, "I wish I hadn't bothered cleaning the house that weekend," then someone else had a mate who'd bought a place on the Saturday before and was planning to get flood insurance first thing Monday.

Adrian's exile hadn't been without incident. He'd organized a fund-raiser and the local TV station asked to mike him up for the day. "I was b.s.'ing with people and by nature I'm a talker anyway and before you knew it we had thousands at the benefit. But I forgot I had the microphone strapped to me and I was saying to people things like, 'Oh yeah, I got some great drugs last night.'

"Then they cut up my interview and moved bits around to make it sound like I said I'd lost everything when I hadn't. My place in the Quarter's okay, though when I saw our factory in Mid-City I just thought, 'Oh my God.' But we're rebuilding."

Kenny said he hadn't been sober for six weeks so he wouldn't have to deal with the stress. "I had four feet of water and I'm trying to laugh about it because Katrina has messed up so many people's lives that otherwise you'd be in shock. My whole street is destroyed and every story you hear is a horror story."

But jokes were flying around like roof tiles in Katrina and we laughed a lot as well. Whether it was a sign we'd all turned the corner or whether it was a defensive mechanism to handle the uncertainty and destruction, I don't know. Perhaps a bit of both.

It also appeared to me that foreigners were dealing with the aftermath better than the Americans. Obviously you'll be more attached to the place you were born, grew up, and spent your life, so one would expect the locals to feel more pain than the ex-pats. But we had the zeal of converts and cared deeply about New Orleans too, and we wouldn't have settled in a city with mosquitoes the size of cockroaches,

cockroaches the size of rats, and rats the size of cats unless we loved it.

My own theory was that we immigrants had packed up our lives and moved once before and so were mentally better equipped to deal with the prospect of being forced to do it again. Julie and I had arrived with only a few boxes; other lads had brought nothing more than a couple of suitcases; Benji had started a new life in America with two Snickers bars in his pocket. Julie's observation the week after the hurricane that if we had to start again it was okay because we'd already done it once was spot on.

In the morning Dave said, "My life's like the *Magical Mystery Tour* at the moment. I woke up, looked around, and thought, 'Where the hell am I today?'" I suggested this may have had less to do with his present nomadic existence and more to do with the number of Heinekens he'd consumed last night.

We went to Tom and Patricia's for breakfast and talked for two hours about the storm. Instead of the good, the bad, and the ugly, it was the odd, the sad, and the funny.

Life in post-Katrina New Orleans was very odd. Patricia ordered medicine overnighted to her, but after three days it hadn't arrived. The couriers advised her to go to the regional depot, but when they got there the building had been washed away by the floodwaters. She called back and got another address and they drove there. The manager at the second location said he had four trucks loaded with parcels but no drivers to deliver them. He let them climb into the vans and they scrambled around amongst hundreds of packages, many of which had contained perishables like meat and frozen fish, until they'd located her pills.

Dave was working as a contractor and the crew had gone to clean a place in New Orleans East. Water had bulldozed sludge and mud three feet deep into the home and turned the living room into a landscape like a battlefield from World War I. They removed four snakes. Then they waded towards a gigantic green plant that had been swept into the corner of the living room, but the chief reined them back. He said it looked like an alligator nest and told them to wait while he reached across and poked at it with a rake. It was a false alarm. But four snakes and an alligator scare *inside* a home! Just weeks before a family had sat there watching TV; now it was like a location on the Discovery Channel.

Then there was the sad. Tom and Patricia's housekeeper, Jackie Brumfield, swam out of her house with her nine-year-old grandson and two daughters, one of whom had cancer while the other was six months pregnant, and they ended up in the Superdome. One of their pals had lost his business and had no flood insurance.

Dave explained how he felt the need to go into his home and "say good-bye" to each ruined item before he could bring himself to throw it away. He'd pick something up, look at it, and remember where he got it, and only then did he have the closure to dump it and move on to the next thing.

And there was humor (albeit black) floating about, if you'll pardon the pun. Tom and Patricia knew a volunteer cat rescue couple who holed up in a three-story building owned by a frail old man who kept dozens of caged birds.

A few hours before Katrina slammed the city the cat rescue couple heard gunshots, and when they investigated a man lay dead in the street. The police eventually turned up, but already overstretched by a mandatory evacuation and an imminent hurricane, they didn't remove the body. Instead they stood him upright, covered his head, and used yellow crime-scene tape to secure him to a lamppost. They left, the levees failed, the area flooded, and the corpse broke loose and drifted away.

The pair rowed around saving cats and brought them back to the house. They were chased higher and higher up the building by the rising water and had their hands full controlling the starving cats, which were attacking the birds. The elderly homeowner died, and just to add an off-the-wall twist to the tale they picked up a Japanese student who flipped out. He sat hunched in a corner nodding his head and repeating over and over, "I am a Rhodes scholar. I am a Rhodes scholar."

Then one afternoon as they stood on the porch the body floated back to the house. Then he floated off again. Then later he floated back. In fact he floated around the neighborhood for days. They got so blasé about the shot man they christened him "Bob" and made jokes like, "Oh look, Bob's back for a drink; it must be cocktail hour."

Dave, meanwhile, had met Ulsterman Gary, a Finn's regular, who had evacuated to a downtown hotel that lost power and practically shut down. Bored guests hung around the function rooms for days, but Gary noticed one guy was always drunk and enquired where he was getting the alcohol. The man took him to the room he shared with his girlfriend where there was a veritable Aladdin's cave of booze. When Gary asked where it came from he told him to come back at midnight and he'd show him.

He took him to the basement where a cooler room on a back-up generator kept wine and beer chilled. He knew the pass code because his girlfriend used to work in the hotel and while Gary held open the door the guy grabbed bottles and cans. As he struggled with the drinks, he almost dropped a bottle and Gary, frightened the noise would alert the staff, leaped forward to grab it. Click. The door locked behind him.

They were shut in a frigid prison and no one knew they were there. After hours hammering and knocking, they thought they were going to die and decided to go out with a bang, so they opened all the expensive alcohol and resolved to drink their way to the afterlife. However, the next morning the girlfriend woke up, guessed where her boyfriend was, and appeared to release two very inept, intoxicated thieves.

Dave had spoken to another Finn's regular, Camille, a half-English, half-Dutch ex-porn star who spent days in insufferable conditions in the Superdome followed by another unbearable spell on the interstate waiting to be evacuated. Eventually, after almost a week of hell, he'd finally gotten on a bus bound for Houston believing his ordeal was over.

At the first truck stop the bus pulled in and three guys got off, held up the shop at gunpoint, and calmly got back on the bus. The cops had been called and surrounded the vehicle, impounding it and arresting the trio. After thinking his nightmare was over Camille was trapped for hours while the officers questioned the passengers and completed their investigation.

When they finally arrived at the Astrodome he assumed the speakers at the entrance were playing music to welcome the evacuees. Instead when he got off he heard a Texan sheriff warning everyone would be searched and threatening serious repercussions for anyone found in possession of contraband items. He said passengers were dumping handfuls of drugs all over the place.

It was time to head back to the Shire. I called at Medhurst's office to give him tins of British baked beans and a box of tea bags as a cheering-up present. He asked if I was playing soccer in Houston, but I hadn't even considered it as it would have felt like a betrayal, like cheating on my wife. Soccer-wise I was married to New Orleans and Finn's, and Houston wasn't a seductive mistress I'd want a wild affair with. It wasn't even a grizzled hag of a landlady I'd have a fumble with while I kipped in her spare room after being kicked out by the wife. I had no intention of breaking my soccer betrothal vows with that Texan tramp.

When I got back Julie showed me pictures from Chalmette a colleague had emailed her. They didn't look real: cars on top of houses, boats on top of garages, vehicles at crazy angles hanging down from buildings, homes as flat as pancakes. It looked like cars had been Photoshopped on top of regular suburban street scenes.

On October 30, Julie drove me to the airport as I was going to Northern Ireland for two weeks. The interstate was twelve lanes wide and in the lane to our right and twenty yards ahead a car was towing a travel trailer. I noticed it suddenly start to swing violently and then three vehicles ahead there was a crash. Everyone squealed to a dead stop. A Hispanic woman jumped out of a damaged car. She pulled a child from the back seat and stood in the middle of the interstate cradling her baby.

I heard the screech of brakes behind us. It was a blinding powder-blue day. The sun was bouncing off every metallic surface. In the rearview mirror I could see a vehicle doing maybe sixty mph plough into an SUV four cars back. The driver didn't realize the traffic had stopped.

When I was young I had two brightly colored plastic toy cars I charged up by pulling a long plastic thread through the motor. A friend and I would send them careering head-on into each other and they were designed so the doors, hood, and trunk would fly off. That was what this crash was like. I watched big chunks of both vehicles scream off and hurtle through the air like little plaything pieces.

We rounded the smash and got out of there as quickly as we could. I couldn't wait to leave Houston.

CHAPTER 29

The Bag Boy

During my road trip with New Stephen while on our initial evacuation, we had visited the Four Corners region. There I had asked a tourist to take our photograph. He said he'd email it when he got home, and it arrived in November. Must have been some holiday. I mention this because New Stephen moved back to Dublin in September but was about to reappear in my life.

The day of our hurried evacuation he'd brought his clothes in an almighty roll-along soft-cover suitcase and stored it on our second floor in case his own place flooded. I'd planned to ship it to him, but it was too large for regular mail and would have cost three hundred dollars to courier, so I packed the contents into a box and sent that but held onto the empty bag.

At the end of my vacation in Northern Ireland, I was flying back to the States from Dublin anyway, so when I left Houston, I put my suitcase inside his (that's how large this bag was) and flew to Belfast, planning to meet him at Dublin Airport on my return journey so we could catch up. But New Stephen is nothing if not laidback, and when I told him I had his suitcase in Northern Ireland he emailed me: "Thanks for bringing the bag back but it's a pain in the backside to get to the airport at 10 A.M. If I promise to meet you at 10 A.M. I'll probably end up going on the lock, hungover to hell, and missing the rendezvous! But if I feel I can make it up I'll give you a bell."

It obviously wasn't preying on his mind then, but it was

an expensive piece of luggage and I knew it wasn't even his but his mother's. I suggested leaving it in the terminal so he could pick it up later rather than face getting there for the crack of 10 A.M. He replied, "Yeah, that'd be fine. My mother really wants that bag back so I suppose I should make the effort to get it back for her. Let me know where you leave it."

It was appropriate the case was devil red because I was about to embark on the trip from hell. I got to the Belfast bus station ticket desk a few minutes before the scheduled 7:30 A.M. departure to Dublin Airport and the staff member ignored me to talk on his cell phone. I managed to interrupt him to ask for a ticket and he stopped chatting long enough to tell me, "Oh, that bus has gone already."

"How come? It's not 7:30."

He shrugged. "I called it," was his confusing answer. He must have been a frustrated sports umpire.

"Where's the next stop?" I could jump in a taxi and get ahead of it.

"Lisburn, but you've no chance of catching it now." It seemed this particular coach was fitted with a space shuttle engine.

As I rifled through my options, a bus with "Dublin Airport" pulled into the station. I was livid. I'd been on the point of dashing for a cab and embarking on a high-speed ten-mile drive and my transport hadn't even arrived, never mind left. The cowardly imbecile didn't have the courage to look at me as I cursed him while he issued my ticket. It went downhill from there.

I was the only passenger. We drove thirty yards then the driver got off and disappeared into the bus garage. We hadn't even left the station! He emerged ten minutes later eating his breakfast. We set off again and had an uneventful forty miles picking up passengers until we reached Newry. It took an hour to crawl through the rush-hour traffic and we parked in the depot at 9:40 A.M., now fifty-five minutes late.

Two employees were waiting at the stop to talk to our driver. One approached his window and asked, "Now, are you sure you know where you are going?"

"Not really. Do I take a left at the old road . . . ?"

"No, no, no. When you get to . . ."

Meanwhile, people were disembarking and asking for their bags from the storage compartment, and while they did this one worker was telling the driver how to release the doors to the luggage bins as the other talked on top of him with directions for a route he'd obviously never driven before. It was a recipe for disaster.

Then a woman said, "That poor couple are getting on the other bus; they have a plane to catch."

"What's that? So have I," I said.

"Oh, love, you'd be better off with the express over there. It's going straight to the airport."

I was still fifty miles away from the airport and should have been checked in by now. I jumped off, pushed old women and children out of the way, grabbed the monster bag, and waved down the driver as he pulled out.

We arrived seventy minutes late as check-in was closing. I handed over my own case then went to the information desk and the girl said I could leave the bag for New Stephen at Lost Property. Unfortunately, though, the office wasn't in the terminal but in a separate building some distance away. "Goddamn you, New Stephen," I thought cheerily. If I took it to Lost Property, I'd miss my flight, but I couldn't bring myself to discard it either.

I returned to the check-in desk, aware that in a post-September 11 world it wasn't the best idea to ask an American airline to look after a case. Especially in an Ulster accent. But it was open, empty, and made of nylon, so once again I explained my predicament and asked if they could store it for a few hours until New Stephen got out of bed. The girl was sympathetic but had to ask her supervisor. She came to the counter, I told the story again, and she said no — then called over a security guard. He asked what the problem was and I went over the situation a further time. He said no.

They told me if I wanted to catch the plane I'd better hurry. Both advised me to dump it in a trash can, but I still couldn't face tossing it away. I asked to check it in as hold luggage but it was too late, though I could do that at the gate. If I made the plane.

I jumped the line at security and ran to American immigration, which in Dublin you clear before boarding. Due to the number of stamps in my passport from my travel agent days the officer was convinced I didn't live in the States. I could hear the last call for my flight as he barraged me with loaded, baited questions like, "Are you still married to the girl you wed to get your green card?"

Eventually I negotiated the interrogation, sprinted to the gate, checked in the monster, and queued to board. I was paged to return to the gate agent. The supervisor and security guard from check-in were waiting for me. "Mr. Rea, how many bags did you check?" asked the supervisor.

"Two."

"But your ticket only shows one."

"Yes, but I've just checked another at the gate. Remember the big red bag I couldn't check in the concourse?"

"Oh right," she answered. I couldn't work out if it was some kind of test or if she was simply a cretin. The security guard stared at me continuously until I got to the Jetway. Then we sat on the ground for an hour.

When we landed in Chicago I was late for my connection to Dallas and still had to pick up my luggage and clear customs. I had less than half an hour until my next flight and of course my own normal-sized suitcase came out in minutes. But there was no sign of the monster, even though in theory it had been the last bag into the hold. I waited and waited.

With fifteen minutes to go, I gave up. I wasn't going to waste a second longer on this cursed case of death and would track it down when I got to Houston. I tore through O'Hare, barged to the top of the security queue again — this time swinging my own bag about like a mace as I hadn't time to visit the checked-luggage bag drop — and got to the gate eight minutes before departure.

I collapsed in front of the agent and panted, "Is the plane still here?"

"YES!"

"Thank God for that." I handed her my ticket.

"Oh, there's no room on this one. We gave away your seat because we thought you weren't coming. Where's your monster bag by the way?"

That last sentence I made up. But the rest is true. I was now on standby and the next three flights to Dallas were full. When I made it to Texas the first connection to Houston didn't have seats either. I finally touched down at 11:00 P.M., twenty-two hours after leaving Belfast.

And guess what? I stood for ages in baggage claim and the red monster never showed. I spent another thirty minutes filling out lost luggage paperwork before I could leave. It was delivered two days later at 4 A.M. What sort of lunatic delivers a case at 4 A.M.! If I hadn't been half asleep I would have said it wasn't mine and told him to send it to New Stephen's address in Dublin.

But my trip to Belfast had been useful because I discovered that Katrina was caused by homosexuals. According to press reports, Maurice Mills, an enlightened twenty-first-century politician with Ian Paisley's Democratic Unionist Party (DUP) from the town of Ballymena, said the hurricane was sent by God to punish New Orleans' tolerance of gays.

He explained: "The recent Hurricane Katrina descended on New Orleans and took many people suddenly into eternity. However, the media failed to report that the hurricane occurred just two days prior to the annual homosexual event called the Southern Decadence Festival. . . .

"Surely this is a warning to nations where such wickedness is increasingly promoted and practiced. This abominable and filthy practice of sodomy has resulted in the great continent of Africa being riddled with AIDS, all at great cost to the nations and innocent children."

Just days after the storm my mate Keith predicted American zealots on the religious right would see New Orleans as a modern-day Sodom and Gomorrah and equate the disaster with a cleansing biblical flood. I should have known the nutters in Ulster would try to beat them to it. There was no point explaining the floodwaters hadn't touched the two gay districts (the Quarter and the Marigny) but had devastated middle-class, family-dominated suburbs like Lakeview.

Within months DUP rising star Paul Berry was forced to resign after arranging to meet a male masseur in a Belfast hotel. Then the party's Dessie Stewart, former mayor of the town of Coleraine, admitted four counts of electoral fraud and punched a photographer on his way into court. Undoubtedly fit to lecture us on morals, these God-fearing paragons of virtue.

Paul and his girlfriend, Jamie, also happened to be in

Belfast to attend a wedding and I showed them the city. Before his visit, Paul had made another trip to New Orleans and found a gang of looters in his apartment. "They'd closed off the street and when I walked in the door two Latinos were carrying out my TV. They froze and looked at each other as if to say, 'What should we do; should we kill this guy?'

"Then one started jabbering in Spanish but I just held up my hands and said, 'It's okay, I just need this,' and took my social security card, which is all I'd returned for anyway. There were eight of them; what was I going to do?"

As the city rebuilt, groups of Hispanics congregated at gas stations and roadsides waiting for homeowners to pick them up and hire them for casual work. Paul stopped to get gas—and six jumped in the back of his truck. He tried to explain he just wanted to fill up, but they didn't listen as they were too busy fighting one another for the chance to earn cash.

He and Jamie came along to the international exhibition game between Northern Ireland and Portugal, but the highlight of their visit was a trip to the electronic state-of-the-art, open-air, pop-up, three-man-at-a-time, overhead-spotlighted, after-dark, public urinal recently installed in Belfast city center. It was an experience every bit as fantastic as it sounds.

CHAPTER 30

Click Your Heels Three Times

We were going home.

While I was in Belfast, Julie's company decided to return to New Orleans at Thanksgiving. Now we had one more week in Houston, just long enough for my Irish friend Jason to visit so I could try on the Pakistan-made Scottish kilt I was to wear at his wedding to a half-English, half-Spanish girl in Mexico.

And long enough to buy Julie's Christmas present: a coat, hat, gloves, and scarf. I'm joking. That was her birthday present. She's a gadget freak so I wanted to get her an iPod nano, and as there was barely a grocery store open in New Orleans, never mind an electronics shop, I had to buy it before moving back. I had a voucher for Best Buy, but none of their nine outlets in the area had any in stock. I called all of them everyday to find out if they had some or if a delivery was scheduled. It was the big-ticket item and they were flying off the shelves; twice I was told they'd received a case in the last twenty-four hours but had already sold out. They were so sought after that secondhand iPods were selling on eBay for more than new models.

But two days before Thanksgiving, I got lucky. After an extraordinarily long nail-biting game of being passed from one department to another, I was told there had been an arrival that morning. They still had six. No they couldn't hold one for me. No they didn't care that I was a Katrina refugee. Or that it was for my invalid great-aunt who had a week to live.

I drove the fifty-three miles like a maniac. By the time I arrived, they had only a couple left. I dropped to my knees in gratitude, kissed the assistant's hand, and left the store singing and dancing. The wife's Christmas present sorted with a month to spare. I was a bloody genius, not to mention a loving husband.

Fast forward to 3 P.M. on Christmas Eve and Julie and I are queuing in our bank. A sign advertises a free iPod nano if you open an account with a certain amount of money.

"Look, dear. Pity we can't do that because you could get one of those fancy iPods," I say smugly.

Julie reads the poster. "Oh, I wouldn't want one of those. They don't have a radio."

This was the closest I've ever come to committing murder.

As Julie and I were preparing to move home, Finn McCool's FC was fitfully reanimating with an average of ten players at Sunday training. Frank the Tank, after tracking down India House owner Mark and offering to help rebuild it for free, was the latest to return. Andy meanwhile promised his "Katrina fridge" to a friend who was going to keep it in his garage for beer. Andy took it outside, went back in to lock his door, and when he returned it had been swiped. Word was Dumpster diver Captain Morgan was the chief suspect.

Erick had mixed news: his apartment complex had escaped with only sporadic wind damage, but his parents' home had three feet of water. "On TV we'd seen people with water past their knees in the area but a friend got into the neighborhood and said there were no watermarks and that gave us hope.

"When we came back it didn't look like anything had happened from the outside, but when my father opened the door . . . the look on his face. I'll never forget it as long as I live. You saw everything, his whole life story, by the expression on his face. Everything he ever worked for was gone just like that. It was a mess.

"I'll never forget the smell and the look of things like the couch I used to sit on when I was a kid, things I saw everyday when I came home from school. It all got pretty emotional. My mum was upset but my dad stayed strong and said, 'It's okay, we'll just start over.'

"My parents came to this country with nothing and couldn't even speak the language, so if anybody can do it, they can. But they lost about 98 percent of everything they ever owned. And so many other people around us experienced the same thing."

People like Mike Mac. He, Marian, and their four boys and baby girl had all moved in with Sean. He said, "As soon as I saw the people out crying on the streets I knew we'd been flooded. I opened the door and everything was ruined. It was the first time we'd seen damage, and it was a poignant moment as up until then we'd been detached from it all.

"But we had insurance and were compensated. My wife and I arrived in America with two cases each, and over thirteen years we gathered so much crap, and the only things I was upset about were photos and sentimental stuff.

"I work at a company with three hundred employees and I reckon a third were left with nothing. One day a visitor asked how I'd got on and I said we'd a bit of flooding in the house and didn't elaborate because the woman beside me lost everything."

After practice the lads occasionally went back with Dave to our place, and some wondered how a "hobbit" like me could afford an attractive, recently renovated house. Dave said I robbed treasure from dragons.

An even more unlikely fairytale was that Adrian met Prince Charles and Camilla on their visit to New Orleans on November 4, when onetime Finn's coach Steve Ebbs stopped by his apartment and invited him along to a royal reception in the Quarter.

"I was in a dirty tee-shirt and was straight from—quite literally—scrubbing crap off the walls at work. We stood in this room and Charlie came out with all his equerries and I thought I'd get busted as I was looking very strange, but he came over and shook my hand.

"I'd called my mum and dad and had the phone on in my pocket so they could hear and it was 7 P.M. on Friday night at home and they'd had a drink. I can talk and fell into conversation with him and Governor Blanco and the mayor. Charlie knew all about insurance and asked what I was doing here.

"Then I went home and ten minutes later I was walking the dog. I always said I'd never cross the road to see the royals, but I did. You know Camilla looks a bit of a dog on TV? Well she's even rougher in real life. It was a bizarre afternoon."

Five days later Rangers played Celtic—and it was on at Finn's. Stephen emailed a photo entitled "We shall not be moved" showing a handful of drinkers including Stevie, Big Rab, and Joy crowded around a TV. They wore face masks, held cans of beer, and were covered in dust. The bar was a shell without doors or walls and the sheetrock had been ripped out, exposing the wooden supporting beams. But at least the satellite was up and running.

Benji's mood had improved and he invited the team to Thanksgiving at his house. Michael replied, "You're having a Thanksgiving party and inviting the British? The whole point of Thanksgiving is to celebrate getting the hell away from them!"

Billy corrected him. "Thanksgiving is about being nice to Native Americans and then screwing up their whole way of life as they knew it. Haven't you seen *Waterworld*, I mean, *Dances with Wolves*?"

Julie and I rose at 5 A.M. on Thanksgiving Day to load up the car and drive from Houston. Relief at breaking free from Texas and the joy of seeing some mates for the first time since the storm made it an unforgettable day. It was ironic the foreigners had such a good time on an American holiday that means nothing to us, and no matter how long I live in this country I don't know if I'll ever experience an equally special Thanksgiving.

We stayed at Benji's all day listening to how New Orleans was now like the Wild West. The National Guard-enforced curfew had trapped two of our crew.

Graeme was caught when he drove a friend home to the Quarter. "I didn't even realize what had happened, then these Humvees swerved in front of me and there were soldiers swarming all over my car. One asked if I'd been drinking and I said, 'Aye, sure, it's Friday night. I've probably had six or seven beers.' Next thing he was calling the cops and I was really, really shocked. I asked if he was getting the police and he said, 'Yes, you've been drinking.' I just thought, 'What a jerk.'"

When the severely stretched NOPD arrived, Graeme could tell immediately they had more pressing matters to deal with than conducting late-night breathalyzer tests. "As soon as the cops got out of the car I knew fine well I wasn't getting a DUI because they were just so tired, so angry and frustrated, and were thinking, 'What are these arseholes doing calling us out for a guy who's had too much to drink?'

"Who was I gonna crash into or run over? The whole city

was deserted. They told me to walk a straight line and I walked the straightest that's ever been walked. He said he had to do something because the Guard had called them all the way across the city, and so I jumped in the car with a $111 ticket for driving without headlights."

Captain Morgan had also forgotten about the curfew and at a roadblock was stopped, questioned, and his ID checked. He too was asked if he'd been drinking.

He replied, "Well, I've had a couple."

The soldier smiled and said, "Yeah right, just a couple. I'll give you a choice. You can either sit here and I'll call the NOPD, or you can pull over into that parking lot and sleep it off until the morning."

He plumped for the latter option and quickly fell asleep. When he awoke in the morning there were six other vehicles parked beside him with drivers blearily rubbing their eyes and starting their engines. He already had a reputation for sleeping in his car as he'd a habit of falling out of Finn's drunk, cranking his ignition to get the heater going, then sleeping with the engine running the whole night.

But his best vehicular-sleeping story was when he hooked up with a girl who had a Scooby-Doo Mystery Machine-type van one summer. They spent the night in the van near a 7-Eleven in a sketchy neighborhood and he woke the next morning hot, sweaty, and dehydrated. Clad only in his underwear, he grabbed a few dollars and went to buy a drink in the store.

He came out to find the girl had cleared off and left him.

Apparently she returned later to pick him up though.

It was an emotional weekend. My euphoria at being home was shattered on Friday by the death of George Best, certainly the most talented soccer player Northern Ireland has ever produced and arguably the greatest player the world has ever seen. The first match I ever went to was his last appearance for Northern Ireland against Holland in 1977, and though I saw him in the flesh a few more times, he was past his peak.

On Saturday, Chelsea traveled to play against Portsmouth and after three months battling to see games, I could now sit on my own sofa in my own living room and watch my team on my own TV. But all I remember about the match is the supporters' show of respect for Bestie.

The next day was a double celebration: my birthday and the resumption of training with Finn McCool's FC after my three months in exile. I was awful. My first touch on the ball was even worse than normal, and I had no stamina and was knackered after five minutes. The only positive was that after ninety-four days I was playing again.

Afterwards we went to Cooter Brown's sports bar to celebrate my birthday amongst National Guard troops and New York cops. We ordered pitchers and pitchers of beer and a load of food and requested FSC be put on one of the many TVs. They refused as they were showing NFL games. We argued that we were a large party who had been there for hours spending a sizeable sum, and eventually they grudgingly put it on a set at the back of the bar and we left our table to sit on stools in the screened-off gambling section. The sooner Finn's reopened the better.

But it felt like peace was being restored to the Force. We reintroduced Thursday training and the email announcing it was sent by Medhurst, not Benji. Finn's threw a party at their building site on December 1 to celebrate the official end of hurricane season.

Finally, it was over. Until next year.

CHAPTER 31

The Surreal Life

Life in New Orleans was very surreal three months after Katrina. Normal everyday rules didn't apply. I felt like a frontiersman or an extra in a *Mad Max* movie. The city's population was estimated to be a tenth of what it was PK (pre-Katrina), a level not seen since the mid-nineteenth century.

Think of an infrastructure and it was missing: schools (thus very few children), hospitals, traffic lights, grocery stores, restaurants, garbagemen. There was no mail delivery. In a poverty-wracked city where a quarter of the population relied on public transportation, there were no streetcars. The 368 buses running in August had been slashed to 44. A full one hundred days after the storm just 64 percent of New Orleans had electricity.

What we did have were cats, lots and lots of cats, prowling and scavenging under the house and in the garden and on the porch. If a mad scientist had crossbred a B movie horror flick with a Western, he would have created life in New Orleans in the winter of 2005.

We also had an abundance of storm chasers, contractors who'd descended on us from all over America looking to make a quick buck. PK the overwhelming majority of license plates about town were from Louisiana, with a few from neighboring Texas or Mississippi. One day in December, I counted plates from seventeen different states. On Christmas Eve, I even spotted one from Alaska. Trucks and lorries and vans and SUVs bullied their way around the city, firing the wrong way down one-way streets and ignoring stop signs. The roads, dangerous enough before the hurricane, now turned into *Death Race 2000.*

And we had plenty of trash. You'd pile it outside your home and hope someday it would be picked up. There were no regular collection dates or schedules, and confusion concerning which agency was responsible for what trash and what was okay to lump together and what had to be separated reigned. Every imaginable kind of human detritus lay on footpaths and sat in Dumpsters and littered roads and besmirched gardens. Domestic waste mingled with flooded clothes, burnt furniture, and abandoned cars. It was a battlefield aftermath, and we'd had our butts royally kicked by Mother Nature.

On Claiborne Avenue a guy set up shop at a flooded gas station forecourt and cut hair with a razor and a little handheld mirror. The last time I'd seen a similar street hairdresser was a decade ago in one of Johannesburg's poorest areas. On one of the tens of thousands of abandoned fridges, someone scrawled, "Welcome to the Third World."

PK the Sunday paper ran a column called "Who's in Town" with the week's conferences and conventions and the number of hotel rooms booked by attendees. But now there was nobody in town. The column was retitled "Who's on TV" and listed the shows featuring politicians talking about the hurricane.

Julie and I settled back into our home. We discovered it was underinsured, but we couldn't increase the coverage until we repaired the roof, which was considerably more damaged than we'd realized. Thankfully we'd had one of the driest three-month spells on record. Seawater, not rainwater, was the city's problem.

However, the storm had knocked out our heating and

Julie was practically suicidal. She'd dress for bed like an igloo-dwelling Eskimo and wouldn't drink after 5 P.M. so she didn't have to get up during the night to pee, as it took an hour to remove the layers.

Getting a workman was nearly impossible unless you wanted to chance one of the cowboys treating post-hurricane Louisiana like the California gold rush (I heard about two homes that hadn't taken water but were then flooded by unqualified plumbers). Luckily I tracked down Ralph Tebbe, who had originally installed our unit and who was coincidentally also working at Finn's. "Are all you Irish guys called Stephen?" he asked.

He lived on the North Shore and had to rebuild part of his own kitchen and roof, and for a week, whenever he went to bed, he lay looking up at the night sky through the missing chunk of his ceiling. I said he should've lit a campfire and cooked beans. He told me I was overdoing the Wild West analogies.

Mark too had returned to New Orleans after his Memphis interlude. "We were in a friend's bed-sit, which became a truck stop as we'd fifteen people stay in the fortnight after the storm. Then we were given a tiny efficiency apartment in half a garage which had been designed by a local recycling artist, so it was very appropriate for us.

"I went to record stores and asked them to donate records and we got tons and tons and melted them into bowls and magazine racks. We made the colored vinyl into lampshades and album covers into clocks and sold them at a show.

"So we just partied in Memphis as there was nothing we could do, but then we met a guy who offered his shopfront and we did really well. Anything to do with Katrina especially sold great."

Like us, he had snuck into the city a few weeks after the

hurricane. "I thought I was coming back to a dead chicken. I got a chicken for my birthday and called it Zulu after the Mardi Gras krewe parading that day. I was planning to eat it but it laid an egg everyday so I kept it and made a dog-box condo for it.

"A friend put it inside our apartment the day before the storm, but when I got back the chicken had gone but the box was still there. It's a bit freaky. I hope somebody ate it. Our place wasn't damaged, but the crackheads in our complex broke down the wall to rob the neighbor's flat because they could do what they liked as there was nobody around.

"Our shop was okay as the landlord hadn't evacuated and barricaded it inside and outside. Every day the National Guard rapped the door and ordered him out, and after four days they said if you don't go now, we'll take you away at gunpoint.

"A mate stayed for the hurricane and with his girlfriend cruised around with shotguns and handguns on their lap and he ended up working for CNN. He has video footage of Walgreens being looted by the cops and when he pans down all the TV reporters are wearing brand-new shoes!"

While civilization crumbled in New Orleans, the world was fascinated by its downfall. Mark couldn't keep up with the demand for the handbags he'd made from MRE packages (MRE stands for Meal, Ready-to-Eat and not More Rubbish from England, as Benji claimed). "I had to go scavenging through the trash at the Superdome because we'd an order for 150 MRE handbags and we only had seven! The Smithsonian Museum even requested one."

When we first moved back I was simply glad to be home and willing to put up with any inconvenience. Sure there was a bit of garbage about, the library was closed, and I couldn't get a letter delivered, but so what? In a few weeks when the billions of dollars of promised aid flowed in everything would be hunky-dory. I expected we'd be back to normal by Christmas, maybe Mardi Gras.

Then nine days after returning I went with Eric, Big Rab, and Captain Morgan to Dave's house in Mid-City. Now I knew why they talked about the area being "nuked." It would be years before this district came back. Smashed homes and wrecked houses, battered boats and vehicles on the roads, cars encrusted with saltwater lines, seven-foot-tall sludge and dirt marks on everything were the new landscape of former neighborhoods.

But what really shocked me was the absence of life. There was nobody around. It was as if aliens had swooped down overnight and kidnapped the human race. The five of us spent hours at Dave's tearing the place to pieces and dumping the debris out on the street. His kitchen, his bathroom, his floor—we ripped every flooded goddamn thing apart and busted the walls back to the studs. Once I heard a chainsaw, but the whole time we saw no one. The neighborhood was empty. Mid-City was in a coma and it wasn't awakening any time soon. Depressing. Deserted. Dead.

No wonder Dave was down. "You look at your home and go, 'Hell.' I can't stay there alone too long, maybe fifteen minutes. I don't like being in it on my own. It's so utterly devastating. I'm dislodged, there's no end in sight, and you feel sorry for yourself.

"I've become intolerant of people not affected who are laughing and joking and having parties and enjoying themselves. I despise anyone who's going on as if nothing happened and find it very irritating, and that includes friends I've had for a long time. The only good thing is we've all been forced to talk to each other about our sentiments and what has gone on and that's been very healthy."

Sean also valued his teammates' support in this alien emotional landscape. "I need to have a drink with the lads. I've had to make big decisions affecting several hundred people at work, and I need a break and a little time to separate things before going home with Mike Mac and his family in the house and dealing with the impact of the hurricane on my wife and daughter.

"A lot of people are upside down but you have to be strong and you can't compensate by not really dealing with it inside. Discussing what you are going through is important, but if you talk about it too much it wears you out and you don't have the strength to deal with it."

Mike Mac said, "Men never talk about feelings and ask each other how we are doing with things, but one night Sean and I sat down and put our cards on the table. I told him we couldn't be living with him too long and he said that he understood that but we could stay as long as we wanted. I felt so much better after that talk, without getting too mushy about it."

While Mid-City was bereft of life, Uptown bulged at the seams. Just like Dave and Brandi had moved in with us, returning evacuees crowded into unflooded areas. Rents in "the sliver by the river" soared to astronomical proportions, and the few services and shops open were continually packed because of the increased population. The severely reduced opening hours due to lack of staff made things worse.

To help you understand what life was like in New Orleans at this time, here's how I spent Tuesday, December 13, 2005.

I start with a trip to the post office and arrive as it opens. Already there is a line, which is split in two, residents mailing stuff and others picking up their post. Four policemen run the operation. I have to stay and queue because later the wait will be even longer.

I inch along the jam-packed interstate to the Home Depot store in Metairie for material to plug yet more holes we've found in the roof. It's still early but the parking lot is full so trucks and vans are parked all along the service road.

Armed guards control the crowds of customers in line. One tells me this branch is now the busiest in the nation. It takes almost an hour to pay for three cans of expanding foam. I pay with cash; credit card machines in the city aren't online yet.

New Stephen has sent me his American cell phone SIM card, so I battle the traffic to the Cingular office. It too is packed and I'm told to sign in and take a seat. Wait time is estimated to be around fifteen minutes. There are no empty chairs and I stand for forty minutes. They aren't interested in trying to get my phone to work and kick me out as quickly as they can.

Next up is Christmas shopping and I go to Best Buy to get Julie a CD. It takes less than sixty seconds to walk in, lift it from the display, and join the check-out line. I count thirty-three people in front of me. I'm there twenty minutes.

I crawl down Veterans to Target to buy an ornament Julie had admired in their Houston outlet. I can't see it anywhere and try to find someone to ask. The only staff member I'm quick enough to grab is harassed and flustered and advises me to go the customer service desk. I am ninth in line.

I'm finally told it's not in stock and they don't know when any goods will be delivered. I ask the girl to check with the Westbank branch, but no stores in the area are making or taking "department calls." She suggests I go home and call them myself.

I drive into the CBD to get some newspaper articles I'd

written scanned onto a disc. Normally, finding a parking space here is a nightmare but now there are no meter maids and the meters aren't working. Vehicles are left at bus stops, in front of twenty-four-hour access garages, and even facing the wrong way on one-way streets.

I park right outside the office and when I return there's a group having a picture taken with National Guard soldiers. They are posing beside a sand-colored armored Humvee with a Christmas tree stuck on the hood.

I head out of downtown, round the now streetcar-less Lee Circle, and stop at a dry cleaners on St. Charles run by an Asian family. I walk into the middle of a heated argument. A six-footer in a suit is holding up a blue-and-white striped shirt and haranguing the middle-aged Chinese woman.

"You've ruined this shirt. Look at it. I bought it after Katrina; it cost me thirty-six dollars and I only wore it once." Three black marks streak down the back.

"Not our fault, not our fault." She claims it was like that when he brought it in. This gets him mad and he turns to me and the other two customers and begins to shout.

"They said my bill was $159! Then they said it was $110." He turns back to the woman. "You have no prices up. I'm going to report you to the Better Business Bureau. You're ripping people off."

"What you want me do? I wash again. We wash over for you." She reaches for the shirt, embarrassed as another customer enters. The man senses weakness.

"No, I want fifty dollars. If you don't give me it, I'm going to report you for price gouging and inflating your charges. And you asked me for cash. You're cheating on your taxes. I'm a lawyer and I'm going to sue you for thirty-six dollars. You hear me? I will . . ."

She tries to interrupt, but by the time a middle-aged

Oriental man I assume is her husband appears from the back, he's worked himself up into such a state he's foaming at the mouth. Now he's using language that I have to surmise is not the standard lexicon taught at American law school, none of which is printable.

I have to wait because it's the only open cleaners around, but I step out onto the pavement for some fresh air. Seconds later the customer smacks out the door, still cursing loudly, and the husband pursues him into the street shaking his fist and shouting in his native language. I go back inside and make sure I get a quote before leaving.

By now it's 4:10 P.M. and I have to collect Julie from work at 5 P.M. I realize I've missed lunch and drive to Café du Monde in the Quarter, near her office, for a coffee and beignet for the first time in five months. I have trouble finding a parking spot, but it's only because there are so many Dumpsters lining the street.

The Quarter, New Orleans' brightest star and visitor beacon, is empty. There are no artists hanging paintings on the fence ringing Jackson Square, no panhandlers, no balloon-animal makers, no performance artists. For the first time today I don't have to queue. There are only four patrons and half the café is shut down. I take my order and sit on the steps by the Moonwalk overlooking St. Louis Cathedral.

Usually there's a train of horse-drawn carriages lined up offering rides around the Quarter. This afternoon there's one. As if this tourist wasteland isn't mournful enough, wafting across from an unseen tuba player comes a dirgeful "rum-a-dum-dum" Christmas tune. I feel like topping myself.

My day started like a packed chaotic scene from a fast-cut Francis Ford Coppola movie such as *Goodfellas,* veered into a foulmouthed argument worthy of Quentin Tarantino's

Pulp Fiction, and built to a tear-jerking climax that would've done Frank Capra proud.

Life in New Orleans was very surreal.

CHAPTER 32

The Real Life

The week after I got back to New Orleans, I went to the Fly to see if anyone was around for pickup. Three guys were hanging about, another ten turned up, and we played a seven-a-side match. But the funny thing was, it was like Katrina had never happened. After such a cataclysmic, life-changing, world-shattering event you'd guess we would have at least mentioned our experiences in passing. With my mates it dominated every conversation, every phone call, every social gathering, and every visit to the pub. But not here. We played the game, went home.

In fact a few weeks later Nick, my erstwhile translator, announced he was moving to Atlanta and pottered off to his car. Someone shouted, "See ya, Nick." That was it. He'd turned out twice a week with the same guys for years and they'd probably never see him again. At least they knew his name, I suppose, which was more than they knew of me.

What did change was that my pickup games began to merge and overlap with the Finn's training sessions, as if I'd mated my dog and cat so I could enjoy them both at the same time. When we reintroduced fitness training on Mondays we were back to a thrice-weekly schedule, but attendance was low and we needed others to bolster numbers and pad out our games, so pickup players from the Fly joined in.

But if any of us harbored doubts about the future viability of Finn McCool's FC they were laid to rest on Sunday, December 11. On a crisp sun-kissed, blue-skied Louisiana morning we had a turnout of sixteen, our biggest for four months. We were back. Our own Captain Marvel Medhurst was also back.

Pickup players lined themselves up to take us on. I knew them from a year and a half of playing at the Fly. Medhurst told them to get lost. He marched onto the pitch and said this was our practice and he was neither prepared to play more than eleven-a-side nor have some of our guys sit out. So as we'd been there first they'd all have to go and play on another field. He came back and shrugged. "They were a bit aggravated, but I don't care because all I care about is our team."

I felt guilty. I had once been the outsider looking for a game. I'd unknowingly shown up at Wispy Hair's training and been annoyed I couldn't take part; actually I'd thought it was downright mean. A few grumbled as they passed and one even muttered something along the lines of, "We'll remember this." Oh, how Katrina had changed the New Orleans pickup football world! The balance of power had shifted. I felt like a Nazi spy in France who'd been rewarded when the Germans invaded.

On the other hand it wasn't as if we'd stopped them playing. There were at least a dozen of them and all they did was walk fifty yards to an empty field and start their own game. And some had been laughing at our older, fatter players and joking about "water breaks." As they had never been particularly friendly to me, I have to admit I was gloating, maybe just a little bit.

At practice, the latest version of the club crest was rejected out of hand, Benji emailing, "The mountains look like shaved pencils." As there were no mountains in it, this may have been one of his wacky baccy-inspired missives. Big Rab suggested our logo should be Macca in a pair of water wings being winched by a helicopter.

After a month in Atlanta, Macca was now in South Bend

near Chicago as coach of the Indiana Invaders. I tracked down a prototype Macca Corinthian figurine made in 1996, when he'd been an English Premiership player with Bolton Wanderers. It was a one-off rarity as they'd decided not to mass-produce him and the owner, Johnny Carson, didn't want to sell. He did, however, email me warm wishes for the future and condolences about his all-time football hero George Best.

Meanwhile, I was about to be plugged back into the Matrix. I got a job.

PK, I'd helped Kenny with his column in a new sports magazine, and a week before the hurricane I'd gone to the launch party in shorts and a tee-shirt thinking it was an informal affair. Everyone else was dressed up so I called Medhurst and asked him to bring me something to wear. In the parking lot I'd changed into his trousers, which had a waist ten inches bigger than mine, and I ended up looking like a reject from an MC Hammer video. Incidentally, I never returned these pants, as I dropped them off to be cleaned two days before the storm and the place was destroyed.

That Saturday in Finn's two days before Katrina hit, Michael had told Kenny he was interested in backing the Shell Shockers financially and they'd arranged to talk about it on Friday. The meeting had obviously been postponed, but Michael had since invested in the club and both of them wanted me to be their media relations officer.

I met Michael to make sure it was a paid position. Kenny had a reputation for charming or coercing people into doing things for free, but his lilting Irish brogue wasn't going to butter too many parsnips in the Rea household. I had hats and scarves to buy for my wife.

Michael asked if I would also be the play-by-play guy. I said yes even though I didn't know what it was, and only found out later it's someone with a microphone who explains to the watching fans exactly what they are seeing. This concept must surely be unique to the States.

So Julie and I went to the Shell Shockers Christmas Party (they definitely needed help; the invite had the wrong year) and then we adjourned to a nearby bar where we met an Irish surgeon from Dundalk called Michael Boyle and his Cuban wife, Dina. He spent the night impersonating his Spanish-speaking in-laws and trying to phone his mother in Ireland (he reckoned she'd be up early for Mass) to find out the name of a hotel in his hometown that neither of us could remember.

Whenever he went to the toilet, his Irish friend Kieran O'Driscoll from Cork would order a drink and put it on Michael's tab. Kieran cornered me to knowledgably discuss the makeup of Northern Ireland's World Cup squads of 1958 and 1982. Then he talked about the Italian club AC Milan. Next he claimed he was a Marxist-Leninist. And a scientist. As our relationship progressed he started singing to me, and his repertoire featured everything from traditional Irish ballads to Italian opera. He was an opera singer too, you see. We gave the three of them a lift to another bar on our way home, and they were so grateful they tried to drag me in to buy me a drink.

When Dave got up the next morning, I was reading an Associated Press report that Pakistan had banned an extremely dangerous sport: kite flying. While the Supreme Court was outlawing the pastime—as it had become increasingly deadly—police outside had tear-gassed five hundred angry enthusiasts. I had also just received a postcard from my pal Blair who'd been to a folk music club run by a cooperative of Filipino dwarves.

Dave then told me a story that began with the words, "My mate who married a cabbage . . ." He clarified that his friend had been a male model in a photo story in the British adult comic book *Viz* and he hadn't literally married a cabbage. I mentioned the singing Irishman and Dave said, "Oh, you must mean Kieran. Did he grab your shoulders and bellow right into your face?"

It turned out that everything Kieran said was true. While in the States on a temporary visa he'd enrolled in a community college and his exam scores had been off the chart. They were so high he'd attracted the attention of the navy who said they'd arrange a green card if he came to work for them as an oceanographer. They'd sent him to NASA. Bloody NASA! And he had taken opera lessons. A Marxist-Leninist opera-singing scientist from Cork who worked for the U.S. space agency. How could I have doubted him?

Between Kieran, the cabbage-marrying bloke, the folk music dwarves, and the deadly kite-flying all in one morning I was finding it increasingly difficult to tell fact from fiction in my life.

Shortly afterward, we visited Julie's family in North Carolina and it almost led to our divorce. The cause was the English Premiership clash between Chelsea and Arsenal on Sunday, December 18.

By now I'd lived stateside eighteen months and had been watching games on American TV for a decade. I knew which channels had the rights to each competition, and if there is one thing I've learned in this country it's how to track down a Chelsea game. It could be my specialized subject on *Jeopardy!*

The pay-per-view potential championship decider kicked off at 11 A.M. and was on in an Irish pub in Charlotte, and I'd agreed to accompany Julie on the visit home on the condition she'd drive me there, as I wasn't insured for her parents' car. On Saturday afternoon her mother said Sunday lunch would be at noon and when I explained I'd be watching the match, Julie, keen to avoid the sixty miles roundtrip, wondered if the contest was on in a closer sports bar.

The relatives crowded around the table all got involved. One after another they suggested pubs to try and my frustration grew exponentially because I knew none were showing the game. I had spent ages on the Web checking which bars had the necessary satellite or cable equipment, and there sure as hell weren't any in Gastonia.

I got increasingly annoyed and exasperated that no one was listening to me as they all innocently assumed if it was as important a sporting event as I was making out, then it was bound to be on locally. Everything had been under control—I knew where I had to go and Julie had said she'd take me—and now I was mad at her for turning this into a big deal, while she was embarrassed by me because I was on the brink of exploding.

Julie's mother decided to put herself in charge of finding a venue nearby. After that avenue was exhausted, she turned to the possibility of getting it on the house TV and scrolled through the onscreen program guide. The game appeared on the schedule on both an English and a Spanish-language channel (under "futbol"), but I explained you couldn't even order it unless you had a digital setup. She insisted on calling the cable company anyway.

When they confirmed what I'd told her, she said, "Try looking under 'futbol.' That's how they spell it in Ireland." I rolled my eyes to Julie, who was looking daggers at me. "Still can't find it? It's being played in Ireland tomorrow, but maybe it's on here today." Even Julie's brother laughed at that.

She finally accepted what I'd been saying for twenty minutes and hung up. "Well, Julie's nephew has a recording of a high school football game he played last week. I'll have him bring that over tomorrow and you could watch that instead."

I knew everyone was only trying to help and save Julie a drive, but I was furious the whole family had been sucked into what was a pointless big production. I shouted at Julie, she shouted back, and it developed into a full-scale row at the kitchen table with her relatives as awkward onlookers.

"All this for a ball game?" asked her mum incredulously. I was seething and went to a bookstore to calm down, but when I returned Julie railed at me for showing her up in front of her family and I blew my top at her for breaking our agreement and the storm brewed up again. Even now it still flares sometimes.

But there was a happy ending. Chelsea won 2-0 and I watched it in the living room after Julie's brother rigged up an illegal hookup. We returned to New Orleans still married, but the following year Thanksgiving weekend coincided with Chelsea playing Manchester United and Julie went home alone. Just in case.

Back home, mail was still sporadic so we sent a Christmas email instead of cards: "Once again we would like to thank you all for your support after Katrina. Until you've been through something like that you really can't explain just how uplifting it is to know that people all over the world are thinking about you.

"Areas of the city still look like a war zone. The devastation is unbelievable, swathes and swathes of homes destroyed. Nobody is living there; there is no sign of life. Whole neighborhoods wiped out. Your friends homeless and jobless. It's like nothing we've ever experienced before.

"But we have a lot to be thankful for . . . and Chelsea finally won the league after 50 years and Northern Ireland beat England at home for the first time in 78 years. So 2005 wasn't all bad news."

But bad news did keep coming. On December 21, four

months after the hurricane, more bodies were found in the Ninth Ward.

With the daily grisly stories it was inevitable some shoppers would be offended by the model Christmas village erected in Lakeside Mall. It featured dolls being winched into helicopters, houses with blue roofs, and overturned toy cars and boats. It was removed after complaints and then reinstated after complaints about it being removed after the first lot of complaints.

The curfew was lifted on December 23 and we celebrated until 5 A.M. in the Kerry, an Irish bar in the Quarter where Stevie was working while Finn's was being renovated. On Christmas Eve, I was out again at a party hosted by Rita Olmo, the mother-in-law of Ray, the long lost friend I'd reunited with in New Orleans shortly after we'd moved. A ninety-four-year-old woman from rural Louisiana who'd been born in Belfast was doing yoga on the floor.

She told me: "We left Northern Ireland when I was a girl. My father was an Orangeman of course. My oh my, when we lived in Chicago and St. Patrick's Day came around he would draw all the shades and sit in the dark and refuse to leave the house.

"But he did start the first church in the area for the Negroes, you know. I suppose he was prejudiced in one way but not another. Isn't that strange?"

I didn't bat an eyelid. Compared to some of my recent conversations this wasn't strange at all.

So after a dramatic, nomadic, and tumultuous year Julie and I got to spend Christmas in the first home we'd bought together. On Boxing Day, the day after Christmas, we had a steady flow of Finn's regulars around to drink mulled wine and watch the five televised English Premiership games. They started arriving at 8 A.M. . . .

CHAPTER 33

Rebuild. Recover.
Re-New Orleans.

On New Year's Day, Julie and I drove around the east of the city. Post-apocalyptic doesn't even begin to describe it.

Buildings had been swept off their foundations by the force of the water. Houses blocked roads, some lay on top of cars, others were tilted on their side. On the blocks nearest the levee break in the Lower Ninth Ward there were only concrete stoops, perhaps a few steps, sometimes a mailbox. One wrecked home had floated from 2600 Law Street to 4800 Law Street. A house on the City Council's list of those marked for demolition was labeled, "Found on Audry Street, address unknown." Imagine not being able to find your home because it had been washed away. Also washed away were thousands of buried coffins, and as scientists worked to identify bodies, the state passed a law making it compulsory for all caskets to carry nameplates.

As I looked at a pile of debris tapering to a point ten feet high outside a flooded structure, it occurred to me that it was an apt metaphor for the pyramidal community we now had in New Orleans.

At the top were those who'd actually benefited from the hurricane, such as out-of-town contractors who had rushed here to make money and lived in fancy executive downtown apartments. Some locals, while lamenting the disaster, were also financially better off than four months ago due to insurance payouts or increase in business. A radio commercial advertised, "Nothing sparkles brighter than a diamond after a storm! Buy something you can share together!"

The next level down had people like Andy, Benji, Mark, and myself who'd hardly been affected. Our house had holes and broken doors and windows and we'd been evacuated for three months, but really we'd been very lucky and escaped relatively unscathed.

Below us were those like Big Rab, Paul, and Captain Morgan whose homes had been damaged and they'd lost a few things, but they were already over it and getting back on track. Captain Morgan said, "The excitement about returning dissipated over time as reality kicked in and I had bad days as that initial energy died off. It's going to take a long time for the city to come back, but I'll get my house fixed up and life will go on."

Then came people like Medhurst, Dave, and Jonathan who had lost their homes, their possessions, their jobs, or all three. A lifetime of irreplaceable mementoes were gone. But at least they were insured, and I'm not making light of their losses when I write that they were educated middle-class guys who would recover.

After that were the thousands of people who lost everything they had ever owned and didn't have flood insurance.

And at the bottom were those who lost family and friends. Their faces were everywhere: on TV, in the newspapers, on the streets. I'm guessing the higher your place on the pyramid the more guilt you felt.

But not everyone with a lofty position felt guilty. Our next-door neighbors sold their house and moved to Houston citing disgust at the scenes in the storm's aftermath. The husband whined about the spray-painted message on the door left by the National Guard when they'd broken in fearing he lay dying. His wife said they'd experienced "terrible trouble with looting." Missing were a ladder and a garden hose nozzle.

I saw a nozzle in the dollar basket of a hardware store the following week and nearly bought it as a gift to help alleviate their great misfortune. I also could have gotten back their ladder as it'd been looted by a certain bed and breakfast owner two blocks up who'd borrowed it and forgotten to return it. I didn't though because I too needed it — to hack away at the next-door neighbor's tree.

Despite his security paranoia he wasn't a bad sort, but he was a bit miserable and nosy and because of our shared alleyway was often telling me to lock the gate or fix that leak or move this box. His tree overhung our backyard and shed thousands of little black berries that were then smashed and trampled into our kitchen, but I couldn't be bothered asking him to do something about it.

Instead, when they said they were off to Texas, I used his ladder to climb up and trim back four branches. It was only a stepladder so I couldn't reach higher than twelve feet. None of the limbs were more than three inches in diameter, and they were hanging over our bloody yard anyway! Thinking I'd never see the neighbors again, I dumped the foliage evidence outside our front door to be picked up on a future indeterminate date.

Unfortunately they came back to collect furniture a few days later. It didn't take Sherlock Holmes to work out the culprit. They stomped into the house and threatened to sue us. I had to listen to how they'd been through hell. On the couch beside me were Dave and seven-months-pregnant Brandi, both homeless. I should've told them to stop their Andy-like whining and thrown them out, but I apologized sincerely and promised I'd never touch their precious branches again. Then made faces behind their backs as they left.

Their racial prejudice (like that of some other locals I spoke to) had been reinforced by the criminal opportunism of some

African-Americans after the hurricane. A commemorative Katrina magazine I bought pictured a grim-faced white man with a shotgun outside Cooter Brown's bar. You assume he was defending it from robbers, but if it had been a black weapon-toting civilian photographed in front of an Uptown bar would the reader presume he was looting?

However, sometimes adversity helped bridge the color divide. Mike Mac told me about an acquaintance trapped on a roof for three days beside an African-American neighbor he'd never spoken to. They passed the time talking, and when help finally arrived the black neighbor insisted they take the white guy first and they ended up together on Causeway Boulevard awaiting evacuation. The black bloke looked after and protected him the whole time they were there, and now that they were both back home they were good friends.

The ethnic makeup of the city had altered dramatically with a huge Latino influx of builders and laborers, and these days a walk to Magazine Street was accompanied by a salsa beat or macarena music blasting from boom boxes as workers hammered away on roofs. Ray and I called into Burger King for lunch and it was mayhem; crowded with dozens of Spanish speakers, it was more like a Mexico City bus station waiting room than a fast-food joint in America.

I told Ray, "I want something light because I have to fit into my kilt in Mexico," possibly the weirdest statement ever spoken in a Burger King in New Orleans. As I was also wearing an orange tee-shirt, blue shoes, and green Santa hat I'd picked up cheap from a drugstore, I shouldn't have been surprised by the server's wary look. Maybe she wrote a book about how bizarre life was in post-Katrina New Orleans and put me in it.

Gangs of Hispanics were turning up for pickup at the Fly

and would swamp us at varying degrees of lateness, launching in with no regard for equal team numbers. Frequently the games descended into muddled pandemonium, which was probably a stereotypical reflection of life in their sometimes chaotic countries.

Then on January 11 we arrived to find padlocks on both the fence around the electricity control box and the handle on the panel where you switch on the floodlights. Nanou, the organizer of the indoor team I had joined before the storm, grabbed a long metal pole but wasn't able to smash off the lock. After years of uninterrupted playing on the same pitch at the same time on the same days, the plug was pulled when the city's population shrank to a scintilla. It was the end of pickup and Finn's midweek training.

The following week I was out of action anyway. My neck was stiff after an indoor game and on Wednesday I asked my doctor about it as I already had an appointment about something else. He x-rayed me and found fluid leaking from a vertebra in my neck and trickling down into my shoulder. I never bothered filling his prescription because it was only mildly uncomfortable and the next day it felt better.

On Friday I thought I was going to die. I've never experienced pain like it in my life.

Apparently the fluid had dripped into a large trigger-point muscle at the top of my back and the tissue's defense mechanism, not recognizing the liquid as being part of my body, attacked it. Ironically, because I was fairly fit with a sizeable portion of muscle mass, the pain was conducted through my body easier. So that was a bit of luck.

The pain shrieked out from my shoulder in great big pounding spasms that shot all the way down the right side of my body. Red-hot lasers sent from the bowels of Hell pulsed for a bit and then contracted back, like a poison-tipped metal robot hand scraping inside my body before clenching into a fist. It was agony. I spent two days in bed wracked by excruciating spastic convulsions.

Julie spoke to the doctor and begged him to prescribe painkillers over the phone, but what saved me was Dave's idea to raid Captain Morgan's medicine cabinet. Whatever he was using to deal with post-Katrina trauma worked on me, though for a few days I shuffled about like a medieval rack torture victim.

With perfect timing New Stephen, whom I hadn't heard from in two months, emailed asking me to track down his ex-landlord and get his guitar back. My attempt was halfhearted; I'd been burned by the monster case.

By that point our house had become something of a stand-in for Finn's. Julie was ecstatic. On January 14 a marathon of four televised English Premiership matches kicked off with the game between Manchester United and Manchester City at 6:45 A.M. and the doorbell woke me at 6:30 A.M. Dave let in Eric and I went down to the kitchen as I'd prepped tea and coffee the night before. With my back to them I asked which they preferred, but when I turned around they'd already opened beers.

When you start drinking that early it's going to get ugly. Dave stopped counting when he hit twenty. While it was still dark, he and Mark cooked breakfast between shouts and screams as their team, City, won. Our neighbor T.J. Iarocci stumbled out of his front door rudely awakened from his Saturday-morning slumber by noisy English soccer fans. Frazzled, disorientated, and unkempt, he looked like he'd just been dumped by the side of a lonely Arizona highway after a particularly rough anal probing by a UFO.

Benji brought plants as a present for Julie, who has a thumb that isn't so much green as blacker than death. It only takes her hours to murder any kind of potted flower or seedling in the yard or the house. I warned him he had passed a death sentence on his gift, but he held out even less hope for the city's recovery.

"Many people have lost their high-paying jobs and everyone is getting out. I don't see the population coming back and everywhere I see decay. It's bad enough now but imagine how different the city would look if the levee had broken left instead of right. What if poor areas like the Lower Ninth had been okay and more homes in the rich white suburbs had gone?

"New Orleans is so dirty now and full of gray neighborhoods with no flowers. One of this city's features was that we had color and even low-class people hired us to work in their back yards and porches. Grannies would buy pansies with their last pennies and no matter how poor people were they made an effort. Now they are only doing up their garden to sell their house."

The following week Manchester United took on Liverpool and it was a Sunday typical of many at this time: we would train in the morning; we would sit around for a bit afterwards; I'd return home and mention to Julie in passing, "Maybe one or two of the lads might be coming around to watch a game"; she'd give me a dirty look and go out shopping when the boys arrived.

It was true that after practice, with no pub to go to, we'd very occasionally have a few drinks and a chat. If it was a sunny Sunday, and let's say three guys had brought beer, this could stretch on into lunch time. Or mid-afternoon. Or late evening.

It was also true that this could get you into trouble. Like the day Dave and I returned to his car to find fourteen missed calls on his cell phone. When we got home Julie and

Brandi ganged up on us like a wrestling tag team and were finishing each other's sentences. In the old British colonial way I went for the divide-and-conquer technique and headed for the shower knowing Julie would follow me.

"Where were you? I thought you'd be back hours ago."

"We had double training because there's a big match next week," I lied. "Anyway, you have Medhurst's number; if you needed me, you could've called him."

"I tried. He wasn't answering either."

"Well, you could've called Andy."

"I did. He didn't know why you weren't home because you'd finished training hours ago and said y'all were just sitting about drinking beer."

Stabbed in the back by that whinging bastard. Benji's next minutes centered on the search for a mole in the camp.

Chapter 34

FEMA McCOOL'S

A year after the first kick-around we finally played a competitive game. Of sorts.

Mike Mac brought a case of beer to training and we sat for hours in semidarkness and decided to enter an indoor squad in the forthcoming ten-week season. Riverside's heavy-duty metal doors, built to withstand 175-mile-per-hour winds, had been ripped from their hinges by Katrina and tossed fifty feet away. The center had been turned into a wind tunnel with many sections battered and damaged, but it was functioning again.

Our uniforms had been washed away from Medhurst's home, but Benji donated a dozen tee-shirts that parodied the city's slogan, "New Orleans: Proud to call it home." These tops featured a swimmer and a flooded house and read, "New Orleans: Proud to swim home."

As the player with the most indoor experience, I was made "wee captain" and put in charge. Benji's minutes had Sean crying, "Yes! Home rule at last!" When despite Medhurst's opposition we had Sunday training moved back an hour from 9 A.M. it further fuelled the teasing that I was trying to undermine his position, and I emailed a spoof press report: "Asked to comment, Panting Paul said: 'To hell with you. This team is full of crap players. They'd be nothing without me.' He then left to batter a dolphin to death and torture a small, playful Labrador puppy.

"Across town Sexy Stephen was met by reporters as he delivered a hot meal to his elderly neighbor. He said: 'I only want what's best for the team. I'd gladly lay down my life for any of them. Even the Frenchie.'

"Asked if he was intending to run for the captaincy he fingered his lucky charm, a small cross given to him by a disabled orphan he met during his mine-clearing work in Cambodia, and replied: 'If public office is thrust upon one then one must put aside selfish concerns and devote oneself to helping people.'"

I suggested meeting fifteen minutes before our match kicked off, but Mark emailed: "We need to get there 30 minutes early so we can get a feel of the ground and, more importantly, a feel of the ball. If you don't then you will look a c — t." We all got there thirty minutes early.

So on January 10 the splinter squad, FEMA McCool's, sashayed onto the (indoor synthetic) field for the first time. We got beat. And I had a stinker.

Our opponents were talented young Latinos on a team called "Brazil, Brazil" so there was no disgrace in losing, especially as half our lot had never even set foot in the place before. We were right in it at 4-3 behind, but then I made mistakes handing them two goals within a minute and we ended up losing 7-3.

After months of nagging I'd finally induced my teammates into forming an indoor team, only to be the worst player on our debut. I was glum. My sole extenuating excuse was that I'd eaten an incredibly stupid pre-game meal of MRE sausage, beans, and rice.

Boxes containing twenty-four different types of MREs were distributed free by the army in New Orleans and we lived on them for weeks. Each came in a separate brown package and was a complete dinner with an appetizer, dessert, powdered flavored drink, and candy and chocolate. To make the main course you filled a pouch with water, placed the packet of food inside, and sealed the top. You propped it upright for fifteen minutes (the instructions suggested using a brick on the battlefield, but we made do with one of Julie's terminally ill houseplants) and a chemical reaction created steam, a hissing noise, and heated the food. A few months before, I would have found it disconcerting if you'd told me I'd be preparing a U.S. military-supplied dinner in the living room. Now nothing seemed out of the ordinary.

It had taken us six attempts to get it right and that was in the comfort of our own home. How the hell they expected infantrymen on maneuvers in Iraq to do it, God only knows. Another drawback was that the meals were full of fat and energy, as soldiers in the field need three times their usual caloric intake to function normally, so I began to resemble Jabba the Hutt.

When I told Billy what I'd eaten seventy minutes before playing, he shook his head and said, "Man, that will lie in your stomach like a lead weight." He was right. I should've had the chicken and pasta.

After our loss, all twelve of us went to the pub to drown our sorrows, but the following week we beat the Honduran team Catcho to record Finn McCool's FC's first-ever competitive victory. We returned to the pub to celebrate.

In contrast to my indoor squad's dazzling success, the outdoor team led by Big Captain Medhurst was going through something of a crisis. We had no floodlit field for weeknight training, no pitch to play games on, and proposed trips to Mandeville and Baton Rouge for matches fell through.

But more damaging and divisive was the internal dispute about new signings. On one wing were players such as Dave, Benji, and of course Andy, who said he didn't want "outsiders, especially if they're Yankee Doodle Dandies."

Some of the lads believed like Eric that we had to broaden our horizons. "We've morphed to the point where we're taking it a lot more seriously than we ever thought we would, and the competitive nature of you ex-pats means you don't want to have some American beating you. Finn's was only ever going to provide the core, but you were never going to get twenty-two players that came into that bar all the time."

Sean agreed but with a caveat: they should be drunks. "I'd prefer people who will integrate with us and have a few beers afterwards. Medhurst may call you a c—t but we still make everyone feel awfully welcome.

"There's no point getting good players who will be a disruptive influence and dissolve our chemistry, because that's what gives us our strength. We have to make a team that can win because if we just have a laugh then we'll get slaughtered and everything will fall apart. This is an important part of our lives right now and that would mess it up."

Others, however, just wanted to win. Billy said, "Get the best players we can and create a really competitive trophy-winning side. When you step onto the field you don't step on to be friends, you step on to win the freakin' game. Go have fun after because it's no fun to lose."

Medhurst agreed. "I'm forty-two and if I buy boots, then I'm serious and the group playing now has always taken it seriously. The point is ultimately to win, and you're not going to be able to do that carrying weaker players.

"We are based around the pub and it's our sponsor. It's the center of our group of friends, it's where we all go, and if there's a meeting it's going to be there. But we've run out of people who go there who can play, and new players will end up coming there with us and we will bring them into our culture."

As I was waiting to get my hair cut one day I had a long, animated discussion on the phone with Benji about recruitment policy. He said, "We are essentially a pub team with a cultural connection with one another and if we picked seven Americans, then the complexion would change. We're together because we're mates and at our age it's not about the glory. We're a gang of foreigners and outsiders and we should aim to keep it that way."

We agreed that our most pressing concern was getting a forward who could score goals to play with Billy, and when I hung up I noticed the bloke beside me was wearing a replica soccer shirt of the Dutch club Ajax. I got to chatting and discovered student James Cook was a twenty-four-year-old attacker who'd just moved to New Orleans, and the best news of all was he'd been born in Belfast and had lived there for a large part of his childhood! I couldn't believe our luck and immediately called back Benji to say I'd found us a foreign forward.

After my trim I went to Finn's to see the Pattersons and Stevie for the first time since Katrina. I parked beside an abandoned van covered in dirt and grime with a smashed front and crumpled roof and went into the pub. They had a lot to do in seven weeks if they were to reopen on St. Patrick's Day.

The storeroom had been converted into the ladies' toilets, the bar had been lengthened, and a fish-and-chip shop was being built in a new room currently no more than a shell. The coolers had arrived that week and just the day before, twenty-two weeks after Katrina, the power had finally come back on. While I was there a steady stream of regulars and neighbors stuck their heads in the door to wish them well.

Despite the hopeful progress at Finn's, Mid-City was still a wreck. There were no working traffic lights, few businesses back, little sign of life. I needed batteries, and when I did find a gas station after a long search for an open store in the area the queue stretched to the door.

Then suddenly, that same afternoon, we had a pitch to play on and a team to play. And that team was Olympiakos.

Michael mentioned that the Shell Shockers had Pan American stadium on Saturday for open trials and that Finn's could use it afterwards. He called an Olympiakos player he knew to ask if they wanted a match, and when he said yes I rang Medhurst, who agreed to the game. Just like that, in a matter of minutes and completely out of the blue, we were all set.

We had neither uniforms nor a coach to pick the team and we'd hardly trained in months. A further handicap was that Eric was off to live in Thailand and his going-away party on Friday was sure to turn into a late night. Graeme, who'd lost heavily against Olympiakos with other clubs, said he'd be delighted to keep the defeat to single figures.

So just like back in August we gathered in a pub (this time Grits) and talked about the following day's game against Olympiakos. Benji took the responsibility of selecting a starting eleven "who have a proven track record of consistent commitment to the club and who attend practices regularly." He picked Mark in goal; Medhurst, Michael, Julien, and Dave at the back; me, him, Graeme, Joe, and Andy in the middle; Billy up front, with Eric, Sean, and Mike Mac on the bench.

On Saturday, January 28, 2006, five months to the day after we were originally due to play, a bunch of old, foreign, overweight drunkards took on one of the best teams in New Orleans. What a fairytale ending it would be if we had won and I had scored the winning goal.

CHAPTER 35

The End Game

With fifteen minutes left I went haring down the middle of the pitch. An Olympiakos player raced beside me. We were on the edge of the penalty box and the ball was out wide right. It was crossed in hard and low. With a determined lunge I threw myself at it and connected with my right foot.

I knew it was a goal as soon as it left my boot. They say in a car accident time slows, you get tunnel vision, and everything happens in slow motion. It was just like that. The goalkeeper didn't even jump as I watched the ball arc over his head and nestle in the back of the net. Unfortunately, the keeper was Mark and I'd just scored in the wrong end. My own goal made it 3-0 to them.

Considering we were a pub team who'd never played a competitive match, it smacked of overkill when they roped in the Shell Shockers' captain, P.J. Kee, to guest for them, and we were 2-0 down at halftime and hadn't managed a shot on target. But the second forty-five minutes were much more even and playing with the wind we had plenty of chances, including a great opportunity in the dying seconds, which I blasted wide. Obviously my finishing was better against my own side.

I was ribbed mercilessly. Kenny even had me call into his radio show two days later under some pretext or other then laughed at me live on air. I, the proud scorer of the first-ever goal in Finn McCool's FC history, was now the scorer of the first-ever own goal as well.

But our ragtag crew hadn't been humiliated despite a few injuries and a heavy drinking session that hadn't ended until 6 A.M. for some, and if Olympiakos was the best amateur club in New Orleans, then we needn't fear anyone.

It also made us realize how much we missed organized games. It reenergized us and gave us the kick up the backside we needed to get going again. Now that we had the use of Pan American, other clubs fell over themselves for the chance to have a run out on one of the few available fields in the city. We went from a team who'd played six games in a year to one that played six games in six weeks!

Dave became coach and his reign began with a 2-1 victory over LA United, the first game I'd missed as I was at Jason's wedding in Mexico. I had another first the following week when I started on the bench because he went for an unchanged lineup against Ipswich. I hadn't really been dropped as such and he was undoubtedly right to stick with a winning team, but that didn't stop me complaining about it. His "betrayal" was all the more galling as he was living with us and I took a knife to the match and pretended to pull it out of my back before handing it to him.

We lost 7-4, but only because we loaned them players, including Juan Kincaid, a local TV sports reporter, who scored four goals against us. We won 3-2 in a rematch and I too played against Finn's after switching sides at halftime when Ipswich suffered two injuries. The next Sunday another first division team, Hellas, beat us 3-2, but my personal performance got Sean's seal of approval.

He emailed: "I thought today that Steve Rea was the best I have seen so far (I know he is indoor captain!) but in all seriousness man of the match for me. But perhaps we need to dig deeper. You all know me, I don't shout or roar or complain but winning is very important to me. We could have and should have won today . . . For me, without winning, it's really just a social club."

The smoldering debate flared up yet again. Once more we devoted hours to discussing if we should keep the "pub team" ethos intact. Benji was still adamant. "We can win but have fun doing it and it's wrong that fat boys like Adrian have been drummed out of the team. It's not necessary to drop people like him, because we can hide him. We've lost the plot a little bit. We should develop club rules so that misunderstandings do not occur in the future."

Mike Mac agreed. "We need to talk about this stuff before it becomes a problem. I support new players but sometimes we can be a bit cliquish, and it would be better to have people show up to practice a few times before they get a run. It does us no good as a team to have players show up for a game, play one time, and never be seen again."

Medhurst saw it in simpler terms: "This is a part-time social thing and although the personalities have to mesh, the important thing is that you've got to be able to play. We have a solid core and are looking to improve; we are like a social club who happen to play football."

One night the indoor squad thrashed out the thorny issue and I emailed the consensus: "Team members are instructed to invite anybody and everybody to training. If they turn up for a few weeks and fit in, then Medhurst and Dave make the decision whether they are eligible for selection."

So it was settled. Until next week.

Julie and I arrived in Belfast on St. Patrick's Day for her first trip back in two years, which meant I missed a 5-2 victory over ICC, the last warmup game before the season started.

Finally. It felt like we'd waited a lifetime.

Epilogue

Today life is slowly coming back to the City of the Dead. Some things are completely different, others haven't changed at all.

Occasionally, I come home and Benji has deposited left-over plants on my doorstep like a landscaping Father Christmas. Julie wraps up warm and painstakingly plants them in the yard, but unfortunately she's still the Dr. Kevorkian of the horticultural world and they die within weeks.

In her defense a family of cats, a mother and four kittens, now live out there and sleep in the soil amongst the flowers. Sometimes I stand at the kitchen window and watch them play for a minute or two. When I take them tuna they devour it then push the empty can around the yard.

There are still cats everywhere. A survey after the hurricane found that 44 percent of the people who didn't evacuate stayed to look after pets, while only 18 percent remained to care for a family member. I guess the post-storm feline proliferation shouldn't be that surprising.

The local TV highlighted Finn McCool's reopening on St. Patrick's Day 2006 as proof of Mid-City's regeneration. The pub was packed and drinkers spilled all the way down the block. The World Cup that year was a financial soccer bonanza with the England and American games in particular attracting such crowds that on a couple of occasions you couldn't physically get through the door. At one match Benji shouted, "Would you all just f — k off and give us our pub back!"

But even now when you drive back from the bar at night only a few scattered houselights herald any sign of life in that district. Street after street is still in darkness. The traffic lights one block from Finn's were only fixed fourteen months after Katrina.

The one-year hurricane anniversary was poignant and a memorial marking the floodwater's height was unveiled in the Lower Ninth Ward. We had a steady stream of friends and family visit us after the storm and we always took them there to show them where the levee broke. I was initially worried that driving around might be akin to rubbernecking at an accident site, but I think it's important that people see the devastation and destruction for themselves. "Show them the Lower Ninth and let them take it back with them," said Mark. He's right. Everyone says the same thing: you don't appreciate the scale of the tragedy until you see it with your own eyes. However, the Lower Ninth looks better every time I go and with each passing day there are signs of progress all over the city. But it feels like the long hard road to recovery is being traveled at a snail's pace.

New Orleans has been hemorrhaging citizens for more than four decades. The 627,000 inhabitants in 1960 had shriveled to 485,000 by 2000, and at the end of the century Louisiana was the only state in the nation decreasing in population. Tens of thousands of evacuees who either lost their homes or who worry about the long-term safety of the damaged levees will never return.

The Times-Picayune quoted Florida International University sociologist Betty Hearn Morrow: "New Orleans will never be the same, that's no question. My guess is that an awful lot of people may not come back." Many thousands of others will not return because as Ray predicted just days after Katrina, they are now in a better place socially and economically.

The same article reported Jefferson Parish planning director Ed Durabb: "Moving is traumatic ... but if you don't have much it could be a good thing. Sometimes a change of scenery can get you out of a hole. Many people were on public assistance here. These folks had a horrible education system. Someplace else they might not be handicapped by a school system in disarray."

The 2000 census found blacks made up 67 percent of the city, but in November 2006 the Louisiana Recovery Authority said that demographic had withered to 43 percent. New Orleans is whiter, richer, and older. Our area was also quieter, as it took two years for the famous green streetcars to once more rumble down St. Charles.

According to the same census, 60 percent of Americans live in the state where they were born but in Louisiana the figure shoots up to 77 percent. I'd bet that rate is even higher for people from New Orleans. The city has a way of holding onto you.

Native son Erick: "Because New Orleans isn't the wealthiest place you develop a strong sense of home. Life is very different here, there's just something about this place. My love for the city got to the point where every time I left, the only thing I thought about when I was gone was wanting to come back."

And the city will come back. Physical, psychological, and political green shoots of regeneration grow on the still-desolate wasteland. Referenda on amendments to consolidate the levee boards and the number of property tax assessors sailed through, and hopefully the days of cronyism and corruption are coming to an end. Billions of dollars of aid are earmarked for the region, but the eyes of the nation are upon us.

Dave and Brandi's odyssey finally ended. They left us when Beckett was born in March 2006 and went to Brandi's dad's then to an apartment at Captain Morgan's place. They moved back in with us for a few weeks before returning to the Captain's at Christmas, finally returning to their home nearly two years after they had been forced from it by Katrina's rising tide of destruction.

Colin never came back and Eric and Graeme have since moved away. Mike Mac returned to Ireland and emailed his good-byes: "If someone had said I would never play for the team, I'd still have come to practice because it was so enjoyable. At the risk of sounding mushy I just want to say, I really enjoyed being part of this team and hanging with a great bunch of lads."

Billy wed Lauren. Julien got engaged to Dominique and never went back to France. He still brings elegance and class to our defense. Frank the Tank married Christie and bought a house in the city. He still brings power and strength to our midfield.

Adrian is no longer part of the team. He said, "When Medhurst gets drunk he says, 'It's not the same without you.' I wasn't committed enough and I just wanted to have a laugh and hang out with my mates. I've regretted staying up until 6 A.M. when my intention was to play, but I'm not going to beat myself up about it.

"But the team was my idea. I really miss it. That first session made me feel alive again. There's nothing better than playing football."

Captain Morgan got drunk and crashed his car. Dave got drunk and crashed Brandi's car. I was sober and crashed Captain Morgan's truck. We were hit by a gun-wielding teenage motorcyclist who'd just been involved in a shootout. Crime continues to be rife in certain areas.

Jonathan and Cathryn missed the city and moved back. He resumed his role as team secretary and she got pregnant. As far as I know the two events are not related.

Macca returned to New Orleans to guest for the Shell Shockers and never bothered returning to South Bend, calling his club and telling them to ship his stuff down. I won a grant from the Tennessee Williams Literary Foundation to interview him about his harrowing hurricane escape.

I finally got to give the monster bag back to New Stephen when he managed to crawl out of bed to meet me in Dublin airport in March 2006. I still speak to Young Stephen regularly and see him when I go home. He plays for his cousin's team and we still talk about nothing else but soccer.

My disdain for the New Orleans Saints disappeared. I'm now a fan and even watch them play in the renovated Superdome when I can. They had a great season when they returned to the city after Katrina, ending just one game short of the Super Bowl, and gave the city a fantastic post-storm boost. I still think American football is the most complicated sport ever invented though.

I missed the FEMA McCool's indoor play-off final when I went home. Benji hatched a plan to make me think a total team meltdown had followed an on-field row and the very future of Finn McCool's FC was in doubt. Conspirators emailed that they were leaving the club and fooled Finn's exiles all around the country called him to find out what had happened.

We lost the final but the next season won the second division with a last-gasp 6-5 victory after being 4-0 down. The long-lost Sebastian, who wandered over to training one evening in July 2006 after three months in Uruguay and six in Texas, scored the winner with four seconds left to secure Finn's first-ever soccer championship of any sort.

By this time Riverside was owned by the Shell Shockers. The Northern Ireland soccer team toured the States and I arranged for coach Lawrie Sanchez to be pictured with a Shockers shirt, while goalkeeping coach Dave Beasant helped us get photographs with John Terry and Jose Mourinho holding the jersey when Chelsea were in Chicago two months later.

Dave's son Nick came to New Orleans to play for the team and when the season ended he turned out for Finn's. A contact at the Irish Football Association donated jerseys to us on the storm's anniversary and our press release made papers and Web sites around the world.

But because I traveled to the Shockers away trips I missed the first competitive game played by Finn McCool's FC and a further three matches in our inaugural season in the Southeastern Louisiana Adult Soccer Association Division Two. With eighteen of our PK twenty-two-man squad, we ended up a kick in the head away from winning the league.

We were playing Uptown United, a strong first division outfit who'd switched to the Islano league before the hurricane and had been made to drop a level when they returned to SELASA. We were only leading 1-0 but absolutely battering them. Then Eric tangled with a Brazilian and next minute they were rolling around on the ground locked together in a homoerotic embrace with neither willing to let go. We all piled in to separate them but couldn't break their bond. Unfortunately Frank's frustration at failing to prize them apart boiled over and he gave the South American a tiny, "friendly" kick right in front of the referee. When the dust settled he was sent off along with the wrestlers. We'd nine men for the whole of the second half, and despite a backs-to-the-wall performance, they equalized and sneaked away with a point. We finished second two points behind them, but we were all convinced that if Frank had stayed on the pitch, we would've won that game and thus the league. I finally scored for the first time in ten months in the last match of the season against the Arab Stars. It was a good strike as well, a half-volley cracked in from outside the box. Honestly.

We had forty at our end-of-season party emceed by Stephen and held at an Indian restaurant. Joe was voted Player of the Year, Benji got the Services to the Club award, and Andy and Paul tied for Most Improved Player. Billy was top scorer and also clinched the highly contested category Most Effective Member of the Hobbit Wall.

We won a large trophy for second place. It wasn't in Finn's ten seconds when Captain Morgan grabbed it and thrust it in the air like a triumphant NASCAR driver on the winner's podium. The ceiling fan chopped the top of it in two. Medhurst was furious.

Now that we'd been promoted there was some discussion as to whether we should even take our place in the top tier. We had a few good players but were basically the same bunch of drunken idiots we'd always been, and we'd need to recruit younger and better or face a weekly hammering. Paul said, "It was always going to get competitive eventually. It was just a matter of when." New players like Jeremy Dwyer, Kevin Muggivan, Christopher Sacco, and Richard Ziegler became important club members both on and off the pitch. Andy, Benji, and Dave still complained about "outsiders."

When the season kicked off on October 1 against Olympiakos there were just thirteen originals on the roster. Our injury-ravaged team was missing Mark in goals and lost 5-1, our biggest defeat ever, and Dave's response was to sack Big Rab and install injured Paul as his assistant. When Dave then resigned later that day, Paul went from crocked reserve to coach in six hours.

I missed our historic first game in Division I after popping a calf muscle and was as gutted as Dave's house. The only positive was my skilled physiotherapist, Kendall

Goodier-Hales, was also able to work loose impacted ligament and tissue damage in my foot; since stubbing it playing beach football in Mexico eight months earlier it would hurt every time I kicked a ball. While injured I had my eyes laser corrected as well.

So kicking without pain and seeing without lenses I felt like a new man when I made my first division debut four games in. We only lost once in the last eight league games and finished third behind Uptown and Olympiakos. In the return fixture against Olympiakos we should have won but tied 1-1, and I was voted man of the match.

We knocked league champions Uptown out of the cup but lost the final to Olympiakos on penalties after another 1-1 tie. Nick Beasant, living up to the reputation English players have for missing penalties, was responsible for our sole miss in the shootout. The turnout at our end-of-season party swelled to seventy. Matt Kelso, a Scottish Shell Shockers coach I'd convinced to come and star for us, was Player of the Year.

We still keep threatening to set up a fund-raising committee and attract sponsorship. We launched a club membership scheme for 2007 and hit the one hundred mark within weeks, but we still can't get up the energy or organization to bring in the money that we could.

We still endlessly analyze the criteria to sign new recruits. We still group together at the bar and talk incessantly about players, the club, tactics, the next game. As Paul said, "On our team we are not short of people who like the sound of their own voice. Win or lose, you're going to get an inquest." I'm sure there have been more in-depth discussions and words written about us than the famous 1960 Real Madrid team or the legendary 1970 Brazil squad.

Life will never be the same for those of us who experienced Katrina. Even if you were like me, one of the lucky few barely impacted materially, it still scarred you mentally. It affected everyone in this city and altered our lives — maybe for a couple of weeks, maybe for three months, maybe for as long as we live.

Personally, I think it humbled me and made me more thankful for what I have. It didn't turn me into Gandhi and I didn't renounce all my worldly possessions and join a monastery, but back in New Orleans I did a bit of reevaluation and donated some stuff to charity. Living for three months in a tiny apartment with only a few possessions, knowing some of your mates lost everything, illuminates how little you actually need day to day.

A catastrophic hurricane also does wonders for making you realize nothing is more important than the safety of your wife. And how important it is to have good friends. The storm scattered us geographically but brought us together emotionally. Finn McCool's FC is no ordinary pub football team like most in Britain and Ireland. Through accident, birth, or choice we've ended up in this red-headed stepson of an American city and we are now closer than ever after our shared evacuation, trauma, and rebirth.

When I transcribed the interviews I'd conducted for this book I had to listen to the tape repeatedly to make out what was being said because there was so much laughter. I'd plan a twenty-minute chat but hours later we'd still be there, guffawing and chuckling at the personalities and incidents that make up the history of Finn McCool's FC. We still joke a lot. We still have a lot of fun.

On January 28, 2007, one year to the day after the Olympiakos friendly, we kicked off our second season in the first division against a team called Arsenal. Medhurst and I were the only survivors in the lineup from the very first game. But that doesn't matter. The team's the thing.

I was captain for the first time because Spurs-supporter Medhurst refused to shake hands with anyone wearing the jersey of their hated London rivals Arsenal. Like in our very first game the final score was 2-2. And I was sent off in the first half. Just like Medhurst in his first game as captain. There's a certain symmetry there.

We paid photographer Larry Graham to re-create Leonardo da Vinci's *Last Supper* and thirteen of us posed in his studio for the ensemble portrait. We had an unveiling at Finn's and it now hangs near the pool table. It was lavishly pictured, meticulously set up, beautifully lit, artistically mounted, and stylishly framed. It looks great and I love it.

But the photograph I love more is the one mentioned in the prologue. That snapshot, taken after our very first game, made it through the storm and the wind and the floodwaters and the looters and is still pinned to the notice board.

Even today, years after it was taken, I frequently find myself sneaking over to take a peek at it yet again.

And it always makes me smile.